The Idolatrous Eye

The Idolatrous Eye

*Iconoclasm and Theater
in Early-Modern England*

MICHAEL O'CONNELL

New York   Oxford

Oxford University Press

2000

Oxford University Press

Oxford   New York

Athens   Auckland   Bangkok   Bogotá   Buenos Aires   Calcutta
Cape Town   Chennai   Dar es Salaam   Delhi   Florence   Hong Kong   Istanbul
Karachi   Kuala Lumpur   Madrid   Melbourne   Mexico City   Mumbai
Nairobi   Paris   São Paulo   Singapore   Taipei   Tokyo   Toronto   Warsaw

and associated companies in
Berlin   Ibadan

Copyright © 2000 by Michael O'Connell

Published by Oxford University Press, Inc.
198 Madison Avenue, New York, New York 10016

Oxford is a registered trademark of Oxford University Press.

Library of Congress Cataloging-in-Publication Data
O'Connell, Michael, 1943–
The idolatrous eye : iconoclasm and theater in early-modern England /
Michael O'Connell
p.   cm.
ISBN 0-19-513205-X
1. Theater—England—History—16th century.   2. Theater—England—
History—17th century.   3. Theater—Religious aspects.   4. Bible
plays—History and criticism.   5. English drama—Early modern and
Elizabethan, 1500–1600—History and criticism.   6. European drama—
Renaissance, 1450–1600—History and criticism.   I. Title.
PN2590.R35028   2000
792′.0942′09031—dc21   99-22941

1 3 5 7 9 8 6 4 2

Printed in the United States of America
on acid-free paper

FOR LISA,

AND FOR KATE AND JEFF,
MEG, ELLEN, AND BRENDAN

Acknowledgments

I have been fortunate in the decade I have been working on this book in the conversation and support of my friends and colleagues at the University of California, Santa Barbara. Lee Bliss, Robert Erickson, Patrick McCarthy, J. Sears McGee, Robert Potter, Mark Rose, Jeffrey Burton Russell, and Everett Zimmerman have read versions of various chapters and through their suggestions and counsel have helped me clarify my arguments. In particular, Richard Helgerson has read draft after draft and has unfailingly supplied me with just the right measure of challenge and support. Mary Kay Duggan was a willing listener and reader during the year we were colleagues at the UC Study Center in London. Also beyond Santa Barbara, Arthur Kinney, Fritz Levy, and Lauro Martines all gave me the benefit of their reading and support at an early stage of the project. In the final stages Malia Wong and David Ziegler provided research and bibliographic assistance. Finally, the book has benefitted from the support and valuable suggestions of the press readers, Sarah Beckwith and Gail McMurray Gibson.

Various institutions have also lent their support. I am most grateful for a University of California President's Fellowship in the Humanities that provided me with the freedom of two quarters to read and write during a crucial stage of the project. The Academic Senate Committee on Research at Santa Barbara has consistently supported my work through research and travel grants. A National Endowment for the Humanities Summer Grant also provided welcome assistance. The Biblioteca Herziana and the Centro Teatro Ateneo of "La Sapienza" accorded me the hospitality of their resources during two pleasant summers in Rome.

An earlier version of chapter 1 appeared in *ELH* and I am grateful to the editors for permission to reprint that material. Portions of chapter 3 appeared as "God's Body: Incarnation, Physical Embodiment, and the Legacy of Biblical Theater in the Sixteenth Century," in *Subjects on the World's Stage,* edited by David Allen and Robert White, which Delaware University Press has allowed me to reprint.

My greatest debt is to my wife, Lisa O'Connell, who, with characteristic generosity, has listened and read and given of her wisdom and good sense at every stage of the project.

Santa Barbara, California   M. O'C.
May 1999

Contents

Introduction   3

ONE   Theater and the Devil's Teats   14

TWO   Word against Image: The Context of
Iconoclasm   36

THREE   God's Body and Incarnational Drama   63

FOUR   The Textualization of God's Body   89

FIVE   "Let the Audience Look to Their Eyes": Jonson and
Shakespeare   116

Notes   145

Bibliography   177

Index   189

The Idolatrous Eye

Decapitated sculpture in Lady Chapel, Ely Cathedral

Lady Chapel, Ely Cathedral

Introduction

The personal origin of my interest in the issues explored in this book goes back about a decade and a half to a moment of wonder that the sculpture lining the walls of the fourteenth-century Lady Chapel of Ely Cathedral had been systematically defaced by iconoclastic hammers. While enough of the intricate foliage decoration and the undulating pattern of nodding ogee arches is left to suggest something of the magnificence the chapel once possessed, the heads and faces of the figures in sculpted scenes of the life and miracles of the Virgin are mutilated. The grace of what remains of the figures and their drapery indicates a high level of sculptural accomplishment, but among the hundreds of figures, not one now remains whole and undamaged (facing page, top).[1] The stained glass of the chapel is gone as well, and the overall impression is a vast, almost bare interior space—the forty-six-foot span is one of the widest stone vaults in England—that has been drained of the warmth and color it once possessed (facing page, bottom).

I had, of course, seen other evidence of iconoclasm dating from the reign of Edward VI, but the stark nature of the damage to this chapel struck me forcibly. What, I wondered, made the representational sculpture and glass adorning the chapel so abhorrent in the late 1540s that it had to be defaced? I had around the same time been fascinated by what seemed to me the curious use of the term "idolatry" in tracts attacking theater in the late 1570s and, early 1580s. What was it that theater shared with the sculpture of the Ely Lady Chapel that made both of them offensive to some people in this thirty-year time span? An obvious answer is that both engage the eye. Theater, though obviously verbal and textual, is also a form of visual art. Clearly the status of visual expression was such that it could, in the midst of a larger culture that valued the image, stimulate suspicion and outright hostility—hostility so thoroughgoing that much of the heritage of medieval English visual art is now simply lost.

I was not alone in my fascination with the issue of iconoclasm in the sixteenth century. Though the first book-length treatment of iconoclasm in England, John Phillips's *The Reformation of Images: Destruction of Art in En-*

gland, 1535–1660, had been published a decade earlier, the 1980s witnessed
the beginning of significant scholarly interest in the question of iconoclasm in
the Reformation.[2] Why the sudden interest in the topic? From one perspective,
of course, there is no need to explain such interest. Iconoclasm was an important social aspect of the Reformation in Europe, far-reaching in its impact on
the national cultures it touched. As such, it is an important topic for social history, one that links large ideological shifts with social practice. Moreover,
iconoclasm can be understood to represent a countervailing aspect of the general culture of the period, which is also the Renaissance, and to our sense that
this was, elsewhere in Europe, a time of an expansive creativity in the visual
arts. Thus the "discovery of iconoclasm," to exaggerate somewhat this scholarly turn, responds to our interest in reconceiving traditional historiography
and the received image of the period.

But I want to suggest that our interest in this literal iconoclasm of the sixteenth century expresses our own preoccupations. It is a striking fact that over
the past two decades our own suspicions of and anxieties about the image
have surfaced, apprehensions that, if not iconoclastic in their result, are pervasive in the culture. They can also be vehement in their expression. Frederic
Jameson, for example, begins his introduction to a book of essays on film with
the assertion that "The visual is *essentially* pornographic, which is to say that
it has its end in rapt, mindless fascination." If film asks us "to stare at the
world as though it were a naked body," we know that our society has begun to
offer us the world "as just such a body, that you can possess visually, and col-
lect the images of." For Jameson the only defense against, the only control of
the essentially physical nature of the cinematic image is to engage it with language.[3] There is implicit in Western culture a deep-seated tension between
language and visual representation, between the word and the image. W. J. T.
Mitchell has recently suggested that "The dialectic of word and image seems
to be a constant in the fabric of signs that a culture weaves around itself."[4]
Both word and image are means of communication; both are vehicles and foci
of expression. They most often appear as complementary ways of conveying
information and understanding, as when a drawing illustrates a text or a cap-
tion identifies a printed photograph. Language seems inevitably to incorporate
the visual in description and metaphor, and visual symbols, even apart from
alphabetic graphemes, frequently indicate the verbal. Metaphors drawn on one
are often used to describe the other; Horace's classic dictum *ut pictura poesis*
finds its modern complement in E. H. Gombrich's emphasis on the "grammar
and semantics" of visual art.[5] But there exists as well a persistent suspicion
that at some level the two are in conflict with one another, that one is superior
to the other in some respect, that one is more precise, more reliable, more subtle, more nuanced, more emotive, even more "natural" than the other. The picture is proverbially worth a thousand words, but is it really, one inevitably
asks, and in what sense? Does the visual image even accomplish the same
thing as the word? It is often asserted that images work more immediately to
produce response, especially of an emotive character, and this alleged immediacy has become common in any discussion of word and image. Modern neu-

rophysiology teaches that language and images are processed by opposite sides of the brain, but this way of constructing our mental experience does not so much explain the tension or conflict as give us yet another metaphor for it; individuals may insist they are "right-brained" or "left-brained" on the analogy of right- or left-handedness, and this is then asserted to explain a predilection for the visual or for language. The tension between word and image is in all likelihood not physiological but cultural; it is not so much that right- or left-brainedness exists as that we find it a useful shorthand in making a value judgment or encouraging a particular way of performing a difficult mental activity. In privileging one faculty over another, or one mode of knowing over another, we are not expressing something essential about human nature but rather taking a side in the long-standing epistemological dialectic of image and word.

I want to propose that this tension becomes conflict when technologies of representation are in a state of transition, when we become acutely aware of, and correspondingly anxious about, the power of one in relation to the other. Clearly the present moment is one such point. A variety of new electronic technologies for the processing and storing of both verbal and visual information, as well as the power and ubiquity of the electronic image (and its recent transformation of film into a medium as accessible as the printed book), combine to render us apprehensive about their cultural and epistemological implications. Contemporary concern for the political and ideological effects of television is only one manifestation. The sensitivity, perhaps hypersensitivity, of post-structuralism to the differences between the written word and spoken language is surely another. There can be little doubt that the recent scholarly interest in the question of images and iconoclasm—and particularly the iconoclasm of the early modern period shared by the present study—can be understood as similarly implicated in this anxiety about the relation of word and image. The subject of sixteenth-century iconoclasm, though in its literal form seemingly remote from present concerns, has in fact a considerable resonance in the cultural moment, a resonance that comes in large measure from anxiety about the image in its electronic form, an anxiety particularly evident in political contexts and commodity culture.[6] In comparison with the word, the image may have come to seem coercive in the response it provokes; its affective power appears to leave no gap for critical reflection, especially in the mass audience at which the electronic image is aimed. By contrast the word is frequently claimed as evocative rather than coercive, as calling forth reflection and allowing the participation of the listener's (or reader's) own subjectivity. Modern critiques privileging word over image not infrequently appear iconophobic, even iconoclastic, in their orientation. Not long ago the Internet quarrels over word and image took the form of partisanship of Lynx, a browser that returns text-only files, and satire or anger at sites in HTML that exclude such text-only browsers. Iconoclasm became momentarily literal by the inclusion of links that caused Netscape, an image-friendly browser, to crash.[7]

The frankly iconoclastic jeremiad of the French Protestant theologian Jacques Ellul, *The Humiliation of the Word*, offers one of the most striking indications that in the past decade the conflict of word and image has indeed broken the surface of modern consciousness.[8] Although the targets of Ellul's iconoclasm—the "idols" of consumerism, state power, and technology—may finally be figurative rather than literal, he directs his animus directly against the proliferation and power of the visual imagery of film, television, and photography and against what he believes has been the corresponding degradation of language. Ellul rather precisely transposes Reformation arguments into a quarrel with late twentieth-century culture and in the process causes us to understand that the conflict unleashed at the Reformation has been extraordinarily enduring in European thought and mental habits, indeed that current anxieties over the technologies of image making still have much to do with the sixteenth-century conflict. Ellul privileges language and hearing and opposes them to sight as the faculty of efficiency that simply ties us to surrounding reality. Sight, he believes, gives us the world as it is, without paradox or ambiguity. By contrast, the word deals with connotation, overtones, the potential and imagined, and with mystery. Only by the word may the world be *interpreted*. The condition of speech and hearing is human presence; it comes from one interiority and penetrates to another. Written language is a diminished version of speech, ceasing to be "multicentered and flowing."[9] The basis of Ellul's radical separation of hearing and sight is theological, grounded on his insistence that God's biblical revelation of himself occurred always through speech. God created through the word and *spoke* to man; Old Testament revelation is never theophany, he insists, never a visual manifestation of divinity.

Even within the context of Christian theological discourse, the doctrine of the incarnation might well be thought a crucial difficulty for Ellul's argument; in it the divine Logos is understood to enter the phenomenological realm of the physical and visual. In Greek Orthodox thought, Ellul admits, the incarnation has a wider significance, transforming humanity and sanctifying the human faculties—and in so doing, making possible a theology of the visual. But Ellul rejects this argument by understanding the incarnation as limited by history: it is the only moment in history "when truth joins reality," where "reality ceases being a diversion from truth and where truth ceases being the fatal judgment on reality." Only at this point can "the Word be *seen*, can sight be *believed*." This possibility "is limited to the period of the incarnation. Once the incarnate life of Christ is completed, the two orders become separate again."[10] By putting it in such starkly temporal terms, Ellul constrains his theological anthropology within very narrow limits. Not historicizing the character of biblical revelation, he understands as essential the logocentric terminology and tropes employed by biblical writers. The consequence here is not only the negative polemical cast of Ellul's analysis but a narrowed sense of the aesthetic and the affective, a narrowing that corresponds to his understanding of the central doctrine of Christianity. Resting as it does on biblicist traditions continuous with the Reformation, Ellul's argument makes clear that at least some of the contemporary quarrel between word and image has its basis in a tradition that reaches back to the iconoclasm of the sixteenth century.

The image has, of course, its defenders both among theologians and cultural historians. Even in its title, Margaret Miles's *Image as Insight* might be understood as an implicit challenge to the line of thought represented by Ellul, for her book responds critically to the idea that religious understanding and experience can inhere solely in verbal expression.[11] Focusing on particular historical instances of the power of images in Western religion, Miles argues that images can be understood as conveying an alternative history, especially of those excluded from the articulate use of language. Language, "regarded as the foundation of a common humanity," establishes a hegemony over cultural understanding and produces a history constantly biased in favor of those skilled in its employment (p. 21). Such hegemony "has foreshortened our historical imagination" and imparts understanding that, in circular fashion, conveys the perspective of the verbally articulate of the past to those of the present (p. 38). She argues throughout for an awareness of the affective and expressive power of the image for those historically on the margins of verbal discourse, especially women. By careful attention to the use of images she vindicates the sense of sight from what Ellul would regard as its predilection toward the merely idolatrous. David Freedberg's richly detailed historical study, *The Power of Images,* dovetails with Miles's in offering an analytic valuation of the force images have exerted, and continue to exert, over imaginative life. Sharing to some extent Ellul's estimation of the psychic power of the image, Freedberg considers the manifold ways in which visual representation has been understood as efficacious in a wide range of religious, moral, juridical, and erotic contexts.[12] Though he is not specifically concerned with the relationship of image and word, his study of response commands attention because of his insistence on the power of images and the role the human form plays in our response to them. Both of these works take the rarer position, in terms of modern theoretical understanding, of maintaining the claims of the image in relation to the word.

Theater does not enter Freedberg's discussion, nor do the kinetic images of film and television, but because much of what emerges from his argument about the phenomenology of the image can be transposed to a consideration of the visual character of theater, I want to pause for a moment over his argument. Where he differs from previous scholarship, particularly art-historical but also of cultural history, is in his willingness to engage seriously the whole question of response to the image. What concerns him is the extraordinarily wide range of human experience in which images have been judged efficacious. Whether in the conception of a well-formed child or to ensure the proper frame of mind of one condemned to death, as the focus of pilgrimage or to give thanks for miraculous deliverance from sickness or danger, to enliven religious meditation, to shame a traitor or criminal, to harm an enemy, to honor a dead or absent ruler, and perhaps above all to make the sacred present and responsive—in all these activities humans have found images to be efficacious, satisfying, potent. Over the centuries images have been treated in ways that frequently startle modern consciousness, as if they conveyed in some essential way the subject portrayed in them or evoked an emotional response suggestive of the subject's actual presence and power. Freedberg refuses to separate such response to images as the work of the "popular imagination" or of "primitive" consciousness; he is not willing to categorize the use of images as an indication of a "magical" cast of thought and therefore alien to modern consciousness. He is concerned rather to see relation and continuity both between what is characterized as "high" and "low" response and between historical periods. Erotic response to images, even in its apparent denial in aesthetically constructed discourse, he suggests, can become an index for understanding how human beings respond to the lifeless image in terms of living presence. What connects the wide variety of contexts in which images demonstrate efficacy is a cognitive process that elides the difference between signifier and signified and fuses them into a kind of identity. Instead of accepting the image as simply an object, one responds to signifier as if it were the signified. It is in fact the very potency of this process, he argues, that creates fear of the image and leads to suppression of the evidence of response, especially in discourse that privileges logocentricity.

One particular point of Freedberg's argument significantly advances our understanding of response to images: in virtually all cases he considers, the issue of the realism of representation emerges as an essential element in the efficacy that the image is understood to have. This is not to say that "realism" is at all times and in all places the same thing but that effective images strive toward an illusionism in much the same way drama does. Freedberg is not discussing the image as art, at least not in terms of its aesthetic status, but in terms of the cognitive processes that make it effective. Like theater, images at the extreme verge of realism—the simulacra in wax museums, the lifelike images of the *sacri monti* of northern Italy that present biblical scenes as emotionally-engaging three-dimensional tableaux, or effigies of a deceased monarch—seem to "colonize" reality by incorporating into the representation elements from the actual world, such as fabric, objects, or eyes made of glass.[13] In these cases the incorporation is material. But in the case of an effective portrait, the "colonization" is metaphoric—or perhaps, in the curious ontological puzzle that representation sets us, some degree "more than" metaphoric—as we insist that the painter or photographer has somehow "captured" the very personality of the subject. It is this element of verisimilitude that binds signifier to signified. Even when the clues are less precise, he suggests, "we still seek to reconstitute the reality of the signified in the sign. Sign fuses with signified to become the only present reality" (p. 245).

Representation sets us an ontological puzzle because in the case of the image we cannot precisely define the relationship that exists between the sign and the signified. With a portrait we may exclaim on the putative identity of image and subject; in the multitude of instances considered by Freedberg, people treat an image as in some sense identical to its prototype. We know of course that in fact they are not identical, that the subject is, or was, alive and that the image is not, even though we may at times choose to ignore this in the character of our response. At the same time the relationship is not simply conventional.[14] In the case of the image, when we use *sign, signifier*, and *signified* on the analogy of Saussurian linguistics, we swerve from its usage there in denying that the relation is simply an arbitrary one, based on an agreed-upon semiotic system. The image, as image, has colonized significant elements of the appearance of the original; the form of the subject appears recognizably in a way that exceeds conventional systems of representation of language or culturally constructed systems of sign and symbol.[15] This is the case even when the appearance of the prototype is conjectural, as when painters represent biblical figures or saints. (And yet, Freedberg reminds us, representations of Christ and the Virgin were sometimes believed to go back to the miraculous images on the napkin of Veronica, the shroud of Turin, or paintings by St. Luke. The issue, of course, is not the actuality of the origin, but what is understood, what is believed.) The element of likeness establishes the possibility of an affective response to the image, a response that chooses to accept it as fictive presence and to accord it imaginatively some provisional elements of presence.

At the center of our response to images, in Freedberg's survey of the evidence, is the human body. And the focus of the body—the elements always attacked by iconoclasts—are the head, the face, and the eyes.[16] What arrests our gaze most forcefully is the image of ourselves; we cannot *not* look, we may say, at a representation of the human body. Images seem always to have as their ultimate goal the "reconstitution of the living body," the creation, at least at the level of response, of the illusion of presence (p. 245). In this, of course, they fall short of theater, in which the illusion of presence is created by actual human bodies standing for other bodies. And yet the shared focus on the body may explain in part why, historically, animus toward images should also become opposition to theatrical representation. A phenomenology of theater to which I shall turn in the first chapter understands the potency of drama as similarly inhering in the representational relationship between actors and those they portray. Like the image in Freedberg's formulation, theater does not deal in mere signs that must be conventionally understood to stand for another reality: one *human body* plays another, and theater similarly "colonizes" reality by taking actual objects and making them play other versions of themselves on the stage.

As will have been evident from my brief summary of Ellul's argument, one source, historically the central source, of the Western tension of word and image is the biblical prohibition in the second commandment of making images of God and the Hebraic predilection for understanding the sacred through language. A strong reticence to seeing the divine as embodied in any object, natural or man-made, characterizes biblical religion, at least from the Deuteronomic period on. Rather than any material object, it is language that encodes and manifests the sacred. When Solomon is represented as expressing the Deuteronomic theory of the temple in the account of its dedication (1 Kings 8:27–30), he is portrayed as emphasizing that God does not dwell on earth—the heavens cannot contain him, much less the temple building. Rather he invokes the divine promise to David, "My name shall be there," and asks that through this verbal pact the place be made efficacious—not that God be *present* but that he *hear* when Israel prays there. It is not presence which manifests the sacred—much less the image of a God who has no materiality to portray—but simply the *name* which he has agreed may be invoked in terms of a place. What is significant is the bracketing through verbal formula of God's presence, the "as if" character of a presence so understood in the aniconic Deuteronomic theology. If the name "dwells" in the temple, it is through a conceptual pact made by the worshipers who acknowledge its provisional character, its "fictionality" we would say. If this were to be put in the terms of Hellenistic thought, the closest equivalent would be to say that the temple was built for the *idea* of God. But the difference between *name* and *idea* is in fact the heart of the matter. The root of *idea* is the verb ἰδεῖν, to see; its original meaning concerned form and visual appearance. A Greek temple would have sought the provisional indwelling of the god through a conceptual pact based on the *eidolon* (a cognate of *idea*), the image. In Hebraic terms *eidolon* becomes the idol, the object of opprobrium.

Christianity, like the Judaism from which it emerged in the middle of the first century, obviously takes its life as well from verbal narratives and teaching; at its center is verbal remembrance—initially oral, but in written form by about 70 C.E.—of the life and teaching of Jesus of Nazareth. But at the same time it is clear that the theoretical passages in the New Testament writings from which the doctrine of the incarnation would be developed imply a significant turn in understanding the sacred in relation to the visual and phenomenal world. The terms εἰκών (icon, image) and ὁμοίοσις or ὁμοιότης (likeness) are used to express the relation of Christ to the Father or of the Christian believer to Christ.[17] The most emphatic use of the term comes in Colossians, where Christ is called "the image of the invisible God, the firstborn of all creation" (Col. 1:15–20). This, and other passages expressing the relationship of Christ to Father in terms of image and vision, take on a high degree of significance as texts defining the doctrine of the incarnation.

What I am proposing is that the iconoclasm of the Reformation was not a mere change in the style and emphasis of the worship of Christian Europe. Rather, it emerged from tensions in the relation of image and word that inhere in the central religious doctrine of Christianity, the incarnation, the belief that God, in taking on a human form, became subject to representation as an image. Elaine Scarry notes the importance of this understanding of the sacred not only to representation but also in conferring authority on human sentience and the human body:

> The centrality of the body is emphatic not only in the original narratives themselves but also in the choices that are unconsciously and communally made about representations of Christ, the "graven images" of Christianity. An act of representation is an act of embodiment. Christ is himself embodied in the scriptures, long before any visual depictions of him. But it is also interesting that centuries of visual representations have made Christ's embodiment more prominent, have made it their central content.[18]

The doctrinal assertion that God took on a human body "confers spiritual authority on human sentience" and at the same time requires that human sentience become authoritative: the watching, seeing, and touching portrayed in the New Testament scriptures put the human senses into a new and significant position vis-à-vis the sacred (Scarry, p. 220). But the understanding of the incarnation has not been static over historical time, and the role accorded sentience and representation are entangled with the logocentrality of its Judaic roots, its dependence on its own foundational texts, and the role of language in centuries of doctrinal formulation.

The focus of this book is drama, an art that is visual and whose medium is the human body, during the time when Europe experienced the greatest outbreak of iconoclasm in its history. I argue that the crisis in the relation of image and word in this period was productive of a deep disjunction in the culture's religious experience, one that could not help but affect theater. European theater since the twelfth century had been a predominantly religious tradition. In England the most developed theatrical practice was the cycle drama, the biblical mystery plays that had been played in towns and cities since the late fourteenth century. The iconoclasm that had struck the painting and sculpture in churches in the late 1530s and 1540s would, two decades later, lead to elimination of this biblical theater as well. In my first chapter I consider two related sets of circumstances. First, the opening of the public theaters in London in the 1570s occasioned attacks on *secular* plays as "idolatrous." Second, in this same decade the religious authorities took action to ban the performance of the 200-year-old cycles of mystery plays in English towns and cities. Such a ban may seem initially surprising, for the plays were biblical and vernacular and in this respect might be understood to accord well with the Reformers' educational program. But the state religious authorities made clear that their objections were to representation itself, to any theatrical representation of the sacred. Similarly, the attacks on the nascent public playhouses as "idolatrous" show a deep suspicion of the powerful visual appeal of theater. The success of the public theaters did not allay the suspicion among its Puritan opponents, as the closing of the theaters in 1642 demonstrates. How did this continuing attack on theater as "idolatrous," I ask, affect the self-understanding of an art that is visual as well as verbal?

My second chapter explores the context of iconoclasm in the contest of word and image, picking up the argument begun above: that the relation between word and image becomes conflictual when the technologies of knowledge and representation are in a state of transition. Beginning with Erasmus' insistence on the importance of *text* for understanding the "philosophia Christi," the chapter traces the implications of the incarnation for the understanding of the image and its uses in religious culture. The theorizing of the image occasioned by the Byzantine iconoclast controversy indicates the centrality of the incarnation to the understanding of image and word, though this would remain only implicit in late-medieval religion. The most significant moment of transition in the technologies of knowledge and representation came with the invention of printing in the fifteenth century and the intersection of print culture with Renaissance humanism. In the Reformation, humanism is implicated in the devaluation of the visual and the physical with a corresponding insistence on word and text in representing the sacred.

The third chapter centers on the centrality of the idea and practice of the body in the Middle Ages, beginning with the Cathar rejection of the body and the material world in the early twelfth century. It argues that drama as a phenomenon in the medieval world is bound up with the issue of physicality and incarnation, specifically that the new emphasis on the body of Christ in the twelfth and thirteenth centuries provides the theoretical underpinning for the return of drama as a mode of representation. In the crucial transformation of Christianity with the founding of the mendicant orders in the early thirteenth century, theater ceases to be Latin, liturgical, and monastic and becomes instead vernacular, performed by lay guilds and confraternities, and centered on cities. I examine the issue of physicality and representation in several theatrical instances: an Umbrian *lauda* of the fourteenth century, the Florentine *sacra rappresentazione,* and the York cycle, in all of which the body of God becomes both thematically and dramaturgically central. The emphasis on the wounded body of Christ in the York cycle may explain something of the reaction to theatrical embodiment in Reformation antitheatricalism. The portrayal of the torture and death of Christ, I suggest, is a significant legacy of the late-medieval theater to Shakespearean tragedy, where an analogous sense of power of the wounded and bloody body emerges.

The fourth chapter traces the Protestant transformation of the biblical play, beginning with John Bale in the late 1530s and ending with George Peele's *David and Bethsabe* late in Elizabeth's reign. The question is, given the altered religious aesthetic, whether a Protestant religious theater was still possible. While Bale does not shrink from the portrayal of God on stage, his theater shows a greater interest in what I term the "textualizing" of God's body, the emphasis on texts and discourse rather than on dramatic embodiment and the affective elements of drama. The representation of the sacred proves increasingly difficult in the second half of the sixteenth century, and after the 1560s, it becomes impossible to portray Christ on the Protestant stage. Only two texts of biblical plays performed in the public theaters survive, Lodge and Greene's *A Looking Glass for London* and Peele's *David and Bethsabe,* but the titles of a handful of lost plays, drawn from either the Old Testament or the Apocrypha, indicate that the power of the two-hundred-year-old tradition of biblical theater was still felt. Henslowe's *Diary* indicates a project of producing six biblical and quasi-biblical plays in 1602, but little more is known of this mysterious final moment of biblical theater in early modern England. Its finality seems conclusive: even Old Testament and Apocryphal subjects had became taboo, and a biblical theater was no longer possible.

My final chapter returns to the question posed in the first chapter, how did the strictures on the visual affect the self-understanding of theater? It explores how Shakespeare and Jonson define their art as one that is both visual and verbal, how their plays respond to the pervasive anxiety about visual experience that characterizes the culture. In this work of definition, the two contrast markedly. Jonson approaches the need for the defense and delineation of theater directly in his prefaces, prologues, and, most tellingly, in his attacks on Puritan opponents. But in his own allegiance with humanist culture, Jonson frequently seems half in agreement with their critique of visual spectacle; he insists on his plays as *poems* and values their textual, printed incarnations over their theatrical life. This lends a certain ambivalence to his attack on his Puritan foes—and suggests anxiety about the very character of theater, even in the midst of such plays as *Bartholomew Fair*, which provide a significant focus on the theatrical body. Shakespeare is keenly aware of the need for definition and defense both of the visual element of theater and of its physicality as well. But by contrast, the self-reflexive moments in such plays as *Midsummer Night's Dream, Hamlet,* and *Troilus and Cressida* indicate a willingness to assert visual experience and spectacle in the economy of theater. The most telling moment in this regard is the final scene in *The Winter's Tale,* when Perdita falls to her knees in self-avowed reverence, indeed worship, of what she takes to be the statue of her long-dead mother. The theatrical coup of this scene, as the statue "returns" to life, indicates Shakespeare's self-conscious willingness to insist on the visual and physical elements of theater. Indeed, he involves even the audience in a moment that would seem to confirm the worst fears of the Puritan antitheatricalists. Shakespeare thus engages the image itself in his self-reflexive meditations on theater, in this confirming himself as a *visual* as well as a verbal artist.

ONE

Theater and the Devil's Teats

In 1583, seven years after the first public theater was built in London, Philip Stubbes colorfully declared that all stage plays are "sucked out of the Devills teates, to nourish us in ydolatry heathenrie and sinne."[1] A few months earlier Stephen Gosson, in his second attack on the stage, compared playgoing with the eating of meat sacrificed to idols, a practice against which St. Paul had cautioned the Corinthians. "If we be carefull that no pollution of idoles enter by the mouth into our bodies," Gosson warned, "how dilligent, how circumspect, how wary ought we to be, that no corruption of idols, enter by the passage of our eyes & eares into the soule?"[2] When, three decades later, Ben Jonson made his Puritan Zeal-of-the-Land Busy call the puppets of Bartholomew Fair a Dagon, "that idol, that heathenish idol . . . a beam in the eye, in the eye of the brethren . . . such as are your stage-players, rhymers, and morris dancers," he reproduced the actual language of those who, finding theater religiously abhorrent, insisted on its idolatrous character.[3] Again and again Elizabethan and Jacobean antitheatrical writers hurl the charge of idolatry against the stage. As late as 1633 William Prynne worried in *Histrio-Mastix*, his thousand-page attack on theater, that if stage plays had propagated idolatry in the past, "they may likewise resuscitate, and foment it now."[4]

The charge of idolatry is strange, for the drama of the public theaters is secular, having nothing obvious to do with worship—and hence with the false worship of idolatry. In Jewish and Christian tradition, the prohibition of idolatry is located of course in the second commandment of the Decalogue: "Thou shalt make thee no graven image, nether anie similitude of things that are in heaven above, nether that are in the earth beneth, nor that are in the waters under the earth. Thou shalt not bowe down to them, nether serve them: for I am the Lord thy God" (Exod. 20:4–5; Geneva Bible translation).[5] Theater does not, of course, involve bowing down, nor is it in any very obvious sense a graven image. The similitude of things in theater is predominantly human, the human body and voice enacting a narrative representation. But behind the attack on theater as idolatry lies a religious preoccupation, a preoccupation that surfaces in an obverse way when Reformed writers attack what they see as the theatricality of Catholic worship. In this John Rainolds, the learned Oxford divine, popular university preacher, and implacable opponent of the theater, was typical when he charged that "Popish priests . . . have transformed the celebrating of the Sacrament of the Lords supper into a Massegame, and all other parts of Ecclesiastical service into theatrical sights."[6] He sees this as precisely analogous to the way the gospel was "played" instead of preached in the traditional religious drama. All of the Elizabethan antitheatrical writers—John Northbrooke, Anthony Munday, William Rankins, Henry Cross, Stubbes, and Gosson—inveigh against what they see as the dangerous moral corruption of the London theaters.[7] But for them there is no question of regulating behavior in the playhouses or censoring what was played on their stages. The institution is corrupt at its heart, and only a complete extirpation of all theaters and playing would satisfy them. In this Northbrooke, in 1577 the first to write against the stage, is typical of those who would follow him: stage plays and interludes "are not tollerable nor sufferable in any common weale, especially where the Gospell is preached," and he would exclude all actors, along with witches, sorcerers, and other notable sinners, from receiving the sacrament at divine service.[8] This religious preoccupation with what theater is, both the worry that theater is idolatry and the characterization of the "idolatry" of Catholic worship as theater, goes some way toward explaining the extraordinary vehemence of the antitheatrical rhetoric and why the writers could not be satisfied with mere reform of the conditions of playing.

In one sense this attack on the nascent public theater should not surprise us. In *The Antitheatrical Prejudice*, Jonas Barish records that the most bitter opposition to the theater coincides with periods when theater most flourishes.[9] In ancient Greece, the accomplishments of the great tragedians brought on Plato's antitheatrical reaction. In seventeenth-century France, the artistry of Racine and Molière evoked the unremitting hostility of the Jansenists. The brilliance of the Restoration theater called out Jeremy Collier's *Short View of the Immorality and Profaneness of the English Stage* (1698), which led to a long list of refutations and counter-refutations over the next twenty-five years. The war against the Elizabethan stage began just a year after James Burbage opened the Theater in 1576 and reached serious proportions even before the major accomplishments of Christopher Marlowe and Shakespeare's early career. The cultural potency of the public theaters, even at this early point, must have been clearly understood.

What is surprising, what requires explanation, is the charge of idolatry and the persistently religious terms in which opponents of the Elizabethan and Jacobean drama formulated their opposition. For them more than mere questions of public morality were at issue. They were touched by a deeper religious anxiety about the very nature of theater and its modes of representation. Nothing more confirms the religious character of this preoccupation than the fate of the medieval biblical drama early in the reign of Elizabeth. In its 150-year ascendancy, the longest uninterrupted theatrical tradition in European history, the medieval drama represented the one exception Barish finds to the pattern of a culturally potent theater evoking an antitheatrical reaction: "Despite the abundance and energy of mediaeval theatrical culture, no sustained body of anti-theatrical writing survives from the Middle Ages" (p. 66). The one medieval attack on the stage he discusses, the fifteenth-century *Tretise of Miraclis Pleyinge*, while representative of at least some Lollard opinion on the question of religious drama, is a unique document and conveys an atypical, and indeed, in its intellectual and political context, a heretical, sense of the role of theater in the culture. Such restrictions as are found in medieval theatrical records are generally quite specific, referring to *ludi inhonesti* and barring them from such particular places as churches and churchyards or forbidding the clergy from acting in them.[10] Barish's explanation of why the vigorous medieval drama was, if not immune, then largely free from attack has an obvious plausibility. The theater of the Middle Ages originated in the ritual of the Church and took its life from the mysteries of faith that maintained the culture. Its central subject was the biblical story of humanity's fall and salvation (Barish, pp. 66–79). But to explain the medieval embrace of the stage thus is to raise immediate questions about the opposition to it that occurs after the Reformation. For not only was much Elizabethan drama based on materials that sustained the culture—most evidently the English history that became a staple of the stage—but, as printed texts, even the fictional works from which stage comedies and romances derived were not subject to comparable attack. The fact that most strangely underscores the religious preoccupation of the antitheatricalists, however, is that it was the biblical drama itself that provoked the most sustained—and successful—opposition. That a popular and vernacular biblical drama should be assailed by the left wing of the English Reformation requires explanation, for in at least as emphatic and explicit a way as in the preceding two centuries, the religious life of the culture took its sustenance from the Bible. On the face of it, nothing would appear to have been more educationally useful to the goals of the Reformers than suitably revised versions of the great cycles of biblical drama that played in English cities and towns. That this drama was Catholic in origin scarcely accounts for its rejection. In the sixteenth century every church building in England had been constructed for Catholic worship, but this proved no inhibition to their being adapted and used for Protestant worship. Similarly, the *Book of Common Prayer* in large part translated and reshaped the liturgy and rites inherited from Catholicism. In nearly all cases, the new wine of the English Reformation was successfully decanted into the old bottles of the Catholic past. But in the case of the biblical drama, the bottle was decisively broken and the pieces hidden away for several centuries. The emergent secular drama, though it not only survived but flourished in the generation of playwrights that emerged in the 1590s, was subjected to a sustained religious attack for the first time in centuries—indeed for the first time, it seems, since some church fathers had warned Christians against Roman drama more than ten centuries before.

    The argument I wish to advance to explain the nature of this antitheatricalism does not so much compete with as complement Barish's. I find Barish persuasive in his account of how anxiety about the fluid, protean self implied by theatricality persists in Western antitheatricalism and reappears at moments when theater emerges as a cultural force.[11] But I want to interrogate the historical specificity of these attacks on the nascent public theaters, particularly the religious content of their concern over theater as idolatry.[12] Such a discussion must be situated in the context of the upheaval that characterized the religious culture of the sixteenth century. Why was the strongest hostility directed toward biblical drama? What was it in the psychological and religious climate of the late sixteenth and early seventeenth centuries that made drama seem so threatening to a significant element of the intellectual elite of English Protestantism? I want to root my answers to these questions in some particulars of the century, most especially in attitudes toward the perceptual faculties, the structuring agents of human knowing, and in the ways these attitudes were suddenly and decisively altered by the Reformation. There occurs a comparatively sudden shift in the way the perceptual faculties were valued and deployed between the late Middle Ages and the culture of the Reformation, a shift that resulted in a profound change not only in the religious aesthetic but in the epistemology of those countries affected by the Reformation critique of religious expression. The psychic anxieties identified by Barish are no doubt significant, but equally important in the historical moment is this alteration of epistemology and aesthetic values that powerfully underlies the opposition to the transformed theater of the late sixteenth century.

The most immediate result of Reformation concern over idolatry was an outbreak of literal iconoclasm that attacked the modes of worship that had evolved in European Christianity over twelve centuries. A number of scholars have recently been concerned with the effects of Reformation iconoclasm on the literary culture of England in this period, and my own argument should be seen in concert with theirs as an attempt to gauge the import of this deeply unsettling, and persistent, movement.[13] I want to insist that the antitheatricalism of the period is a subset of the iconoclasm that begins about a half a century before and continues unabated along with it. The suppression of the medieval biblical drama should be understood as an iconoclast victory just as much as the destruction of rood screens, painting, and sculpture. An analogous, though temporary, victory would be the closing of the public theaters in 1642. But I want to advance the further suggestion that iconoclasm itself is symptomatic of a larger change occurring in the consciousness of Europe.

Because of what may seem an excessive concern for the theater as a sordid venue of sexual temptation in the discourse of the antitheatrical writers, it is tempting to see them as aberrant or eccentric. And to a modern eye a fear of homosexuality may well appear to lurk in their disgust at the practice of cross-dressing, of boys playing women's parts. The rhetorical vehemence frequently encountered in their tracts may also strike one as excessive, and there is admittedly something both excessive and obsessive about the 1,006-page overkill of Prynne's *Histrio-Mastix*. Recent critical discussions of the tracts have yielded interesting results concerning their implications for the ways gender and class were constructed in the period.[14] But I want to resist Stephen Orgel's characterization of them as "pathological." The concerns of the antitheatrical writers are too consistent and too frequently repeated for us to suppose that we are dealing merely with an expression of the eccentric or pathological. Moreover, they were writing on behalf of and to a sizable body of readers, a readership constituted by an identifiable religious orientation, who found them cogent and persuasive rather than aberrant. Prynne's publisher would scarcely have risked his capital if he had not thought the massive book would find readership sufficient to garner a profit commensurate with the ambition of the project. Opposition to the theater occurred not only in the tracts' and books' sometimes feverish pages but among the respected leaders of the city of London. If nothing else, the closing of the theaters in 1642 requires us to realize the seriousness of the discourse in the preceding sixty years. The playwrights themselves, of course, took the attacks seriously, and in *The Alchemist* and *Bartholomew Fair* Ben Jonson fought back with stage satire aimed directly at his antitheatrical opponents.

But an even more significant result is to be found in the way the identity of the drama itself was shaped in response to the attack upon it as idolatry, especially by its most self-conscious practitioners. Identity, whether in individuals or cultural structures, comes not only of what fosters but what opposes. I want to suggest that the drama that emerged in the latter half of the reign of Elizabeth assumed something of the character it did, not in spite of but because of, the attack upon it. Drama became the most culturally potent artistic medium in the Elizabethan and Jacobean periods; no other art, even those with greater prestige, could compete with it as the medium through which values were tested and inscribed. The control over it which the central government insisted on is but one measure of its potency; its patronage by powerful aristocrats, and by the monarchy itself under James, is another. What characterizes this theater above all is its seriousness. For all the carnivalesque spirit that surrounded the institution, its association with the locales of bear-baiting and bawdy houses and the marginal social status assigned to players, the stage remained, as it had been since the early fifteenth century, the place where the deepest preoccupations of the culture found expression and representation. Its cultural position, in fact, insured that it would be a site of religious contestation. Sensing at some level the potential force of theater, the opposition succeeded in reinforcing its power in the very act of attempting to demonize it. Attacked as "idolatrous," the theater became self-conscious about its own modes of representation, its own phenomenology. Goaded as irreligious, the "schoole-house" and "chappel" of Satan in Anthony Munday's characterization,[15] the stage became the secular space where issues of power and politics, as well as morality and identity, were most potently enacted.[16] In continually pointing up the unseemly competition between the pulpit and the stage, the antitheatrical writers insured that the players would understand something about the cultural gravity, as well as the power, of their medium.

I

In part the charge of idolatry came *ex origine*: Northbrooke and Gosson both argue that plays were first devised to honor the false gods of Greece and Rome at their festivals and because of this retain the taint of idolatry. Prynne would sharpen this line of attack by insisting that since these false gods were disguises of the devil, plays therefore represented devil worship from the beginning.[17] In this argument they were repeating what Tertullian had written in his *De Spectaculis* early in the third century when he had warned Christians not to attend the games or theaters because both were part of the idolatry of paganism.[18] Tertullian's position represented rigorism—he was clearly writing in opposition to Christians who did *not* feel it was wrong to go to the theater or stadium—but it was literally correct; the ancient spectacles were under the aegis of the state religion. For the English antitheatricalists some fifteen centuries later, the argument clearly becomes tropological; if the London playhouses could be said to be dedicated to Venus or Bacchus, this figuratively expressed what the writers felt was the character of the activity there. More significantly, plays were idolatrous in an etymological sense: they were εἴδωλα, *imagines*, images, things seen. "For the eye," Gosson writes, "beesides the beautie of the houses, and the Stages [the playwright] sendeth in Gearish appearell, maskes, vauting, tumbling, dauncing of gigges, galiardes, morisces, hobbehorses; showing of judgeling castes, nothing forgot, that might serve to set out the matter with pompe, or rather the beholders with varietie of pleasure."[19] Its appeal to the eye, they are persuaded, is what makes theater so vivid, so effective in fixing itself in the mind. Anthony Munday voices what is a common fear—as well as a backhanded tribute to the power—of the stage:

> There commeth much evil in at the ears, but more at the eies, by these two open windowes death breaketh into the soul. Nothing entereth in more effectuallie into the memorie, than that which commeth by seeing, things heard do lightlie pass awaie, but the tokens of that which wee have seen, saith Petrarch, sticke fast in us whether we will or no.[20]

Theater, they are convinced, overpowers by the fulness of its sensual appeal. One is surrounded by the visual sumptuousness of the playhouse itself, by the motion and gesture of the actors' bodies, and by the aural richness of poetic speech. In emphasizing the role of the eye in the theater, these writers were glimpsing, in negative terms, something of the phenomenology of theater, that it engrosses its participants by its very physicality. To seek out the experience of theater, Gosson adds, is "to spend our studie in things that are meere natural," and to do so is to be "carnally minded."[21] Once inside the playhouse, one's carnality, one's corporeality, places one on the margins of participation in the physical enactment occurring a few yards away; sharing the actors' space, the spectator cannot escape some form of bodily participation in what is occurring.

But it is the appeal to the eye that figures most prominently in the antithe-atricalists' anxiety about theater as idolatry. A modern phenomenologist of theater may allow us to see why this anxiety could associate images and the-ater under the notion of idolatry. In *Great Reckonings in Little Rooms,* Bert States specifies the creation of *presence* as the essential work of theater. In defining the work of art, Heidegger insists that a sculpture of a god "lets the god be present and thus *is* the god himself." He does not, of course, intend the literal presence of the god, but "a presence that makes it unnecessary to refer elsewhere for the god." Similarly, theater makes present "the truth of the god" on stage; the stage does not merely *refer* to a reality beyond itself, nor should we take this "truth" in some vacant and abstract sense.[22] Theatrical presence is not mere sign but a use of corporeality to "body forth" the fiction it portrays. Elements of stage performance—actors, their costumes and props—are not mere counters pointing semiotically toward something they are not. Rather, the actor playing the king is a man who portrays another man who was king. To be Shakespearean about it, one could say that the actor is a man portraying another man who "played the king" in a political sense. The stage throne is a chair portraying another chair. When Falstaff puts a cushion on his head to play the king in his own improvised drama in *Henry IV, Part 1,* the audience laughs because the actor playing the king in the play itself does not wear a semiotically neutral sign, like Falstaff's cushion, but a crown that must *ap-pear,* whatever its material reality, like a crown. Inevitably the playwright will play upon the representational limits available to him, but his art must make use of one reality to re-present, to make present, another reality. The con-sciousness of these sixteenth-century antitheatrical writers had been formed, as I shall suggest in the following chapter, by revulsion against the possibility of seeing a god within the physical presence of a statue or a painting; such a mode of seeing for them was the very essence of idolatry. A similar assertion of presence in the seeing of theater thus raises the analogous possibility of idolatry, even if the context is not specifically religious.

II

But as I have suggested, one context for the stage at the opening of the public theaters *was* religious, the relatively sudden ending of the traditional biblical theater. With a curious symmetry, the final performances of at least three cy-cles coincides with the decade in which the first of the public theaters was es-tablished in London.[23] While the record does not allow full certainty, it has been argued that the religious drama was suppressed by an explicit policy of the Elizabethan church and government.[24] Whether or not such an intention existed *as policy*, it is clearly the case that individual bishops and archbishops, most likely at the direction of the crown, oversaw the elimination of play cy-cles in the late 1560s and through the 1570s. The first generation of English reformers had attempted to use the power of the theater for persuasive and polemical aims. In the late 1530s and 1540s, the period of John Bale's dramatic activity, Cromwell and Cranmer had fostered Protestant interludes and moralities as a means of publicizing reformed doctrine.[25] And Martin Bucer, the reformer of Strassburg who sojourned in England from 1549 until his death in 1551, had promoted the recreational and educational use of plays. In his *De Regno Christi*, dedicated to Edward VI, Bucer suggested that Old Testament subjects could be used to create morally edifying works for an amateur (and probably academic) stage.[26] Moreover, the civic records during this time point to the clear possibility that even the traditional cycle plays might be adapted to Protestant use.

The records surrounding the York play indicate that it was normal practice in the mid-sixteenth century for individual pageants to be revised and adapted. The register of the play, the master copy that the city held, illustrates the extent, if not the exact nature, of this process of revision. Since early in the century, it was expected that the Common Clerk or his deputy would be present at the first station to check the performance of the play against the register. John Clerke, the assistant to the Common Clerk in the mid-sixteenth century, made between 100 and 120 marginal notations in the manuscript, most of them indications that passages had been changed from what had been recorded when the master copy had been made between 1463 and 1477.[27] His annotations illustrate moreover that eight separate pageants were at this point being played in substantially different versions from what had been recorded earlier and that two more pageants contained substantial revisions or additions. Neither of the pageants newly registered by Clerke, the Fullers' "Adam and Eve in the Garden" (in 1558/1559) or the Masons and the Labourers' "Purification" (in 1567), shows a markedly Protestant character. And the plays which survive in their original versions, but which Clerke's marginalia indicate had been replaced by never-recorded revised versions, do not contain material of so obviously a Catholic character that would have required replacement to conform to Reformed doctrine.[28] But some of the revisions occur in plays where the role of the Virgin is significant, as in the "Annunciation and Visitation," where the doctor's substantial prologue emphasizes Marian symbolism from the prophets. It is altogether likely that some portion of the mid-century revision that Clerke records was designed to bring the theology, and perhaps the imaginative character of some pageants, into line with recent doctrinal shifts. But the point to be made is that revision within individual pageants, or even the occasional recasting of entire pageants, was an expected part of the life of the play, that pageants considered in need of updating for whatever reason could be rewritten without the guilds' needing to seek authorization. It was simply the role of the Common Clerk and his deputy to keep up with and to record, as best they could, the most current version of the individual pageants. As far as the city was concerned, the play itself was a living organism, expected to change and adapt itself to conditions—economic or theological—within the city.

City records, moreover, show that performance of the York cycle as a whole was indeed being tailored to meet expectations engendered by the Reformation. In its first performance after Edward's accession, in 1548, the city council specified that "Certen pagyaunt*es*" were to be omitted, "That is to say/ the deying of o*ur* Lady / assumpc*ion* of o*ur* Lady / and Coronac*ion* of o*ur* Lady."[29] The following year the same exception was made. Because of plague, the play was not given in 1550, but again in 1551 the three Marian plays were omitted, and the guilds responsible for them were ordered to give their pageant money to the mayor for the use of guilds that needed additional financial support. By 1553 the Weavers, who had given the Assumption play, were allowed to take over the play (either Christ's Appearance to Mary Magdalene or The Supper at Emmaus[30]), that had been given by the Sledmen, the latter guild having fallen on hard times. The following year, however, after Mary Tudor's accession and the return of Catholicism, the plays that had been omitted were again played by the guilds that had previously owned them, a state of affairs that continued throughout Mary's reign. But when the cycle was performed for the first time in Elizabeth's reign in 1561, the three plays on the Virgin were again omitted, as they were in subsequent Elizabethan performances.[31] Another indication of apparent ongoing revision to conform the play to Reformed doctrine is found in the register at the Last Supper pageant, where the leaf of the manuscript that should contain the institution of the Eucharist is missing, a passage of some fifty-three lines; the lacuna suggests that this scene had also been, or was in the process of being, adapted.[32]

But in spite of revision, both actual and potential, the fate of the cycle plays both at York and elsewhere indicates clearly the difficulty felt by the second generation of Reformers, particularly the faction that would evolve toward Puritanism, in squaring the stage with religious objectives. Like the *Book of Common Prayer*—and with even less theological strain[33]—the the plays might well have been adapted to the Reformation if the impulse to use them had existed among the influential members of the Elizabethan Church. But from the surviving record it is evident that the antipathy toward biblical drama ran far deeper than mere disagreement with specific doctrinal formulations. The clearest indication of this comes from the record of the suppression of the York and Chester plays, where the surviving documents illustrate that attempts by the civic authorities to alter their traditional cycle to conform to doctrinal change were met by a firm ecclesiastical determination to end their performance altogether, however they were revised.

In 1568 York attempted to stage the Creed Play instead of the Corpus Christi cycle, and to that end cautiously sent the text to Matthew Hutton, the strongly Protestant dean of the Cathedral, for his approval; in the absence of an archbishop in the see of York at this time, it seems likely that the dean's advice was authoritative in ecclesiastical matters. But Hutton did not approve and advised the Lord Mayor and aldermen that the play not be performed:

> I haue pervsed the bokez that your Lordshipp with your brethren sent me
> and as I finde manie thinges that I muche like because of thantiquitie, so see
> I manie thinges, that I can not allowe, because they be Disagreinge from the
> senceritie of the gospell, the which thinges, yf they shuld either be altogether
> cancelled, or altered into other matter, the whole drift of the play shuld be al-

tered, and therefore I dare not put my pen vnto it, because I want bothe skill, and leasure, to amende it, thoghe in goodwill I assure you . yf I were worthie to geue you lordshipp and your right worshipfull brethren consell: suerlie mine advise shuld be, that it shuld not be plaid. ffor thoghe it was plausible 40 yeares ago, & wold now also of the ignorant sort be well liked: yet now in this happie time of the gospell, I knowe the learned will mislike it and how the state will beare with it I knowe not.[34]

With the last clause in particular Hutton conveys the impression that he is acting not only on his own authority but from a sense that it was actual policy at this point to discourage performance of the traditional religious drama. While he professes an antiquarian interest, he advises that the play simply cannot accord with reformed religious sensibility. Interestingly, the city did manage to stage the Corpus Christi cycle the following year; perhaps the play's length and complexity made its vetting by the dean impractical. Or perhaps the city had learned a lesson and did not submit the play text for his approval. But its performance that year, 1569, was the last.

The coup de grace for the drama at York appears to have come the following year, when Edmund Grindal was appointed archbishop. A Marian exile in Strassburg and a Calvinist in theology, Grindal had as bishop of London urged the banning of plays during the plague of 1564, adding significantly that it would suit him if plays were banned permanently because of their profanation of the Word of God.[35] Grindal's task in the North was the more thorough establishment of Protestantism, and it is in this context that the active role he took in the suppression of the biblical drama needs to be understood. The drama was merely one element in the complex of worship and religious practice—including religious art, rood screens, altars, mass vestments, and candlesticks in the churches themselves, and the gestures and rites surviving in the liturgy—that were to be discovered and eliminated in the episcopal visitations.[36] In 1572 the civic authorities proceeded cautiously, calling for their Paternoster play to be "perused, amended, and corrected" before it was played that year. While is it not clear who did the perusing, amending, and correcting, it seems likely that the vetting was internal, by the city authorities themselves, for a month after it was played, Archbishop Grindal called for the copy of the play to be delivered to him. What he thought of it is not recorded, but some three years later a delegation of citizens went to the archbishop to ask for the return of "all suche ye play book*es* as p*er*teyne to the cittie now in his grac*es* Custodie." (Possibly the Creed play had also been impounded after it had been given to Hutton in 1568.) The citizens' hope was that the archbishop would appoint two or three "sufficiently learned to correcte the same wherein by the lawe of this Realme they ar to be reformed."[37] But nothing more is heard of these books. In 1579, some two years after Grindal had been translated to Canterbury, an attempt was made once again to revive the Corpus Christi cycle. The city council agreed that the play should be performed that year, and it was decided that the book be sent to both the new archbishop, Edwin Sandys, and the dean "to correct, if that my L*ord* Archebishop doo well like theron." But the play was not given. The following year the council "did earnestly request" the mayor that the play be given, and the mayor promised that he and the aldermen would consider the request.[38] But again nothing came of their efforts, and possibly the attempt to have the Corpus Christi plays overseen and amended had resulted in the impounding of that text as well.[39] Clearly what was wanted by the ecclesiastical authorities of York—and, it seems likely, by the advanced Protestants in the hierarchy generally—was not a biblical drama in conformity with reformed theology, but no biblical drama at all.

The record at Chester shows a similar pattern of revision and adaptation, followed by opposition and final suppression. In the pre-Reformation Banns the "worshipful wives" of the city were charged to bring forth the Assumption of the Virgin, but reference to this play is missing in the post-Reformation Banns as well as in the manuscripts that record the cycle and in other documents concerned with its late performances.[40] It must be assumed that the play dropped from the cycle either in the reign of Edward VI or early in Elizabeth's reign. In addition, there is evidence that the pageant portraying the Last Supper was altered in relation to the cycle as a whole. In both the pre- and post-Reformation Banns, the Bakers were assigned this pageant. But their charter of 1552–1553 erases notation of their involvement in the cycle. Moreover, records of the Shoemakers' guild indicate that their play was altered in 1550 to extend its subject from Jesus' entry into Jerusalem to Judas's plot and the arrest of Jesus. Together, these records suggest that the Last Supper pageant was omitted at this time and that the Shoemakers' play was extended to bridge the gap.[41] There is also evidence of alteration of the Smiths' play that indicates a change of focus away from the Purification of the Virgin; in the post-Reformation Banns, the play is called "Christ among the Doctors," and cast lists from 1554 suggest that this emphasis in the pageant, evident in the text, may have come after 1548.[42] Stronger city control of the overall text of the cycle than at York may have made guild initiative in revising the cycle more difficult, but it seems clear that adaptation of the cycle was being undertaken.

The records also show strong civic support for the plays in the face of opposition from both ecclesiastical and government officials. In relation to York, there appears to have been more opposition to the cycle developing in the city itself in the 1560s, even though the mayors and a majority of the city council continued to support it strongly. Alerted by some within the city, Archbishop Grindal sent a letter to stop the performance of the cycle there in 1572, but the mayor, John Hankey, allowed the plays to go forward with the claim that the archbishop's injunction had come too late. There may have also been a split in the ecclesiastical establishment in Chester, as the bishop of Chester is noted in opposition to the performance, but the dean and chapter of the cathedral provided a barrel of beer for the players.[43] Three years later another mayor, Sir John Savage, took the precaution of having the plays corrected and amended before he allowed them to be performed again. Opposition had developed in the Council, and as a concession to those who opposed performance, it was agreed that the cycle should be played at Midsummer, rather than in the week following Whitsunday, in the hope that this secular occasion would make the plays less objectionable on religious grounds.[44] Some of the plays were omitted because it was feared they might be objectionable "for the superstition that was in them."[45] But Savage was acting against a direct prohibition from Grindal and the earl of Huntington, Lord President of the North. As he came out of the Common Hall on the day his mayoralty ended, Savage was served by a pursuivant from York summoning him before the Privy Council to answer for his apparent defiance; Hankey was served by the same pursuivant for his offense three years earlier.[46] From London Savage requested a letter that would clear Hankey and him from the charge before the Privy Council that both mayors had acted on their own in sponsoring the plays. The succeeding mayor, writing for the City Council, complied readily, stating that both had been acting legally on behalf of the aldermen and the Council of the city in consideration of "dyvers good and great consideracions redoundinge to the comen wealthe, benefite, and profitte" that the city derived from the performance of its ancient cycle plays.[47] The benefit to the citizens of Chester, as of York, was as much economic as spiritual, for the plays, whether given at a religious or secular occasion, were the focus of a civic celebration that brought people to the cities from the surrounding region.[48] That benefit notwithstanding, the Privy Council had clearly made its point. After the performance of 1575, Chester made no further attempt to play its cycle.

Surviving records for a number of other Northern, Midlands, and East Anglian plays and play cycles, though silent on the circumstances, show a similar pattern of suspension of performance after the mid to late 1560s. In Newcastle-upon-Tyne the Corpus Christi plays were given in 1561 and 1568; there is no indication what occurred after this date, only references in guild records of 1575, 1578, 1579, and 1581 to the plays' "antientlie" performed by the city with the apparent expectation that they would be performed again.[49] In Norwich the Corpus Christi play was given with some regularity to 1546, then apparently suspended until 1565 when it was performed again in a revised form.[50] The surviving Norwich pageant gives evidence that this revision was meant to adapt to Reformation circumstances; the Paradise play of the Grocers exists in two versions, the one performed in 1565 noted as "newely renuid and accordynge unto the Skripture."[51] But the plays were not given again after this performance. In Lincoln the Corpus Christi play is attested until 1554. After this date a Tobias play was mounted at Whitsuntide, but this play too was ended after its final performance in 1569. Most hauntingly of all—because it was the best-known play cycle in England—the Coventry records show annual performances, save for the plague years of 1564 and 1575, until 1579. But then the following year, a cryptic notation appears in the City Annals between reference to an earthquake and the pointing of the cathedral steeples: "And this yeare the padgins were layd downe."[52] But no record survives indicating that the plays would never be seen again, nor does there appear any hint of the reasons for the cycle's demise. One can only suppose that the forces that had ended performance in the North had finally caught up to the most popular and longest enduring of the cycles. In 1584 "a new play of the Destruction of Ierusalem," a tragedy by John Smith of St. John's College, Oxford, was performed as a non-biblical alternative to the Corpus Christi play.[53] In some cases the civic officials may have moved performance of their plays from the time of the now-suspended feast of Corpus Christi to what they hoped was the more acceptable celebration of Whitsuntide some ten days earlier, which would similarly allow for fine weather and plenty of daylight but would not imply association with the old Catholic Eucharistic feast: Some towns had effected this change before the Reformation, probably to avoid competition with the Corpus Christi procession, but the move would have become even more prudent after 1548. Even apart from religious considerations, an additional motive for concern about large gatherings of people that the play performances would have drawn to regional centers came in the autumn of 1569 with the revolt of the Northern earls. But the opposition to the playing of the traditional cycles was too widespread and enduring for that to have been the dominant motivation for ending them.[54]

In the conflicts over the plays between the civic and ecclesiastical authorities, it is evident that the motivations of the latter were sufficiently strong for them to have acted against citizen interests, interests that were both economic and social—and to have acted in potential violation of the liberties of the cities. What those motivations were becomes apparent in a record that indicates suppression of the Wakefield play. The manuscript of Wakefield contains an indication that this cycle as well was being adapted to Reformed conditions (or had been subjected to post-Reformation censorship); a twelve-page gap occurs, truncating the end of the Ascension play and the beginning of the Last Judgment play, the place the Pentecost and Marian plays would have occupied.[55] On May 27, 1576, Hutton, the dean of York, issued an order that announced the decision to forbid the performance of the cycle planned for Whitsuntide of that year. In it he expressed what must be a central reason behind the suppression of the biblical theater:

> This daie vpon intelligence geven to the saide Commissioners that it is meant and purposed that in the towne of Wakefeld shalbe plaied this yere in Whitsonweke next or thereaboutes a plaie commonlie called Corpus Christi plaie which hath been heretofore vsed there; Wherein thy ar done tundrestand that there be many thinges vsed which tende to the Derogation of the Maiestie and glorie of god the prophanation of the Sacramentes and the maunteynaunce of superstition and idolatrie; The said commissioners Decred a lettre to be written and sent to the Balyffe Burgesses and other the inhabitantes of the said towne of Wakefeld that in the said playe no Pageant be vsed or set furthe wherein the Maiestye of god the father god the sonne or god the holie ghoste or the administration of either the sacramentes of Baptisme or of the lordes Supper be counterfeyted or represented; or anythinge plaied which tende to the maintenaunce of superstition and idolatrie or which be contraie to the lawes of god or of the Realme.[56]

The real issue, then—and a confirmation of the charge of idolatry—is here given as *representation*. If we can generalize from Hutton's order on Wakefield, the charges against the cycle plays are that they *represent* God and *coun-*

terfeit the life of Christ and institution of the sacraments. This explains why the guilds and aldermen of the various towns were fighting a losing battle in attempting to preserve their plays by adjusting the doctrine expressed in them and excising the Marian pageants. For the final sticking point was not Marian, ecclesiastical, or eucharistic dogma, but the physical portrayal of the divine. It may have been just possible to reduce the God of the Old Testament plays to an offstage voice. In fact the post-Reformation Banns of the Chester cycle envision just such a solution. The Banns exhibit some embarrassment about the dramaturgy of the play and at their conclusion suggest that if good players and a witty, sophisticated playwright were composing it, the actors playing God would simply be heard from the clouds as a voice and not seen. Imagine that the mask, the "face-gilte" worn by the actor, is the heavenly cloud, the Banns suggest—simply listen to the voice and do not imagine that God is appearing in a human shape.[57] But there was of course no way that the heart of the cycles—the life, death, and resurrection of Christ—could have been performed without an actor portraying Christ. (Even Bucer's positive recommendations of a biblical drama a generation earlier had envisioned only the portrayal of moral stories from the Old Testament; he does not include anything from the New Testament, much less the life of Christ, among the possible subjects for stage representation.) The real center of the altered religious aesthetic that separates the latter half of the sixteenth century from a time forty or fifty years earlier, when images had been a focus of devotion and the mystery cycles had been played without interference—and indeed that separated the civic authorities, even in the 1560s and 1570s, from their eccesiastical governors— is the *physical, visual* portrayal of the sacred. The essential minimum of the cycles was the embodiment and enactment of Christ. Matthew Hutton's order forbidding the Wakefield performance indicates that this had become the central difficulty for the plays in the new Reformed aesthetic.

III

While inveighing against theater in general, the London antitheatrical writers save their most enthusiastic invective for the religious stage. Munday considers it "of all abuses . . . the most undecent and intollerable" that sacred matters should be profaned by actors.[58] What disturbs the polemicists is not only that Scripture is enacted but that it is treated with artistic licence. In bringing biblical narratives to stage life, the playwrights of the mystery cycles had been free to elaborate and humanize the figures of sacred history. Both comedy and pathos served to make the narratives emotionally present to the audience. In the York play Noah's wife decides at the last minute that she wants nothing to do with shipboard life, and the scene of domestic comedy makes the patriarch's family, at one level, reassuringly familiar. And while he is a comic figure in some of the cycles, the York Joseph reacts with an understandable jealousy and anger at his apparent betrayal by the pregnant Mary. Such elaboration was hardly ornamental or extraneous, but in fact crucial to realization of biblical narrative on stage. Northbrooke, in the late 1570s, reprehends this elaboration as a mingling of scurrility with divinity. (At the same time, he confirms that the plays remained popular by remarking that their long continuance had "stricken a blinde zeale in the heartes of the people, that they shame not to say and affirme openly, that Playes are as good as Sermons, and they learne as much or more at a Playe, than they doe at Gods worde preached."[59]) To Munday the elaboration means that "the reverend word of God, & histories of the Bible set forth on the stage by these blasphemous plaiers, are so corrupted with their gestures of scur-rilitie, and so interlaced with uncleane, and whorish speeches, that it is not possible to drawe anie profite out of the doctrine of their spiritual moralities" (p. 103). Stubbes similarly reprehends "the bawdry, scurrility, wanton showes, and uncomely gestures" that profane the word of God in the religious drama.[60] If none of the mystery cycles had survived—and there is perhaps an element of chance in the survival of the four extant cycles—we might imagine from such polemical sixteenth-century descriptions that some bizarre form of biblical pornography had been served up on the medieval stage.

These attitudes toward the biblical drama, expressed officially by the sup-pression by ecclesiastical authorities and unofficially by the invective of the antitheatrical writers, stand diametrically opposed to those which had pre-vailed in the previous hundred and fifty years. In fact, it is only in the past half century, when the plays have again been performed and their dramatic power has begun to be rediscovered, that we have emerged from the 350-year-long shadow of this Elizabethan condemnation.[61] Behind the condemnation, I shall argue in the next chapter, lies a two-fold alteration in sensibility. There is first of all the vigorous rejection of the idea that either God, whether in transcen-dence or in the human immanence expressed in Christ, or the sacred events of biblical history should be physically represented. And second—really the re-verse of the same coin—there is a new literalism in the attitude toward Scrip-ture. As Walter Ong has argued, the Bible was present to medieval culture in a largely oral mode: "the culture as a whole assimilated the biblical word not verbatim but as oral culture typically assimilates a message, thematically and formulaically, tribally rather than individually, by contrast with post-typographic culture."[62] The biblical drama of the mystery cycles was less con-cerned with *literal* fidelity to the words of Scripture than with emotional en-gagement with its patterns of fall and redemption, judgment and salvation, with making *present* the life of the biblical narrative. The Chester portrayal of Abraham and Isaac, for example, is elaborated from a brief and strikingly un-emotive scriptural text into a dialogue that emphasizes the human pathos of their situation and Isaac's self-submission to his father's terrible duty. At the end of the play its prefigurement of the Father's sacrifice of *his* Son is made explicit, and the theological pattern is thereby given an emotional emphasis it would not otherwise possess. The Brome play on the same subject goes so far as to dispense with the typological interpretation and to elaborate even further the emotional pathos, which is explicitly related to pain suffered by mothers in the loss of their own children.

With the Reformation comes the insistence on *sola scriptura*, on what is written—and only what is written. God's self-revelation is to be found in the exact words of a *text*. Ong links this to the development of typography, which made exact, unvarying texts possible and lent thereby an increased confidence to the "word-in-space." A consequence was an alteration of the psychological structures for assimilating the word.[63] The written, now printed, word became the norm of truth. In the case of the mystery plays, the words of the biblical text had been simply a point of departure for dramatic elaboration, though this elaboration was consonant with traditions of interpretation. But this elaboration would clearly become suspect when religious truth was perceived to reside in exact texts. Bryan Crockett has rightly insisted that such a statement needs to be qualified by reference to Protestant preaching; the word did not remain inert on the printed page, but was enlivened by the voice of the preacher who performed and interpreted it to his auditors.[64] The role of print culture was to give new confidence to the verbal formulation of God's self-revelation, to provide the word of God, spoken and preached, with a secure grounding and to winnow it from the accretions of myth and tradition. This altered status of the word stands behind Reformation anxiety about biblical representation generally. David Rogers, son of the archdeacon of Chester Cathedral, continuing his father's memorial of the history of the city, gave thanks in 1609 that with the disappearance of the plays, "neither wee nor oure posterities after us maye nevar see the like abomination of desolation with such a clowde of ignorance to defile with so highe a hand the moste sacred scriptures of God."[65] His metaphoric "abomination of desolation" from the Book of Daniel (11:31) ties the religious theater to the idolatrous statue which had defiled the Temple; the biblical word here fulfills the role of the Temple. The new status of the word stands in particular behind the intense dislike on the part of the antitheatrical writers for the interpolations and adaptations of biblical narrative in the cycle plays. Stubbes manifests this in the extraordinary interpretation he gives to the beginning of John's Gospel in order to condemn players of religious drama: "In the first of *John* we are taught, *that the word is God, and God is the word.* Wherefore, whosoever abuseth the majesty of God in the same, maketh a mocking stocke of him, and purchaseth to himself eternal damnation."[66] The abuse worthy of damnation that Stubbes discovers in the mystery plays is not, of course, anything that to modern sensibility smacks of blasphemy or irreligious mockery; it is simply the attempt to make the biblical narratives physically immediate and expressive, to render them emotionally accessible. To the medieval sensibility they clearly were more narrative, more story, than text. To Stubbes it is a text that has been tampered with—amplified, versified, then enacted with all the visual and aural embellishment, all the corporeality, that actors must use to create presence. His antipathy to such enactment leads him to the heterodox identification of the *Logos* of John's Gospel with the word of Scripture, rather than with the preexistent Christ; he confuses signifier with signified and turns the words of the text into the Word toward which words only point. In doing so he gives merely slight exaggeration to the role the Reformers had assigned Scripture as the sole connecting link between man and

God: only in the words of a written, now printed, text was the Word to be encountered. Expressed in the heightened form Stubbes here gives it (and common enough in polemical contexts[67]), the position becomes *logolatry*, the re-
verse of the coin of *idolatry* of which late-medieval and Counter-Reformation
Catholicism stood accused by the Reformation.

IV

From the foregoing it could appear that the split in aesthetic and epistemological orientation occurred neatly along confessional lines in the sixteenth
century and that opposition to theater was a Protestant, or perhaps a radically
Protestant, position, in relation to which a Catholicism still linked to the visual
culture of the late Middle Ages would sustain both theater and theatricality. In
one sense it is true that the division occurs with the onset of the Reformation,
which, as the following chapter will argue, decisively rejected the visual culture that had fostered the cycle plays. Catholicism, at the end of the final ses-
sion of the Council of Trent in 1563, confirmed its acceptance of visual art in
devotional practice. And it is evident that the English antitheatricalists, from
Northbrooke to Prynne, would for the most part articulate their own position
in terms of the schism within Christianity. But with a strange simultaneity, antitheatrical attitudes also emerged in the Catholic Reform. Carlo Borromeo,
from virtually the beginning of his famed tenure as cardinal-archbishop of
Milan (1565–1584), was an implacable foe of all theatrical activity. Most of
his activity and declarations were directed against the *commedia dell'arte* and
the activities of festival that surrounded it. Like the English antitheatrical writers, he saw pagan origins and practices behind theatrical performances and for
this reason condemned them all as contrivances of the devil. In 1573 he insisted that preachers condemn "theatrical performances, plays, and things of
this nature which take their origins from pagan practices and are contrary to
Christian teaching."[68] It was particularly unfitting, he believed, that such activities take place on Sundays and during the sacred periods of Lent or on feast
days. And like his Protestant contemporaries in London he paid theater the
backhanded compliment of its being far more dangerous in that it was sensu-
ous and physical in its representational character. "How much more does that
which the eyes see penetrate into the spirit than does that which we only read
of in books!" he declared in a sermon preached in 1583. "How much more seriously does the living voice injure the minds of the young than that which is
dead and printed in books!"[69]

But what is most telling in this Milanese correspondence with the London
antitheatricalism is Borromeo's opposition to *sacre rappresentazioni*, the traditional Italian religious theater. At the very beginning of his tenure as archbishop—analogous to Edmund Grindal at York some six years later—he ordered "that henceforth the Passion of the Savior not be acted in either a sacred
or prophane location," but that instead it should be expounded by preachers

with gravity and learning. He likewise ordered that the martyrdom and deeds of the saints not be acted, but "piously narrated," so that the "auditors" would be moved to imitation, veneration, and invocation.[70] In 1584 he sharply reprimanded the friars of the convent of Santa Maria delle Grazie, who had organized a *Rappresentazione del Martirio de' Ss. Giovanni e Paolo*. Borromeo's motivations in opposing the *sacre rappresentazioni* both correspond to and differ significantly from the motivations of the English antitheatricalists. He gives as his reason for forbidding portrayals of the Passion and the lives of the saints, "the human perversity" that has caused "much offensiveness, even much laughter, and contempt" to be part of the representations. In this he echoes, and in fact anticipates, the English antitheatricalists who objected to what they saw as the ribaldry and buffoonery that were a part of the traditional English biblical theater. The Catholic Reform had similarly become concerned about the legendary and purely imaginative material that had been incorporated into scriptural and historically documented traditions, and it shared to an extent in the new literalism which characterized Reformation attitudes toward biblical texts. Borromeo, for example, forbade the painting of nonscriptural legends or those not approved by the church, and he gave orders that his suffragan bishops should call together artists to warn them about what to avoid as well as to see that they not proceed in their artistic activity without consent of the parish priest. Doubtful images must be judged by bishops with the assistance of learned men.[71]

While Borromeo does manifest apprehension about images and the lust of the eye, he differs from the English antitheatricalism in not formulating his apprehension in terms of a more generalized fear of idolatry. At the same time he forbids *sacre rappresentazioni* of the Passion, he recommends that preachers use the visual aid of the "image of the crucified Savior" and "other pious actions" which the church approves. This difference emerges tellingly in the use of the visual and the theatrical in the religious devotion of the period. Ferdinando Taviani notes how the "Theater of the Forty Hours," the exposition of the Eucharist for the adoration of the faithful, employed draperies and special effects of lighting and music to produce a theatrical scene. The devotion was first introduced at the time of carnival in 1556 to draw the populace "with the magnificence of sacred spectacle" from "obscene comedies."[72] Borromeo's friend Gabriele Palleoti, archbishop of Bologna (1566–1597), wrote his *Discorso intorno alle immagine sacre e profane* (1582) in a spirit far more sympathetic to visual art than Borromeo could summon in order to establish guidelines for proper artistic representation, in particular to direct painters away from material that was merely legendary and towards what could be found in the biblical texts and verifiable history.[73] The ultimate result of such post-Tridentine efforts as Palleoti's would be a significant expansion through the seventeenth century of the repertory of biblical scenes, especially from the Old Testament, that painters illustrated. Analogously, even Borromeo appears to have approved of the commissioning of a new play, significantly not a traditional *rappresentazione* but one based on an Old Testament subject, on the sons of Jacob for the Collegio Borromeo at Pavia, of which his nephew Fed-

erico was principal. Such a play would presumably have followed the biblical
narrative strictly and not introduced extraneous elements (Taviani, p. 8).

Borromeo's antitheatricalism, while echoed in the Rome of Pius V, was
not universal, or perhaps even predominant, in Italian culture in the late sixteenth century. Theater flourished in many courts and cities. In Florence in
particular, and in other places in Tuscany, the quattrocento *sacra rappresentazione* transmuted into the neoclassical *tragedia sacra*. Beginning with the
anonymous *Saul* of 1566, these biblical dramas and accounts of martyrdom
(including a large number of virgin martyrs) expressed the spiritual ideals of
the Catholic Reform. Louise Clubb has recently suggested that there were
probably hundreds of such plays written in the late cinquecento and early sei-
cento.[74] In the emergent baroque of the seventeenth century, Italy would become a culture based significantly on the image—indeed it seems in many
ways the mirror image of the aniconic verbal culture of England. To some extent Protestant iconoclasm can be seen historically to have functioned as
provocation to stimulate this culture of the image; if the Reformation had
called into question the use of the physical to express the sacred, then baroque
Catholicism responded by insisting upon the physical, by employing the
image in increasingly theatrical ways to portray a different sense of the sacred.[75] Not only the settings for worship in churches, but even elements of the
cityscape—piazzas, façades of palazzi, entire vistas—became in a sense "theaters." Given this development in the seventeenth century, Cardinal Borromeo's antitheatricalism in the decades between 1565 and 1585 may seem
anomalous.

The baroque age, however, did not immediately follow the Council of
Trent. In the thirty or forty years between the conclusion of the Council and
the first manifestations of the baroque sensibility in religious and secular art,
there intervened several decades of anxious uncertainty about the role of the
image. Reformation iconoclasm, while failing to persuade iconodule Catholicism, had raised questions about the status and use of the image that could not
be simply dismissed. It is to this postconciliar period of anxiety that Borromeo's assault on theater, even religious theater, belongs. Its curious symmetry with the contemporaneous antitheatricalism of English Protestant writers
and ecclesiastics indicates a moment of anxiety and critical reflection on the
question of theatricality that transcended specific differences in the historical
conditions of the theaters. A new moral seriousness, especially in regard to
sexual morality, was also shared on both sides of the Reformation divide, and
this too would have the effect of creating anxiety about the carnivalesque
spirit of play associated with theater.

The common denominator on both sides of the Reformation divide is the
human body, the body as depicted in art and the body as employed on stage.
The anxiety that the representation of biblical narrative would transgress what
the text warrants inevitably implicates the bodies of skilled actors, for any enactment must exceed textual limitation, just as any dramatic script based even
on a canonical text would require the addition of narrative and incident. Between the eye and the image, whether painted, sculpted, or realized kinetically

on stage, intervened both a new rigor toward representation and an emphasis on language and text. At issue was where the eye could be legitimately directed. The first century of printing was also a century of extraordinary innovation in visual representation: the discovery of perspective, the recovery of the ancient art of sculpting lifelike human forms from marble, new technologies of creating vivid effects of color (including oil paint), and artists' employment of anatomies to gain a sense of the inner structure of the body. The image experienced extraordinary development in its representational capability just prior to and through the sixteenth century. What could the eye look upon with impunity? Should the extensive new claims of the printed word engross the eye's attention? With extraordinary suddenness the second commandment of the Decalogue arrested Europe's attention.

V

Leveled as it was against both the medieval biblical drama and the nascent secular stage of the Elizabethan public theaters, the charge of idolatry stands as a curious bridge between the two. While it has a more evident applicability to the biblical drama in its association with religious representation and the Catholic past, the term makes certain assertions about secular theater as well. First and most strangely, it arbitrarily assigns a religious dimension to drama that makes no claims in this direction. Not content simply to insist on the immorality of the stage, the antitheatricalists use the term *idolatry* to suggest that theater has something of the status of false religion. By calling the theater the "chappel of Satan," as Anthony Munday does, and by asserting of the players that "the divell is adored as God amongst them, whome they make their idoll as the Israelites did by their golden calfe in Horebbe," as William Rankins does, or seeing plays competing with sermons for an audience, as most of the writers do, they set theater into a system of signification that opposes it to true Protestant worship and aligns it with the falsity of idolatrous, Catholic, worship.[76] The other idolatrous spectacle that draws forth similar opprobrium is the Catholic Mass. There is, to be sure, a degree of rhetorical play in this defining of theater as false religion; the writers do not appear to mean to make secular theater equivalent to the Mass, and the assertion of devil worship is no doubt meant rhetorically (though one recalls the persistent story of the extra devil who appeared in a performance of *Doctor Faustus*). And yet the rhetoric is seriously meant. A persistent association of terminology links theater with Catholic ceremonial. Prynne goes furthest in this direction in his worry that if stage plays have propagated idolatry before, "they may likewise resuscitate, and foment it now."[77] For him the association is even literal; he insists that Catholics are much devoted to theatrical spectacles, and conversely most of the present-day English actors, he has been credibly informed, are "professed Papists" (pp. 72, 142). He describes the Jesuits as a "histrionicall infernal Society" who have used the acting out of biblical stories, instead of preaching them, to convert the natives of the New World.[78] The effect of such associations is difficult to gauge. It surely made a difference in the conferring of patronage to the players; by the early seventeenth century those aligned with the Puritans, both among the gentry and the nobility, were disinclined to lend support to an institution defined in opposition to the true worship of God. But such associations also contributed in various ways to apprehension of the seriousness of the theater as an institution. Those both inside and outside the theater, averse to alliance with the Puritans, would have understood the gravity of the charge of idolatry.

Unwilling to accept the characterization of theater as false religion, they understood the necessity of insisting on the role that theater had traditionally held, even in the marginal social status assigned it. That role was not simply entertainment, though it surely included this, but to embody and give presence to the central myths of the culture. If the religious myths could no longer receive such embodiment, their transpositions in the secular theater would nevertheless retain centrality and cultural force. At the same time such ideological opposition clarified the ideological role of theater, its ability to address the sorts of questions being addressed in print and in sermons. Bryan Crockett notes that Robert Milles, in attacking theater (and Ben Jonson) in a Paul's Cross sermon of 1611, "registers the relative success with which the defenders of the theater argued their case"; in expressing his horror that people say plays are as good as sermons, Milles in effect tempted his auditors to agree with such a sentiment.[79] Paul's Cross was the central venue for the performance of the word of God. An attack on the stage from Paul's Cross was perhaps the most sincere acknowledgment of significance the Bankside and Blackfriars could receive.

A second, and more serious, assertion implied by the charge of idolatry against the secular theater was that its visual character rendered it suspect. This is the more significant charge because it involves both the phenomenal character of theater and the crisis of the image in the sixteenth century. Several antitheatrical writers make the point that there is no harm in reading plays—that the real danger comes in the experience of seeing them performed on the stage. Gosson defends St. Gregory Nazianzus, the fourth-century theologian, and George Buchanan, the contemporary Scots Neo-Latin poet, from the opprobrium of being playwrights on the ground that they wrote only to be read. St. Gregory, he anachronistically asserts, detested the corruption of Corpus Christi plays and wrote the Passion of Christ in verse so that it would delight in the reading. So did Buchanan in his play on John the Baptist. But, Gosson insists, "every play to the worldes end, if it be presented up on the Stage, shall carry that brand on his backe to make him knowne, which the devil clapt on, at the first beginning, that is, idolatrie."[80] Even Prynne agrees that one may lawfully read a play. It is the *seeing* that brings one under the spell of "that flexanimous rhetorical Stage-elocution, that lively action and representation of the Players themselves which put life and vigor into these their Enterludes, and make them pierce more deeply into the Spectators eyes, their eares and lewde affections."[81] This appears to be the significant sequence: eyes, ears, affections. Reading obviously involves the eyes, but only to take in the symbols that properly pertain to the ear; it may be the indirection of this process that is understood to give reflection and judgment their opening. But seeing the "lively action and representation" that the players create and hearing speech directly, carrying the very emphasis and emotive expressiveness that they have in life—these are what so potently affect the emotions, whether the spectator wills it or not.

Theater is obviously an art which requires both seeing and hearing, both visual image and language. Only minimalist experimentation attempts to separate them. But as we have seen, the antitheatrical writers of the English Reformation saw the primary danger in the sense of sight: seeing is what leads the emotions beyond the individual's control. In their terminology one only *hears* a sermon. We may object that such hearing also involves a seeing and a responding to corporeal human presence, that the charismatic preachers who could hold their auditory for the length of a sixteenth-century sermon must have been accomplished actors even in spite of themselves. And this is doubtless true. There is a tension and inconsistency in these objections to an art that was as necessary to the pulpit as to the stage. That this was not perceived and that the objections to the theater center upon elements of spectacle are a clear function of the crisis in the relation of image and word born of the Reformation. This crisis, I shall argue in the next chapter, was not one of mere style but had significant theological and epistemological ramifications. Because this crisis, through the charge of idolatry, bears upon the stage in a double way, in the elimination of the traditional biblical theater and in its effect on the self-definition of the secular theater that replaced it, it will be necessary to consider it in some detail. What I intend to show is that this crisis in the relation of image and word involved as well a crisis in the self-understanding of the Christianity that formed Europe's consciousness.

TWO

Word against Image

The Context of Iconoclasm

There is a theologically startling moment in Erasmus' "Paraclesis," the introduction to his *editio princeps* of the Greek New Testament. In his eagerness
for the "philosophy of Christ," presented now in the original language and in
his new Latin translation, Erasmus goes so far as to wonder whether the Christ
portrayed in the printed gospels does not live "more effectively" than when he
dwelt among men.[1] For Christ's contemporaries, Erasmus asserts, saw and
heard less than readers may see and hear in the text Erasmus has just edited.
The written gospels "bring you the living image of His holy mind and the
speaking, healing, dying, rising Christ himself, and thus they render Him so
fully present *that you would see less if you gazed upon Him with your very
eyes*" (my emphasis).[2] This startling devaluation of the actual incarnation in
comparison with the textual record of it may not be a fully considered position
of Erasmus. In context it seems rather an expression of the enthusiasm of presenting the first typographical edition of the Greek New Testament to Europe.
But it is an illustration, and a characteristic one at that, of the intensity of Erasmus' conviction that Christ was to be encountered most fully in the word, and
not in any visual, material form.[3]

Erasmus himself was never an actual iconoclast, and he was not unresponsive to visual art. Late in his life he would react with shocked distaste at
the violence and disorder of iconoclasm in Basel.[4] The colloquy *The Godly
Feast* (1522) shows a sensitivity to artistic decoration, and the host of the
feast, Eusebius, points out a statue of Christ in his garden and various frescoes
of religious and secular topics, including moralized portrayals of natural history. But even this example may confirm Erasmus' suspicion of visual devotion, for included in the colloquy is a criticism of richly decorated churches,
and part of the point of the decoration of Eusebius' villa may be that it is a private house, not a church; the paintings indeed are meant for instruction and
meditation, not veneration. Moreover, many of the pictures "speak" in verbal

labels painted beneath, frequently trilingually in Latin, Greek, and Hebrew; visual images are thereby mediated by learned verbal accompaniment. Elsewhere, Erasmus shows himself suspicious of the devotional use of art and offers the opinion that it would be preferable to have no images but the crucifix in churches.

A similarly revealing moment in this contest of word and image occurs in Erasmus' catechism for adults. The student in the dialogue wonders whether the implication in the second commandment (in the pre-Reformation ordering) that honor should be given to the *name* of God might not conflict with the prohibition of idolatry in the first commandment.[5] For a word naming God is as much a created thing as an image, and in honoring a word one may perhaps be giving idolatrous worship to a human object. The master, Erasmus' spokesman, answers this easily: one does not bow one's head or knees to the word or to the voice of man, but to Him whom the word signifies; a word is an arbitrary sign, nothing like the thing represented, and there is no peril that a word should be taken for that which it represents. It is necessary, moreover, that God should be declared, and for this use speech was given to humanity. But one of the traditional defenses of images, expressed for example by Reginald Pecock, the fifteenth-century English theologian, was precisely the same: the veneration of an image is meant for, and passes to, the person represented, and no sane person would actually believe the image is the same as the person it portrays.[6] Later, Thomas More, while not addressing himself to his friend's argument, would stand Erasmus' position on its head: if we agree to revere the verbal symbol for God, it is illogical to fear idolatry in revering visual symbols.[7] In both cases, he insists, the human mind has the power to distinguish between the signifiers it creates and the signified, even when the mode of signification, as in the case of the image, involves visual resemblance. In the case of Erasmus' argument, a sophisticated understanding of the verbal mode of signification may appear to result in a kind of almost wilful misunderstanding of the visual. There is implicit in his position a recognition that response to the image differs in a significant way from response to the word—that, as David Freedberg insists, the image tends to efface difference and fuse the relation of signifier to signified.[8] Here it would appear that Erasmus' promotion of transformative new modes of verbal representation, particularly typographic, tends to a rejection of the other visual modes. In regard to Erasmus' logocentrism, Marjorie O'Rourke Boyle notes the changed emphasis in the modes of representation: "The religious pedagogy of the medieval centuries, which relied on the visual image, is succeeded by the humanist doctrine of the published text. . . . The humanist persuasion that an eloquent text orates reality expands in Erasmus to a lively faith in the real presence of Christ as text."[9] For Erasmus—and for humanism more generally—"Christ as text" replaces the painted, sculpted Christ. For succeeding reformers Christ's real presence as text would also eclipse his real presence in the visible, tactile Eucharist.

What lies behind this comparatively sudden shift from visual, sensible, "incarnational" modes of late-medieval religious experience to the logocentric modes of the 1520s and 1530s? Why for Erasmus and the humanist reformers who follow him does "Christ as text" replace the sacramental Christ, the visualized Christ, who a decade before had been the focus of devotion? In a comparatively short period of time, and in much of Europe, attitudes would shift so dramatically that what had before been created by highly developed artistic expression would, a few years later, be destroyed as a religious abomination. A full answer to this question will require a survey of the challenges to representation from late antiquity to the sixteenth century and the ways those challenges responded to and in turn shaped varying conceptions of the incarnation. Some Reformation scholarship has seen a bland inevitability in the iconoclasm that emerged so suddenly in the 1520s and in the upheaval of Europe's religious structures, as if these modes of understanding the sacred fell simply of their own weight and metamorphosed into something reassuringly like our own. This scholarship has frequently contented itself with the explanations given by the contemporary proponents of iconoclasm, without seeing the strangeness of this sudden change in perceptual and aesthetic habits as well as in religious attitudes. I want to suggest that the reasons are more complex in their intellectual dimensions—and at the same time perhaps simpler in the way they correspond both to psychological changes that accompanied the altered technologies for representing language and thought and in the perceptual habits that had to respond to those changes.

I

The best-known pre-Reformation challenge to images in Western Christianity came at the end of the sixth century when Serenus, bishop of Marseilles, removed and destroyed images in a church to prevent their worship. Gregory the Great commended his concern about idolatry, but forbade the removal and destruction of images. In doing so, he established what would become the classic defense of the use of images in the West: "For pictures are used in churches so that those who are unlettered at least may read upon the walls what they cannot read in books." Their instructive, non-idolatrous use should be encouraged so that the illiterate may have a source of knowledge of history.[10] This defense of images, though it would prevail in the Western church, remained theoretically underdeveloped. One difficulty is that it is essentially negative; it sees images as supplying a deficiency, but it does not argue that they may have a positive position among all worshippers. Presumably the literate do not need images; should they therefore not use them? Another difficulty is that it fails to address the affective character of the image and the hold that it may have, legitimately or not, on the viewer's imaginative powers. In what precisely does idolatry consist? Gregory's defense makes no mention of a concern that the illiterate were unable to make the distinction between image and prototype. Did such a concern lie behind Serenus' iconoclastic impulse?

In the East the more serious challenge in the series of iconoclastic controversies of the eighth and ninth centuries would stimulate a more subtle and theoretically developed defense. Stephen Gero has called these controversies "an undeniable foreshadowing of some aspects of the Protestant Reformation."[11] And indeed at their peak in the 760s and 770s the attacks against images extended also, almost inevitably one may feel, to the doctrine of the intercession of the saints and the cult of relics. It is worth considering how the theory of the image is here more fully developed and articulated because it is precisely what in the European Middle Ages would underlie the understanding of images and their use but remain largely unformulated. The origins of the Iconoclast Controversy remain obscure. This comes in large part from the fact that each side was so thorough in its attack. The iconoclasts began by destroying all the icons they could find, in fact leaving very little for art historians to study; when the iconophiles in turn triumphed at the Second Nicean Council in 787, they confiscated all iconoclast literature, so that only citations in iconophile treatises preserve their opponents' arguments.[12] Nevertheless, it appears evident that issues of power between church and ruler were involved, that one element of the conflict lay in the fact that images represented a locus of power that could be either centered upon the empire and its ruler or diffused in the worship of the church. At the same time the great external threat to Byzantine society lay in the forces of iconoclastic Islam. While scarcely a cause, it may well be that the Islamic confrontation helped precipitate the crisis in the Christian empire.[13] In any case, in the explicit terms in which it was fought, the controversy became a contest over the interpretation of the central doctrine of Christianity, the incarnation—and in a way similar, I want to suggest, to the way it would be contested in the Reformation. Though narrowly focused on the role of images in worship and devotion, it embraced the key issues of Christology that had preoccupied Christianity in the early centuries, particularly the way in which the humanity of Christ was to be understood.[14]

John of Damascus (who died before 754) and Theodore of Studios (759–826) are the important theorists of this relation between the incarnation and visual representation. John first applied to images the distinction made by St. Augustine between the worship owed to God alone (λατρεία, in Latin, *latria*) and that accorded to other human beings (προσκυνησίς, *proskynesis*, literally "bowing down," or δουλεία, in Latin, *dulia*), a distinction accepted by the Second Nicean Council in 787.[15] But more significant is the revaluation of the visible and material world that he constructs from his understanding how the incarnation decisively alters humanity's relation to the divine. He historicizes the prohibition of idolatry by arguing that before the incarnation the immeasurable, uncircumscribed, invisible God could never be depicted; hence, John believes, came the prohibition of idolatry. But now that God has taken human nature and human flesh and has conversed with human beings, it is possible to make an image of the God who has been seen. It is at this point that John makes use of the *latria/dulia* distinction. "I do not *worship* matter; I *worship* the Creator of matter who became matter for my sake, who willed to take his abode in matter; who worked out my salvation through matter. Never will I cease *honoring* the matter which wrought my salvation! I *honor* it, but not as God. . . . Because of this I salute all remaining matter with reverence, because God has filled it with His grace and power."[16] To despise images because they are material things is to fall into the Manichaeism of despising what God has not only created but hallowed by entering. Since the divine nature has assumed human nature, a permanent change has been effected in the latter, even in its corporeal materiality; in Old Testament law a dead body was considered unclean, but now the body of a Christian saint is honored in death.[17] Because the Word became flesh he is like other men in everything but sin and "partakes of our nature without mingling or confusion." The corollary for John of Damascus is that "He has deified our flesh forever, and has sanctified us by surrendering His Godhead to our flesh without confusion."

Theodore takes the relation of Christ's incarnation to physical representation one step further. He believes that the transformation of human corporeality in the incarnation not only makes possible but *requires* representation.[18] It is evident that John, perhaps responding as well to an attack on the cult of the saints, is concerned not just with the narrow question of why images should be allowed but with the larger implications for the relation of the divine to the visible and the physical. The incarnation is not limited to one moment in history and to the single human/divine person of Christ, but spills over, as it were, into all subsequent time and in a particular way into the martyrs and saints who have imitated him. Quoting Romans 8:17, John calls the saints "heirs of God and co-heirs with Christ" who will also share in the divine glory. Shall they not also, he asks, receive a share of glory from the church on earth? "In struggling against evil they have shed their blood; they have imitated Christ who shed his Blood for them by shedding their blood for Him."[19] The incarnation thus becomes for John, and generally for Eastern Christianity, a permanent element of the human economy, transforming human possibility as well as human corporeality.

Neither John of Damascus nor Theodore of Studios allow any sharp distinction between word and icon in their understanding of the image.[20] For John the written word and material objects are equally "images." God had the law engraved on tablets of stone and desired that the lives of the patriarchs be recorded; similarly, he commanded that sacred objects, like the jar of manna and Aaron's staff, be kept in the ark for memorial purposes.[21] The spoken word seems equally to partake of this sense of the image, for he notes that a sermon, "by the art of rhetoric," memorializes saints or the acts of God just as the painter does with his brush. Theodore accuses his iconoclast opponents of illogic when they object that images portray Christ's human humility although he is now in glory. Why not, he asks, also forbid the telling of the story, that is, the writing and reading of the Gospels, since they also recount his humility?[22] Word and visual image portray with equal legitimacy, he insists, the memory of the human incarnation of Christ. John also understands images as essential to human psychology. Since humans are fashioned of body and soul, the soul depends upon the physical; humans cannot think without images, just as they must physically listen to perceptible words to understand spiritual things. So also bodily sight raises the believer to spiritual contemplation.[23] The Old Testament made the intangible nature of God accessible to human understanding by clothing it in form and making it available through verbal images. "A certain perception takes place in the brain, prompted by the bodily senses, which is then transmitted to the faculties of discernment and adds to the treasury of knowledge something that was not there before." The "eloquent Gregory," John notes, warns that the mind which is determined to ignore corporeal things "will find itself weakened and frustrated."[24]

None of this positive account of the visual, material world, or of the human body, would be developed in the West until the twelfth century, and even then it would not be articulated explicitly in terms of representation and the image. The Iconoclastic Controversy was replayed, briefly and inconclusively but with some consequences for the Reformation, at the court of Charlemagne in the early ninth century.[25] This occurred after the Council of Frankfort (794) rejected the conclusions both of the iconoclastic Council of Hiereia (754) and of the Second Nicean Council (787). It appears in part that the Carolingian theologians, working in Latin, misunderstood the conclusions of Nicea, which had been badly translated; the distinction between *latreia* and *proskynesis* or *doulia* had not been understood for lack of Latin equivalents. It is likely that differing traditions of liturgy and devotion in the West also played a part. The *Libri Carolini*, which stated the Frankish position, adopted an intermediate position between iconoclasm and the veneration of icons practiced in the East: while the iconoclasts, it asserted, were mistaken to assume that all images were idols, the iconophiles were wrong to insist on the adoration (*adoratio*) of images. If this represented a misunderstanding of *doulia*, it also reflects the practice of the Western Church in which the veneration of images was not an established feature of worship. Images rather were to serve as ornaments of churches and as means of memorializing Christ and the saints. This clearly has more in common with Gregory the Great's position than with the more developed theoretical speculations over the incarnation of the Eastern theologians. In all likelihood, the Carolingian theologians were entirely unaware of this theorizing, which had not been translated and for which there was no equivalent in the Western Church. Rosamond McKitterick notes that while the Carolingians used painting in their manuscripts, it was, finally, a culture in which the text was primary and the written word was considered "more reliable, more truthful, more unambiguous."[26]

II

The Gregorian and Nicean defenses of images would remain largely effective in the Western Church until the fifteenth century. In tracing medieval instances of opposition to images in the Western Church, W. R. Jones concludes that they were isolated attacks by religious radicals on a system of devotion which most Europeans found emotionally and doctrinally satisfying.[27] Even the Lollardy of England in the late fourteenth and early fifteenth centuries would not significantly contravene such a judgment, for its practical consequences, in terms of its actual effect on worship and modes of devotion, were limited. Nevertheless, Lollard opposition to religious representation, as the most serious challenge to images in Europe prior to the Reformation, deserves serious consideration, not least because the English Reformers would see precedent for many of their own practices and attitudes in Lollardy. Whether or not the movement prepared the way for the Reformation in England to any serious extent, scholars have understood some degree of historical connection between the two. But more importantly for my argument, significant analogies exist between Lollard opposition to images and Reformation iconoclasm, in particular because tensions between image and word become evident in each period. Because the Lollard movement—as well as the social and political conditions surrounding it—has left more secure traces than Byzantine iconoclasm, it is possible to understand something of the way in which anxieties about images are bound up in changing attitudes toward, and uses of, language. In both the Lollard movement and the Reformation, altering social contexts for verbal understanding and new structures of verbal representation combine to bring on a crisis in the status of the image.

Though they disagree on nearly every aspect of it, historians are persuaded that a significant increase in literacy in England occurred from the second half of the fourteenth through the fifteenth century. How great the increase was, how it can be measured, even what literacy means in this period all remain indeterminate. A century later, in 1533, Thomas More estimated that between 50 and 60 percent of the English could read: "people farre more than four partes of all the whole dyvyded into tenne, could never read englysche yet."[28] While some historians have seen this as optimistic, others have judged it useful evidence. F. R. H. Du Boulay has estimated a 30 percent rate of literacy in the fifteenth century.[29] Literacy certainly was greater in the commercial centers. In a sampling of 116 male Londoners who gave evidence in consistory court between 1467 and 1476, Silvia Thrupp found a 40 percent rate of Latin literacy; on this basis she suggests a vernacular reading literacy of 50 percent among London laymen in 1470.[30] By contrast, Jo Ann Hoeppner Moran guesses at an overall rate of 15 percent for Northern England and a 13 to 14 percent rate for the laity there. From the evidence of wills, she believes that most members of the nobility and gentry were literate in the fourteenth century; by the end of the fifteenth century "literacy had become more common at the middle level of lay society and was not altogether absent even among the very poor."[31] While all estimates have a large element of uncertainty about them, there is a general agreement that literacy for all classes was increasing in England in the period from the late fourteenth through the early sixteenth century.

The significance for visual representation of this expanded access to texts lies in the central Western defense of images, that they were the books of the illiterate. What would this definition mean for those who were newly literate or had texts opened to them by intimates who had become literate? One potential reaction must have been an impulse to reject the substitute in favor of the real thing. This reaction is reflected in the first of fifteen objections to images and pilgrimages answered by Reginald Pecock in his *Repressor*. The Lollards had insisted that since images served as "remembrauncis" of God's mercies and punishments, of Christ's life and passion, and of the lives of the saints, and that since these benefits may be had through Scripture, written accounts of the saints, as well as devotional literature, images, and pilgrimages were superfluous and therefore dispensable. To the expected reaction that not all people could read, they answered that "alle men and wommen in her yongthe" should be taught to read in their native language.[32] Another reaction must have been to critique the image on the basis of knowledge of the text, a reaction that can be seen in a Lollard discussion of images and pilgrimages: "sith thes ymagis ben bokis of lewid men to sture them on the mynde of Cristis passion, and techen by her peyntur, veyn glorie that is hangid on hem [is] an opyn errour ayenus Cristis gospel."[33] Any image that is so adorned should be burned or put away, "as bokis shulden be yif they made mencion and taughten that Crist was naylid on the crosse with thus mych gold and silver and precious clothis, as a breeche of gold endentid with perry [i.e., decorated with precious stones], and schoon of silver and a croune frettid ful of precious iewelis; and also that Ion Baptist was clothid with a mantil of gold and golden heer as sum men peynten hym." So too images of the apostles and other saints, who lived in poverty and penitence and despised the vanity of worldly life, should be destroyed if they portray them in settings of pomp and wealth. For men portray the saints as living the same worldly lives they themselves lead, entirely falsifying the saints' lives in order to comfort themselves. "And by this falsnesse sclaunderen thei Crist and his seyntis, and bryngen the symple puple in errour of bileve, and to waste temporal godis and leeve dedis of charite to her pore neyeboris that ben nedy and miysese, made to the ymage and lickenesse of God, and so make the puple to breke the heestis of God for her owne wynnyngis." That the Gregorian defense was a two-edged sword that could also be turned back against images is shown as well in a tract that summarized Lollard charges:

> Though ymages maad truli that representen verili the povert and the passioun of jhesu crist and othere seyntis, ben leful & the bokis of lewid men bi gregori and othere doctouris, netheles false ymages that representen worldli glorie & pride of the world as if crist and othere seyntis hadden lyvid thus and deservid blisse bi glorie & pompe of the world ben false bokis and worthy to ben amendid or to be burnt, as bokis of opin errour or of opin eresie agens cristene feith.[34]

There are, perhaps, two possible consequences of such a critique. One would be a rejection of artistic idealization, portrayals of Christ and the Virgin enthroned in glory and surrounded by a heavenly court of saints, in favor of intensely realistic portrayals of the Gospel events—the humility of the nativity, the suffering Christ, the pietà. And such is, of course, the direction taken by much Northern European art, best known in the work of Flemish painters of the fifteenth and sixteenth centuries. The other would be a rejection of images altogether (with the possible exception of "a pore crusifix, by the cause to have mynde on the harde passioun and bittere deth that Crist suffrid wilfully for the synne of man"[35]) in favor of a greater verbal knowledge of the scriptures. This is the direction taken by Lollardy, with the consequence that the "image and likeness of God" to which one's offerings should be made is not the material fabric of the church but the bodies of the poor, a theme repeated over and over in Lollard critiques of images.[36] The poor are the "quicke ymages of God," as opposed to the "dede stones and rotun stokkis" of artistic representation.

To assert the role of literacy in this Lollard critique of images, however, is only half the story of verbal transformation in the period. The other factor, obviously related, was a new medium for religious discourse, indeed virtually a new technology of communication: English prose. Literacy *and* the use of the written vernacular in religious discourse, though not coterminous with the Lollard heresy, become virtually inseparable from it. By the middle of the fifteenth century any use of the vernacular in a religious text could draw suspicion; one of the ironies of this situation is that Reginald Pecock, the learned Oxford opponent of the Lollards, would himself arouse suspicion and be charged with error because of his decision to do battle with the Lollards on their own ground, in English prose.[37] Anne Hudson notes that Lollard texts used the vernacular for the discussion of theological and political topics in ways that had not been attempted since the days of Aelfric in the tenth century.[38] The English vernacular was achieving a new status generally in the second half of the fourteenth century. In 1362 the Parliament agreed that pleadings in the King's courts should be made in English. The earliest surviving English deed dates from 1376, the earliest English will from 1387. The first surviving English letters are dated 1392–1393; after this letters in English become common.[39] In 1362 Ranulph Higden had complained in his *Polychronicon* that English children, "ayenst the usage and manere of alle othere naciouns," were forced to leave their native language and construe their Latin grammar in French; when John Trevisa came to translate Higden's book into English in 1385, he could add that "now . . . in alle gramere scoles of Englond, children leveth Frensche and construeth and lerneth an Englisch."[40] Although the language of Richard's court continued to be Anglo-Norman French, English was coming to be used more and more in aristocratic circles. In 1394 Archbishop Thomas Arundel noted in his funeral sermon for Richard's queen, Anne of Bohemia, that although she was not herself English, she was happy to have the four Gospels to read in English. But perhaps the most telling indication of the political status of English came in 1377 when the Lord Chancellor warned Parliament that the French were preparing for war and that, with the Spanish and Scots, the French "make us surrounded on all sides so that [they] can destroy our lord the king and his realm of England, and drive out the English language." This threat to English was repeated again in the Merciless Parliament of 1388.[41] Increasing numbers of people commissioned vernacular books in the late fourteenth century, copies both of newly written works and of translations into the vernacular.[42]

Though biblical translation into English is not new with the Wycliffites—

since the thirteenth century there had been numerous metrical versions, mainly paraphrases and summaries, of individual books of the Bible—what is new is that the two Wycliffite versions are complete and that they attempt to render the text literally by means of English prose. Indeed the literalness of the first version has been a puzzle to scholars. At times it is so literal as to be virtually unintelligible without recourse to the Latin original. The later version, which is partly a revision of the first (though in some respects independent of it), translates with far more regard for English idiom but also with a continuing concern for precise rendering of the Vulgate, not simply paraphrase.[43] Importantly for my argument, the prologue to this version speaks of translation itself as a new, unfamiliar, and somewhat complex technology, something that needs not only rhetorical justification but considerable technical explanation as well:

> First it is to knowe that the best translating is, out of Latyn into English, to translate aftir the sentence and not oneli aftir the wordis, so that the sentence be as opin either openere in English as in Latyn, and go not fer fro the lettre; and if the lettre mai not be suid in the translating, let the sentence evere be hool and open, for the wordis owen to serve to the entent and sentence, and ellis the wordis ben superflu either false. In translating into English, manie resolucions moun make the sentence open, as an ablatif case absolute may be resolvid into these thre wordis, with convenable verbe, *the while, for, if,* as gramariens seyn; as thus *the maistir redinge, I stonde,* mai be resolvid thus, *while the maistir redith, I stonde,* either *if the maistir redith,* etc., either *for the maisti*r, etc.; and sumtyme it wolde acorde wel with the sentence to be resolvid into *whanne,* either into *aftirward,* thus, *whanne the maistir red, I stood,* either *aftir the maistir red, I stood*; and sumtyme it mai wel be resolvid into a verbe of the same tens, as othere been in the same resoun, and into this word *et,* that is, *and* in English, as thus *arescentibus hominibus prae timore,* that is *and men shulen wexe drie for drede.*[44]

The translator then goes on to discuss the translation of participles, relative pronouns, the allowable repetition in English of a word given just once in the Latin, the adverbs *autem* and *vero,* and the need to alter Latin syntax to achieve proper English idiom. Translation from Latin into English, clearly, is not a familiar activity, not one in which *anything* may be taken for granted. And yet, the writer insists, it is an essential process. Christ commanded that the gospel be preached in all the world. "Also Crist seith of the Iewis that crieden Osanna to him in the temple that, though thei were stille, stoonis shulen crie, and by stoonis he understondith hethen men that worshipiden stoonis for her goddis. And we Englische men ben comen of hethen men, therefore we ben understonden by these stoonis, that shulden crie hooly writ." Though covetous clergy may despise and attempt to hide the scriptures, "yit the lewid puple crieth aftir holi writ, to kunne it, and kepe it with greet cost and peril of here lif."[45]

Promotion of the vernacular and opposition to images and pilgrimages go hand in hand as the two most consistent hallmarks of Lollardy.[46] Are they related in some intrinsic way? Similarly to what I argued above on the question of literacy and images, the use of the vernacular allowed the "lewid," whether literate or not, some entry into the essential narratives of Christianity independent of the *biblia pauperum* of religious art. It gave them then access to a mode of knowing that had been the traditional privilege of the learned, the clergy. Such access may well have seemed all the more attractive and necessary in view of the anticlericalism that underlay much Lollardy. At the same time, because of the more explicit communicative power of language, verbal formulas and verbal narratives may have seemed to offer more certain and precise understanding than the less determinate modes of meaning in visual art. This is not to deny the relevance of the social critique connected to the attack on images, that it was better to make offerings for the relief of God's image reflected in the poor than to cause images to be painted or sculpted; as Aston notes, this radical critique and the ways it was carried out bring us "near the heart of what much Lollardy was about" (p. 126). But even this appears to come of a new and direct encounter with the texts of the Gospels themselves; frequently these texts are used to critique what is felt to be contemporary abuse. Similarly, the attack on images is based on literal readings of the second commandment and other Old Testament attacks on idolatry. The heady newness of this encounter with the Bible in the native tongue, and with vernacular religious discourse generally, appears to fuel much of what was most powerful in Lollardy. The attack on images seems intimately bound up with, indeed a consequence of, this alteration in the linguistic sphere.

III

This sense of opposition between verbal and visual modes will reappear a century later in the more forceful and decisive iconoclasm of the Reformation. In order to understand why the Lollard challenge to images was comparatively ineffective and why the sixteenth-century opposition achieved such widespread diffusion so quickly, it is important to understand the systemic character of late-medieval Christianity, then what assailed that system so powerfully in the Reformation. While Lollardy was, of course, a significant challenge to religious authority in early fifteenth-century England, its spread was geographically limited. But more importantly, it ran counter to a general religious culture in which worship and devotion tended strongly toward physical manifestation—the sacramental system of the Church, elaborate ceremonials, processions, pilgrimages, devotions to the saints and veneration of their relics, painting and sculpture, and a vigorous tradition of religious drama. Much of this expression can be seen as interlocking. The cult of the saints was tied to vivid interest in relics, for example; the cult of relics in turn fostered pilgrimages, the object of which was the sight of the saint's bones and the richly decorated tomb that held them. When shrines of the Virgin became the major centers of pilgrimage, as they did in the late Middle Ages, it was usually an image that provided the focus of devotion.[47] The cult of the saints also went hand in hand with the development, particularly in the fifteenth century, of vividly rendered paintings and statues. The interconnectedness of these various elements rests on the new understanding of the humanity of the incarnate Christ that came in what has been called the philosophical and theological renaissance of the twelfth century. I shall describe this movement in more detail in the following chapter when I argue that the impetus for theater itself came of the new concern for corporeality of which these developments were part. This revaluation of Christ's humanity underlay the way in which religious experience would come to valorize materiality and the physical expression of spiritual concerns. The most significant doctrinal focus of this revaluation was the declaration of the Fourth Lateran Council in 1215 that, in the consecration of the mass, the Eucharist becomes substantially the body and blood of Christ under the appearances of bread and wine. In 1264 Pope Urban IV lent the doctrine devotional support by instituting the feast of Corpus Christi to celebrate the bodily presence of Christ. Interest in the body of Christ was not, of course, limited to this sacramental expression; over the next three centuries the portrayal of the body of Christ would stand at the center of European art. This focus on the humanity of Christ spilled over, in a sense, into the cult of the saints, those human beings understood to have followed him with extraordinary fidelity and to have become in turn mediators of the divine presence. In late medieval practice for the dedication of an altar, even in a parish church, it became obligatory for it to contain the relic of a martyr.[48] As the symbolic enactment of Christ's sacrifice on Calvary, the mass would thus be performed over or near the remains of a martyr who had in his own death reenacted this sacrifice. This association of relics with the Mass implies an imaginative understanding that theology would not fully articulate—and perhaps could not endorse—that the martyred saint in some way became a participant in Christ's redemption. The effect of this renewed emphasis on the humanity of Christ is what may be called an *incarnational* sense of religious experience, a mode of apprehension and an aesthetic in which the spiritual is incarnated in forms immediately accessible to human senses and emotions. The fifteenth-century devotional painting of Northern Europe illustrates this most clearly; events in the life of Christ or in the lives of the Virgin and saints are portrayed in such a way as to render them accessible to immediate emotional experience. The sorrow on the face of the Virgin in a deposition from the cross is that of a mother who has lost her son, and the vividness of the painted image conveys that with psychological immediacy, the visual seeming to bypass verbal expression in its effect. A similar religious aesthetic, uniting the visual and the verbal, is apparent in the enacted emotions of the characters in the vernacular religious drama.

Clearly visual experience plays a central role in this incarnational sense of the necessary linkage of the spiritual with the material. Visual worship of the Eucharist, which would so deeply trouble the reformers, is a striking feature of late-medieval sacramental devotion. To *see* the host became a principal concern of worshippers and in cities the devout would sometimes go from church to church to witness the elevation as often as possible. Glass chalices

were called for so that the laity might also see the wine which had been conse-
crated the blood of Christ. The practice of elevating the host, making it visible
to the congregation, became widespread in public worship about the middle of
the thirteenth century.[49] The monstrance, for displaying the host, came into
use in the following century. The widespread use of visual images is of course
one of the most characteristic elements of the religious culture of the fourteenth and fifteenth centuries, a use that goes far beyond their function as a
biblia pauperum and is integral to the devotional structures of high and low, as
well as of lay and clerical, elements of society. Vision in fact was philosophi-
cally the most privileged of the senses.[50] For St. Bonaventure light is the
prime element of creation and underlies all of sense perception. In its purity it
is apprehended by the sense of sight; when mixed with air it becomes sound,
with vapor it becomes odor, with liquid taste, with earth touch. Light is also
the central metaphor for all human knowledge: God is the source of light,
himself invisible but becoming visible in the incarnation.[51] As Otto von Simson argues, a theology of light was the theoretical foundation of the luminos-
ity that characterizes the gothic architecture of Northern Europe.[52] Basing itself on the Gospel of John, the theology identified the light of Christ with the
divine creative force. Thus what had earlier been painted or portrayed in mosaic in the image of the Christos Pantocrator was given new symbolic expression in the light that literally enlightens the world imaged in the church's
physical structure. Gothic cathedrals and monastery churches, moreover, were
conceived according to geometric principles by which the architects understood they were imitating the Creator; using such principles, they believed
they were applying the very laws that order heaven and earth. In this way the
building would not only become a model of the cosmos in its imitation of the
order of the visible world, but would express an image of the perfection of the
spiritual world. The fabric of the material church could thereby portray the
spiritual church, the universal church, or mystical body of Christ, that encompasses heaven and earth and extends in time from the creation to the last judgment.[53] The system of relation, then, between the spiritual and the physical,
between the divine and the human, was materialized and made visible
throughout the fabric of the church, to be experienced not only in the stone,
glass, and wood, but in the light and space and in what was felt to be the struc-
tural perfection of such a building.

I have emphasized the systematic character of late-medieval religion and
its rationale in the incarnation that was central to its self-understanding because modern scholarship has frequently tended to see the causes of the Reformation in what it has taken to be the excesses of medieval practice. The underlying notion is that late-medieval religion fell of its own weight, that the
practices of "popular religion," such as the reverencing of relics, pilgrimages,
and devotions that seem superstitious to modern rationalism, must have
evoked, sooner or later, the opposition that came in the Reformation. From
this perspective, there seems, then, a kind of inevitability in the rejection of
images, a reaction to what is judged the simple excess of their use. Carlos M.
N. Eire, for example, begins his valuable study of German, Swiss, and French

iconoclasm by employing the metaphor of an earthquake fault in which building pressure causes the destruction that follows:

> Like some impressive city perched on a quivering fault line, the edifice of
> late medieval religion rested on shaky ground. Beneath the deceptively calm
> and firm exterior, a complex series of imperceptible movements were build-
> ing up pressure, mounting strain to the breaking point. Though some con-
> temporaries may have felt minor tremors, or suspected that major quake was
> long overdue, no one could predict when and where disaster would strike, or
> how much damage would be done.[54]

In this reading of causes, the excesses of popular devotion, resting on a naive
literalism of belief that is unchecked or even encouraged by ecclesiastical authorities, grew until they provoked the expected reaction by the rational, purifying forces of the Reformation. These forces oppose what is seen as the superstitious, half-magical elements of popular Catholic piety. But in the period
there is no evidence, aside from occasional cautions against the excesses of
pilgrimages and relic-mongering, that the educated did not derive equal satisfaction from modes of worship and devotion in which the visual and the sensible played an important part. Princes and churchmen, as well as the humble,
made pilgrimages. Even Erasmus made at least one pilgrimage to Walsingham, where a statue of the Virgin was the focus of devotion, perhaps before
his attitude toward pilgrimages, relics, and the cult of the saints took a negative turn.[55] In England the veneration of images and the cult of the saints was
defended against the Lollards by such learned theologians as Pecock and Walter Hilton. And aside from the austere Cistercians, monastery churches were
not less given to visual elaboration than cathedral or parish churches, and indeed they were more likely than the latter to possess important relics. The difference, if there is one, is more a matter of the understanding of the theological underpinnings than a basic disagreement about the forms of religious
expression. But even such differences of understanding should not be over-
stated. The study by Victor and Edith Turner of modern centers of pilgrimage
has found that even among the poor and unlettered there is a surprising knowledge of the basic theology of images and pilgrimage.[56] Rather than a split between sophisticated and illiterate believers, it is altogether more probable that
a community of understanding existed, that in this period as well as in the Reformation, the learned instructed the unlearned. Moreover, most of the testimony about the excess, and about the naivety and superstition that accompany
it, comes from its contemporary critics, beginning with Erasmus and continuing into the polemics of the Reformers themselves. What we have, then, is a
situation analogous to that of the Byzantine Iconoclast Controversy. There
the iconophile victors destroyed the arguments of the iconoclasts, so that modern understanding of the latter is limited to their refutation by the iconophiles.
In the case of the Reformation, the iconophile arguments were not destroyed,
but a continuity of the logocentric tendencies inherent in Renaissance humanism and the Reformation so ties our own scholarship to that period that only
with some effort can the necessary skepticism be maintained toward the pole-

mical exaggeration unleashed in the conflict. In order to find some intimation of the psychological penetration of the late medieval sensibility, modern sensibility needs to turn rather to the art that survived iconoclasm and attempt to see its meanings and purposes. What we discover there are attitudes and perspectives different from our own, but not at all equivalent to "superstition."[57]

When iconoclasm begins in the 1520s, it is with such suddenness and intensity that there is no question of checking abuses and reforming excesses. It is directed against the entire *system* of worship and devotion and aims to replace it with a radically different system based on verbal structures. The seemingly disparate Reformation challenges to images, relics, the cult of the saints, liturgical ceremony, sacraments, the real presence in the Eucharist, and religious theater are themselves interconnected by their underlying target, the incarnational structure of late-medieval religion. Though they did not always express it as such, it is against a *system* that the reformers would formulate their attack. It should be apparent that these challenges must be understood as aimed ultimately at more than the superficial elements of religious expression—that behind them, as in the Iconoclast Controversy of the eighth and ninth centuries, lay the question of how God is to be experienced. Is the divine to be understood as continually incarnated through sacralized elements of the human and physical world? Does the incarnation of Christ, as John of Damascus thought, so decisively transform the phenomenal world that it may provide access to the sacred? Or is it idolatrous to seek the divine in the physical, the Creator in the creature? Is the incarnation to be understood as focused in an entirely unique way on the historical period of Christ's life and experienced primarily in language through texts that may be traced back to historical contact with him? Without itself fully articulating the connections, the Reformation would attack the diverse manifestations of the incarnationalism of medieval religion—and so potently that much of the substance of its critique still influences our attempts to understand the iconoclasm, both literal and figurative, that began in the 1520s. At the same time, it should be understood that the theory both of this incarnationalism and of the image were underdeveloped in the West. No body of theory had been developed to explain, either to the period itself or to later centuries, the relation of the image to the incarnation, as occurred some eight centuries earlier in the Eastern Church. The Western Church did not find its John of Damascus or Theodore of Studios to theorize and justify its visual practices.

IV

As a complex social phenomenon, Reformation iconoclasm resists the attempt to trace it to a single, definitive cause. Nevertheless it represents the major moment of conflict between word and image in the West and as such, I want to argue, stems ultimately from the tension between them inherent in the religious culture. What transformed this tension into outright conflict—and causes it to differ significantly from the Lollard challenge a century earlier—

was the logocentrism of the humanist program which emerged in the late fifteenth and early sixteenth centuries, a logocentrism that was in turn decisively
empowered by the new technology of print. Printing, of course, was the major
factor in transmitting humanism and transforming it from intellectual fashion
to a movement of far-reaching political and social consequence. Indeed, the
printing press is the technology which separates the limited, unsuccessful reform of Lollardy in England from the Reformation that it so closely resembles
in theoretical aims. New attitudes toward the vernacular and increased literacy, I have argued, were implicated in Lollard opposition to images. Analogous ideas about the status of texts and the significance of language in shaping
political and moral culture were given European-wide currency by a humanism that suddenly found itself able to make and disseminate hundreds of
copies in the approximate time a single copy had previously taken. Printing altered not only the availability of the written word but the very ways in which
Europeans thought and assimilated language. The fact that hundreds of unvarying copies could be made of a single text immensely increased confidence
in the written word.[58] Moreover, the lower prices of printed books meant that
their ownership would no longer be confined to the wealthy, but that even the
bourgeois and yeoman classes could possess them. Whole categories of
printed works, chapbooks, ballads, and the like could be directed to an even
broader social spectrum. The greatest changes, of course, would come in the
availability, the uses, and the understanding of the Bible. It is scarcely a wonder that humanists and Reformers could envision the printing press as a divine
gift, a heaven-descended grace that at once enabled their scholarship and amplified the reach of their pens many times over.

That Reformation opposition to images was inextricably bound up with
the logocentrism of the humanist program is apparent from a brief tracing of
its history. Significantly, Luther's attitude toward the aesthetics of worship, toward visual art and, in particular, toward music, would remain largely positive, while the attitudes of his followers who were more directly influenced by
humanism turned sharply negative. Carl C. Christensen notes that Luther's
early comments on the value of art for worship reflect a certain skepticism but
that by 1522, perhaps in reaction to the first iconoclastic incidents in Wittenburg, he began to view religious art more positively.[59] His consistent position
was to classify religious art among the *adiaphora*, things neither commanded
nor forbidden but that individual Christians were free to use or not. In practice, though, he saw the utility of images to human psychology; he continued
to value the crucifix and images of the Virgin and thought that representations
of biblical scenes had much value. It is no accident that within the Protestantism stemming from Lutheran influence there would remain, as Christensen notes, both incentive and scope for visual art.[60]

It is in Luther's follower, Andreas Bodenstein von Karlstadt, and in the
Swiss reformer Huldrych Zwingli that the Reformation takes an iconoclastic
turn. Both men were heavily influenced by the logocentric theology of Erasmus, which was a potent force in clarifying and making explicit those tendencies toward a word-centered religious culture released by typography. As early

as the *Enchiridion Militis Christiani* (1503) Erasmus critiqued the cult of the saints and the veneration of relics by contrasting the corporeality of traditional devotion with a spirituality formed by the reading of Scripture. What is implicit there would be developed and elaborated throughout his career: the vividness and power of Christ's image as it is discovered in the text of Scripture and a consequent depreciation of the efficacy of the visually-rendered image. Actual iconoclasm in the Reformation begins with Karlstadt, who first transformed the Erasmian critique into an assault, both verbal and actual, on what he understood as the evil—not merely the misguidedness—of medieval devotion.[61] After writing against images through much of 1521, Karlstadt published his influential tract, "On the Abolition of Images," in early 1522. In Luther's absence from Wittenburg, Karlstadt had assumed an authoritative position in the city, and the council agreed to remove images from the churches at a specified time. Before this could occur, a group of citizens, apparently incited by the preaching of Karlstadt and his colleague Gabriel Zwilling, took the matter into their own hands, and iconoclastic rioting ensued in Wittenburg. But Luther's return shortly thereafter put an end to both the illicit and the legally sanctioned iconoclasm at Wittenburg. Karlstadt, though forced to leave the city, continued to develop what Eire calls "a fully revolutionary concept of iconoclastic violence."[62] He taught the necessity for action against "idolatry," even in the absence of official sanction.

It is in Zwingli's career in Zurich that one most fully sees the transformation of Erasmian logocentrism into full iconoclastic expression. Educated in humanist discipline, Zwingli was a thorough-going Erasmian before he became a reformer. He spent two years immersed in the study of Erasmus' works; later he dated his conviction that Christ was the sole mediator between God and man from his reading of Erasmus' devotional poem, "The Complaint of Jesus."[63] Through the rigor and consistency in his attitudes toward the aesthetics of worship, the Erasmian hegemony of word over image becomes cultural fact. Zwingli and Karlstadt set in motion the forces to which Erasmus had most prominently given voice; but all three appear to be indicators, "barometric needles," pointing toward a tendency in the culture toward a word-centered epistemology.

In January 1519 Zwingli began his tenure as "people's priest" in the Great Minster of Zurich in good humanist fashion by giving a series of discourses on the Gospel of Matthew, expounding "the complete plain text without any of the accretions of scholastic interpretation."[64] More discourses on the New Testament followed, based always on the principle of *sola scriptura*. Zwingli began the Reformation in Zurich the same year with an attack on the cult of the saints. Much of what followed—attacks on fasting, clerical celibacy, the mass and the Eucharist, the papacy, and episcopal authority—fit the Lutheran mold, though Zwingli was always careful to insist on his independence from Luther. His first original contribution to the course of the Reformation came in January 1523 when, in the first of his *Sixty-Seven Conclusions* (for public disputation in Zurich), he attacked the use of music in worship. This attack comes in the context of a rigorously logical discussion of prayer, in which he maintains that no prayer can be pleasing to God but that which comes directly from the heart. All choral singing, therefore, artificial and public as it is, cannot be true prayer. He also finds that music is nowhere commanded in Scripture to be part of worship. As might be expected, the real issue is the split between text and music in liturgical performance. One cannot concentrate on the full sense of the words and sing properly; the music divides both performer and listener from verbal content and thus cannot be true prayer.[65] What is fascinating about Zwingli's rejection of music in worship is that he was not a tone-deaf despiser of an art he could not understand or enjoy but, as Garside has shown (pp. 7–26, 73–77), particularly adept in music and able to play a variety of instruments well. Equally significant is how quickly and completely Zurich was convinced of the correctness of Zwingli's rejection of musical worship: a year later, by decree of the ruling council, the organs were silenced, and a year after that Mass was sung for the last time and replaced with an entirely spoken communion service. In 1527 the organs, like the images three years before, were completely removed from the churches and destroyed. Though vocal music was again permitted after 1598, organs would not be returned to the churches of Zurich until well into the nineteenth century.[66]

Zwingli's rejection of images came later in the same year (1523) that he attacked music in worship and seems connected to it; it was the product of the same rigorous logic and scriptural literalism which he had applied to prayer. It is not known whether he was directly influenced by Karlstadt, but the latter exerted some influence on Ludwig Haetzer, who published a tract against images in Zurich just as Zwingli began preaching against them.[67] Zwingli argued that the second commandment (in the Reformation numbering) had forbidden *all* images as idolatrous, and in his prohibition he applied the commandment not only to churches but to all public places and even to private homes.[68] Only visual representations of historic events were excepted, and these could not be placed in churches. Though Zwingli's position on images was not unopposed, the response of the ruling council was even swifter than with music. Within a few weeks it was decreed that all the paintings with moving panels be shut and that no images or reliquaries be carried in procession. Six months later, in June 1524, the removal of all images in churches was ordered. Zwingli and the two other "people's priests" worked with the city architect to supervise the removal of images from all the churches of the city.[69] Every statue was taken down from its niche and broken up, all paintings were detached and burned, all frescoes were chipped off, all crucifixes were removed, and every vessel, image, and votive lamp on the altars was taken down and melted. Even the carved choir stalls were removed and burned. Then the walls were whitewashed. When the operation was completed, a recalcitrant Zuricher who had made his pilgrimage to Compostella said of the Great Minster, "There was nothing at all inside and it was hideous." But Zwingli could exult, "In Zurich we have churches which are positively luminous; the walls are beautifully white!"[70] The Word could now be read and preached with no competition from the idolatrous eye. Zwingli's attitudes toward devotional music and art were, as Garside has argued, part of a comprehensive understanding of worship (pp. 39–43). He aimed to eliminate everything sensual from worship that he could. As such, his own system of religious expression represents a rather precise inversion of the late-medieval system, one in which the word-centered activities of the public reading of and preaching on scripture replaced the ceremonial and the sacramental.

Iconoclasm spread quickly among the Swiss states. Bern followed Zurich in January 1528, St. Gall a month later; Toggenburg abolished images in the fall of that year, and Schaffhausen a year later. Basel experienced some iconoclasm from 1525 and after intense and destructive rioting in February 1529 accepted iconoclast policy as a *fait accompli*. Neuchâtel saw iconoclast riots in October 1530, and within two weeks the Reformed party was victorious and the city swept of its images. A similar but more prolonged struggle occurred in Geneva; after sporadic iconoclasm beginning in 1532, riots in August 1535 decisively accomplished abolishment of images there.[71] In the German lands, cities as far removed from Switzerland as the Hanseatic cities of Stralsund and Braunschweig experienced iconoclasm in 1525 and 1528, respectively. Strassburg saw various acts of iconoclasm beginning in 1524 and finally abolished images in February 1530, apparently responding to the need to ally itself with Zurich and other Swiss cities against the emperor.[72] Patterns of iconoclasm show sufficient complexity that no single explanation can account for its spread. On the one hand, in the early and mid 1520s iconoclast incidents appear to arise in so many places at once—and in places as politically diverse and as far removed as the Swiss states, Hanseatic cities, and English towns—that one is tempted to suspect that psychosocial factors, a kind of iconoclast *zeitgeist*, must have played a part. But while the typical perpetrators of iconoclast incidents and the leaders of iconoclast riots were urban artisans, and it was frequently citizens who pressured the municipal councils for reform, behind both groups were humanist reformers who had been preaching the dangers of idolatry. In this rapid spread of iconoclast sentiment, printing clearly played a major new role. If print culture was a factor in creating the mental climate of humanist logocentrism, it quite clearly had as significant a part in the dissemination both of the Erasmian critique of medieval devotion and of the ideas of Karlstadt, Haetzer, and, most importantly, Zwingli. After Zwingli, and influenced in part by him, Calvin would become the major opponent of images and the entire system of late medieval religion.[73] Remarkable in Calvin's critique, in fact, is his synthetic understanding of the way the image underlies this system; his attacks not only on images themselves but on relics, ceremonies, and the mass are grounded on his understanding that a consistent idolatry underlies the entire structure.[74]

In the actual practice of iconoclasm, quite specific influences can frequently be traced, particularly in the Swiss Reformation. A city's or region's experience of iconoclasm was determined by the character of the Reformation there and by whose ideas predominated. Nuremberg presents a good example of this. Some comparatively minor iconoclastic destruction occurred there in the mid-1520s, but the Lutheran character of its reform checked this and finally preserved most of the city's rich artistic heritage.[75] Scotland provides another example, but in the opposite direction: the influence of Calvin on John

Knox set the extreme iconoclastic direction of the Scottish Reformation. Calvin's influence also predominated in France, and iconoclasm became the policy of the Huguenot leaders in the 1560s.[76] Similarly, it was Calvinist preaching that led to the extraordinary outbreak of iconoclast rioting in the Netherlands in the summer of 1566.[77]

V

In England, the movement toward a fully iconoclastic religious structure would happen with a gradual and stepwise progression typical of the course of the Reformation there, a process in which ironies and reversals are frequently apparent. In *Utopia*, published some twenty years before any officially sanctioned iconoclasm, Thomas More has his Utopians worship in churches which are dark—for "they think that excessive light makes the thoughts wander"— and completely free of images.[78] But this was in 1516, when humanists could still construct their own imaginative worlds free of the possibility that someone would enact them in the parish church. In the next decade More, in his *Dialogue concerning Heresies* (1529; revised in 1531), would become the fierce defender of images, relics, and the cult of the saints against Tyndale and the whole tendency of Reformation iconoclasm. By the end of the 1520s, iconoclast incidents had become common enough in England to arouse official concern. Some of the incidents may have come in response to the preaching of Thomas Bilney, who in 1531, and after a recantation that was itself subsequently recanted, became the first to suffer martyrdom for his iconoclastic views.[79] More effective in the long run was Hugh Latimer, who would gradually move toward a fully iconoclastic position—and toward actual iconoclasm in his own diocese. By 1536, when Latimer, newly named bishop of Worcester, attacked images and relics before Convocation, the political climate was already such that Convocation would readily agree to regulate images more strictly.[80] The beginning of the dissolution of the monasteries that same year can be seen as the first outbreak of widespread iconoclasm in England. The dissolution was obviously the result of numerous political, religious, and economic factors, but that iconoclastic sentiment was prominent among them is indicated by the fate of the buildings and the way the furnishings were discarded. Most of the 650 monastic churches, former images of the heavenly kingdom and symbolic models of the cosmos, were systematically dismantled or allowed to collapse when stripped of their roof lead and timber. Clearly the symbolic system and the habits of perception that had fostered it, while still enjoying considerable support in some quarters, had become seriously attenuated by the late 1530s.[81] A similar indication of these changes appears in the virtual cessation in the building and rebuilding of parish churches in England after the 1520s. The previous century had witnessed a vigorous program of ecclesiastical building, still apparent in the numerous perpendicular gothic parish churches spread throughout England. The construction and renovation continued into the first three decades of the sixteenth century, then abruptly ended. This near general halt in church building would last a century and a half, until the latter half of the seventeenth century.[82]

In a series of steps England would move toward a position of total iconoclasm by the middle of the sixteenth century. Convocation's initial decision in 1536 to regulate images put the Church in a Lutheran-like position of "a qualified acceptance of church imagery," allowing their proper use but cautioning against veneration and the abuse of idolatry. A royal Injunction issued by Thomas Cromwell a month later took a more sharply critical tone toward the question of images, ordering preachers not to "set forth or extol any images, relics, or miracles for any superstition or lucre, nor allure the people by any enticements to the pilgrimage of any saint, otherwise than is permitted in the Articles lately put forth."[83] The following year saw the first injunction which allowed official iconoclasm, though in practice the injunction would prove ambiguous and confusing. Parish clergy were ordered to remove any images which were "abused" by being subject to pilgrimage or offerings, and it was forbidden to use candles before images. While such a directive would clearly give scope to an iconoclastic clergyman, it left open to controversy what an "abused" image might be. But this same year also saw official action against England's most important pilgrimage sites, including the destruction of the Virgin of Walsingham and the shrine of Becket at Canterbury. Still, those of a more radical disposition to abolish images altogether would remain frustrated and unsatisfied through the remainder of Henry's reign.

This changed early in Edward VI's reign under the protectorate of Somerset. Initially, in 1547, the injunction of 1538 was reiterated, with the added directive that clergy were not only to remove but to destroy any "abused" image. A distinction continued to be made between images that were used merely as "remembraunces" and those that were idolatrous, but in practice the distinction was impossible to maintain. In London the iconoclasm was general; the images in St. Paul's and in most of the parish churches were pulled down and broken, and many of the churches were whitewashed. In some respects the royal directive of iconoclasm went beyond Zwingli's Zurich: even stained glass windows were included among the images that could be subject to abuse and therefore could be destroyed, an element Eamon Duffy calls "heavy with portent for the outlawing of all imagery whatsoever."[84] Finally, in February 1548, the Privy Council ordered Archbishop Cranmer to see that *all* images in the churches were removed and destroyed. Officially at least, the process which began legally a decade before—and illegally in the individual acts of destruction some twenty years earlier—must have seemed complete. After Somerset's fall, the order was made statute law in the same bill that established the *Book of Common Prayer*.[85] In some cases, images were withdrawn to be hidden away against the possibility of a future reversal of iconoclast policy, but the more general response was the destruction of statues—their decapitation, as in the Lady Chapel at Ely, or the scratching out of their faces, as in the rood screens at Ranworth (Norfolk) and Southwold (Suffolk), to prevent their recognition. Stone altars, which contained martyrs' relics, were removed and replaced with wooden communion tables. Much stained glass was removed, though often it was saved for want of a clear replacement to keep out the weather. In some cases the word literally effaced the image: frescoes and painted rood screens were whitewashed and then covered with scriptural verses. In the Norfolk church of St. Mary's Priory in Binham, the old painted figures have since become visible beneath the whitewash and texts from Tyndale's New Testament.[86]

The thorough, though temporary, reversal of iconoclast policy in Mary's reign returned such statues and paintings, vestments, candlesticks, vessels, and altars as had been hidden away; ceremonial vessels and vestments that could not be recovered had to be purchased anew.[87] Parishes were ordered to replace their rood lofts, which contained the carved crucifixes and figures of the Virgin and St. John. Catholic ceremonial was restored for a period of time roughly equal to the period in which it had been abolished under Edward. What English men and women thought of this zigzagging in the practices of their parish churches is as impossible to determine as their reactions to the reversal of doctrine and the executions for heresy. At the very least, the altered appearances of things made concrete for them the theological ideas that were swirling about and for which some at least were willing to die.

One final and, as it happened, permanent change awaited them. Elizabeth's accession, after some initial uncertainty, brought a return to the fully iconoclastic policies enacted under Edward. The rood lofts were again removed, and stone altars were replaced with wooden communion tables placed in the nave or the east end of the church. Such statues as had been put back or refashioned were again taken out, candles extinguished, and whitewash again applied. The only visual embellishment allowed was the royal arms above the rood screen where the crucifix had once stood. The speed and the thoroughness with which this was accomplished might vary according to the enthusiasm with which the parish had embraced the original changes and, with them, the Reformation. There was considerable local variation in what iconoclasm accomplished; as Aston notes, there were still enough "idolatrous" survivals of the old devotion in the 1640s to attract "the ferocious attention of Interregnum iconoclasts," not all of them restorations by Laud.[88] But much iconoclasm occurred following Elizabeth's Injunctions of 1559, enough indeed to cause the queen concern that funeral monuments might be defaced in the general zeal to remove images of saints. Elizabeth herself appears to have preferred a more Lutheran policy on images, treating them as *adiaphora* and retaining crucifixes and the rood loft. Much to the consternation of her more iconoclastic bishops, the most influential of whom had sojourned in the purified centers of the Continental Reformation, she retained a crucifix and candles in her private chapel. But given the opinions of these bishops, there was no avoiding a return to the thorough iconoclasm of 1548. In 1561 a volume was published translating four sermons of Calvin insisting that there can be no compromise on the question of images, clearly an attempt to press an uncompromisingly iconoclast policy on the queen.[89] The twenty-second of the Thirty-nine Articles may seem to endorse a return to the Henrician position of

repudiating as "a fond thing" the "worshipping and adoration, as well of images as of relics," rather than forbidding images altogether. But the second of
the Elizabethan *Homilies*, "Against Peril of Idolatry, and superfluous Decking
of Churches," establishes a thoroughly iconoclastic policy.[90] In practice the
only exception to the complete iconoclasm of the Elizabethan church was
stained glass windows. In his *Description of England* William Harrison says
that "the stories in glass windows" were excepted from the general removal of
the monuments of idolatry "for want of sufficient store of new stuff and by
reason of extreme charge that should grow by the alteration of the same into
white panes throughout the realm." Windows were therefore "not altogether
abolished in most places at once but little and little suffered to decay, that
white glass may be provided and set up in their rooms."[91] After the iconoclasm at the beginning of Elizabeth's reign, neglect and the depredations of
covetous gentry later became the nemesis of the church fabric; opposition to
idolatry was a frequent pretense for raiding the ornamentation of country
churches.[92] By some accounts the state of Elizabethan churches was such that
if a Rip van Winkle had returned from the 1520s and 1530s, he might have
suspected that the worshippers had gone collectively blind.

VI

What are the implications of this struggle between what I have described as a
culture of the image and a culture of the word in the sixteenth century? It
should be understood first, I would insist, as primarily a clash between religious systems, one based on an incarnational structure of religious understanding and the other resting on the logocentric assumptions of Renaissance
humanism empowered by print culture. In the case of England the contest
meant the official replacement, though by no means total or unambiguous in
the culture at large, of one system by the other. There, as in much of Northern
Europe, Reformation iconoclasm brought to an end a semiotic and symbolic
field for apprehending and imagining the sacred. What would be gained was
an increasingly sophisticated use of verbal modes of knowing and expressing,
the fruit of which in England would be a religious culture based on the vernacular Bible and on preaching, a culture that finds aesthetic expression, for
example, in the poetry of Donne, Herbert, Vaughan, Marvell, and Milton.[93]
What was lost was a visual aesthetic that had materialized religious concepts
and experience in traditions of painting, sculpture in stone and alabaster, wood
carving, stained glass, and theatrical performance. Recent discussions of
iconoclasm have frequently tended to replicate those of the sixteenth century
in focusing narrowly on the question of idolatry rather than on the total repertoire of response to the visual. Consequently it is important to emphasize that
the art itself was bound up in the hermeneutics of the religious culture;
painters and sculptors were themselves interpreters of the subjects they fash-

ioned. While Renaissance styles had not yet penetrated from Italy into England before the onset of iconoclasm, the engagement with the visual must have been closer to the complexity that Michael Baxandall has described of fifteenth-century Italy.[94] Visual art had become increasingly interpretive and reflective, coming from artists who were active participants in the process of creating meaning. The visual was not simply a means of devotion but an epistemology, a mode of knowing, interpreting, and reflecting upon central understandings of the culture. Artists and their public were collaborators in this process of affective negotiation between the present and the narratives and doctrines of religious tradition.[95]

An important aspect of this visual epistemology was *particularity*. At the center of the iconoclast case that the image itself is worshipped has always been the charge that a particular image commands more devotion than another: because one statue or one painting draws more veneration than others of the same subject, the iconophile defense—that it is not the representation itself that is worshipped but what it represents—cannot be true. But in their work on pilgrimage, Victor and Edith Turner argue that the imaginative energy of the object of pilgrimage is never directed with a kind of pure transference to the signified, but that energy is bound up in the signifier and its history within the culture. Also involved is the historical particularity of the pilgrims themselves and their relation to the object:

> The more particular the form of the symbol-vehicle (and the more attention is paid to its form), the likelier the signifier is to take on a life of its own, apart from its intended or original meaning, or "signified." New significance may then be generated as devotees associate the particularized, personalized image with their own hopes and sorrows as members of a particular community with a specific history. . . . The original signified is not completely replaced, but rather fused with and partially altered by the new signified; or it may coexist with the new as part of a mosaic of meaning. The "new" signified may not in fact be historically new, but may represent a resurgence of archaic ideas and beliefs. It is not idolatrous worship of the signifier at the expense of the signified, that is here in question—as theological polemic has too often asserted. Rather it is the creation of a semantic arena in which a multiplicity of signifieds—original, new, archaic—are for time in conflict.[96]

The Turners' argument that "an area of multivocality," an entire semantic field, stands behind a particular image may not allay the iconoclast suspicion that the material image, in its aesthetic and historic particularity, is itself implicated in the devotion. But such an understanding makes one realize that the terms of the debate, either idolatry pure and simple or a transparent image through which Christ or the saint is apprehended, do not respond to the complexity of the phenomenal process of embodying the sacred. The particularity of a certain image, its history of veneration and its claimed response to the concerns of a community, may give rise to the appearance of elements of magic in its use—that if a certain image is treated in a certain way, the saint represented will respond. But rather than magic, what is at work is response to its multivocality, response to the complex layers of cultural meaning bound up in the object of devotion and its site.

Particularity in fact is one of the hallmarks of late-medieval devotion, one that was a consistent target of humanist and iconoclast attack. Rather than the transcendent, the universal, or the global, late-medieval piety appears to have prized the immanent, the familiar, the local, the idiosyncratic. A painting done for a guild would feature the symbols and patron saint of the guild; donors appear in prayerful devotion at the side of paintings commissioned by families. While some pilgrimage sites were objects of a European-wide veneration, most developed out of a religious devotion that was decidedly local. The Virgin of Walsingham and Becket's shrine at Canterbury were the foci of a particularly English devotion.[97] The cult of the saints itself can be understood to emerge from local particularity. In the early church revered figures became saints for specific communities long before Roman canonization would attempt to centralize and universalize the process. Even then specific and local devotion would remain the norm.[98] A saint was not merely one mediator of God's favor among many, but one who, because his or her life was lived in a particular place or because the relics had come to rest in a particular place, would command the attention and affection of a locale. Patronage of crafts was another powerful sort of particularity. The original reasons for the patronage mattered less than the history, the *investment,* we would say, of the devotion of a particular craft to the saint and the sense that the saint favored those who practiced it. While the localized attention or devotion to the particular saint has frequently enough met the official skepticism and disapproval of centralized religious authority, when seen in terms of an incarnational understanding that insists on a tied humanity between Christ and the saints, there is perhaps nothing more primitive about such a notion than the common preference for family and friends before humanity in general.

The Reformation in England was, on the contrary, a centripetal force, taking its direction from the crown and expressing itself most vigorously at the center of national power. In the late 1530s its forces were aligning themselves against the various regional focuses of pilgrimage and the veneration of local saints, their images and shrines. In February of 1538 the rood of Boxley in Kent was brought to London and destroyed at Paul's Cross. In May the Welsh statue of Derfel Gadarn was burned at Smithfield. Images from the shrines at Walsingham and Ipswich were burned in Chelsea in July. Each of these public humiliations of a local image, extracted from its site of pilgrimage and brought to the center of national power, was accompanied by a sermon by a leading churchman who argued the necessity of the event.[99]

Particularlity and regionalism were similarly hallmarks of medieval drama. The cycle plays were local phenomena, centered in the towns and patronized by the guilds and town magistracy. Like the pilgrimage shrines, they drew upon the surrounding towns, villages, and countryside for their audiences. Internally, all the surviving cycles show considerable interest in localizing the portrayal of biblical narrative. Self-conscious anachronisms and local place references—and in the case of York, sometimes semi-serious relationships between dramatic subject and the guild presenting it—punctuate the cycles and give a strong sense of the way the individual town wished to link itself to the sacralized narrative. Each of the individual pageants was the property of a guild; its proprietary character rested not only in the possession of a text and stage properties but in the history of the guild's sponsorship and acting of its roles. The plays were also significant to the economy and prestige of provincial capitals. Mervyn James has argued that both the feast of Corpus Christi and the plays that accompanied its celebration were expressions of a tension between social wholeness and social differentiation in these regional communities; the plays were the central occasion "on which the urban community could effectively present and define itself in relation to the outside world."[100] It is for these reasons of local interest that the guilds and aldermen of the towns fought to keep their cycle plays against the forces aligned against them in the 1560s and 1570s. The pressures that in the 1530s were directed against the local shrines that were the foci of pilgrimage would, after the reestablishment and consolidation of the Reformation a generation later, be brought to bear upon the cycle drama in York, Chester, Wakefield, and Coventry, and very likely against that of Norwich and Newcastle as well.

The central significance of Reformation iconoclasm for drama in England lies in the anxiety it generated toward the visual and with it toward visual modes of understanding and interpreting. The first two decades of Elizabeth's reign saw a consolidation of the iconoclasm that had began in the late 1530s, had reached a highwater mark in the reign of Edward VI, and was briefly reversed under Mary. The churchmen who had sojourned on the continent brought back a more thoroughgoing and Calvinist Protestantism; they would see their task as the more complete establishment of a word-centered Christianity and a correspondingly complete extirpation of the survivals of the incarnationalism of late-medieval religious culture. The major play cycles still being performed at the beginning of Elizabeth's reign should be understood as the last significant survivals of that culture. Their suppression between 1565 and 1579 represents the major iconoclast victory of the reign and, as I shall argue in chapter 4, marks an important shift in the focus of theatrical activity. The cycles were not of course the only regional theatrical activity; traveling companies performing interludes and moralities also toured the market and cathedral towns. Their activity would prove more readily adapted to reformed aims.[101] But these first two decades of Elizabeth's reign involve a double redirection of theatrical activity, away from the regional centers, where the cycles had been centered in the previous century and a half, and away from the religious character of those cycles toward secular setting and subjects. As I suggested in chapter 1, this occurred amid much anxiety about the visual, "idolatrous" character of theater and was accomplished amid the nearly complete victory of an aniconic Protestantism over the field of a highly visual late-medieval religious expression. If theater was to remain a significant structure for rendering the culture's sense of what was most central to it, as it had been in the previous 150-year period, it had of necessity to engage this aniconic turn. But its "idolatry" inhered in more than its visual character. I shall argue in the next chapter that the phenomenology itself of theater had roots in the incarnational elements of late-medieval culture and in the role the body had played in the origins of religious theater.

THREE

God's Body and Incarnational Drama

In my opening chapter I presented the charge of "idolatry" leveled by the opponents of the emerging public theaters as a strange one, requiring explanation. The strangeness derives from the perspective of subsequent cultural understanding, in which theater is understood as a secular institution, having an
ideological dimension surely, but aesthetic and recreational in its purposes.
From the perspective I have sketched in the last chapter—that of a long and
potent tradition of the visual image understood as conveying an incarnated
sense of the divine and of the attack on that tradition by the logocentrism of
the Reformation—that strangeness diminishes. Media are notoriously inseparable from the ideological messages they convey, and early-modern theater
was not only visual and iconic but tied to a two-century history of religious
use. The attacks upon the beginnings of the public theater and its fate in 1642
make amply clear that the stage was not viewed solely as a neutral cultural institution, purely secular and aesthetic. To an influential part of the intellectual
elite it was an antagonist of and competitor with the progressive religious culture. To the most vocal and articulate of that elite it appeared aligned with the
religiously atavistic, dangerously so, and able to appeal to sensibilities that
properly should have atrophied in the reform of religion. The popularity of the
London theaters testifies to the survival of those sensibilities, even as the reform was successful in eliminating them from worship. But the status of theater was fraught with ambiguity in the late sixteenth and early seventeenth
centuries. Though its roots lay deep in the centuries in which it had performed
a religious function, it was no longer religious, certainly not in the same sense,
and yet it could not claim a well defined aesthetic or professional status. Patronized by aristocracy and licensed by the crown, it was nevertheless kept literally at the margins of urban space—and figuratively at the margins of the
culture.[1]

    I argued in the opening chapter that the discourse of the antitheatrical
writers of the 1570s and 1580s, in fastening on the term *idolatry* to impugn
drama, was aligning it with the rejected visual culture of late medieval religion. In this chapter I want to extend that argument to encompass the larger

phenomenology of theater, to suggest that its very corporeality was invested in
a legacy of incarnational understanding that had its grounding in the medieval
religious theater. What makes drama what it is, clearly, is the impersonation
by actual persons of the figures of a narrative. In the realm of the sacred it was
precisely the fact of impersonation that drew the mistrust of the Reformers
and caused them to end the performances of the biblical plays. This was expressed most clearly in the decree of the ecclesiastical commission of York
in 1576 that no play or pageant be played wherein either the persons of the
Trinity or the administration of the sacraments "be counterfeyted or represented." Concern for physical representation, "any thinge plaied" which
would tend to the "maintenauce of superstition and idolatrie," stood significantly behind the refusal of the ecclesiastical authorities to allow even revised,
Protestantized, versions of the mystery cycles.[2] The sticking point was the
physical portrayal of the sacred. In thus objecting to the cycle plays, they were
in part objecting to the dramatic medium itself, the medium through which it
is arguable the Scriptures had been hitherto most widely known in the culture.
The belief that such impersonation was transgressive, indeed that it was potentially blasphemous, represents a radical shift of position between pre- and
post-Reformation Christianity. Physicality and divine enfleshment, I shall
argue, were not only an important preoccupation of the medieval biblical theater but its intellectual root.[3] Impersonation, the phenomenology of drama,
then, can be understood as intimately tied to this concern for the corporeal.

The vernacular English cycles of biblical drama were, of course, initially
performed on the feast of the Body of Christ, Corpus Christi. V. A. Kolve first
argued for the significance of this fact in *The Play Called Corpus Christi*.[4]
More recent formulations, by enlarging the conception of Corpus Christi, have
introduced a broader sense of the interconnectedness of the feast and the
plays. Mervyn James argues that Corpus Christi represents "society seen in
terms of body" and that this concept of body provided urban society with "a
mythology and a ritual in terms of which the opposites of social wholeness
and social differentiation could be both affirmed and also brought into a creative tension."[5] Peter W. Travis sees the thirteenth-century veneration of the
Eucharist as expressive of the characteristically medieval sense of the inter-
penetration of the sacred and the secular; like the eucharistic host, the drama
attempted "a far-reaching unification of the sacred and the secular, of Christ
and the community of the faithful."[6] If the genius of the feast was that it mag-
nified the already polysemous symbolic character of the sacrament, the Corpus Christi play analogously became "a type of sacred action performed in
order to evoke, express, and sustain the community's faith in the ultimate
meaning of Christ's presence in their lives" (p. 12). More recently Sarah
Beckwith has elaborated this sense of the way Corpus Christi was available to
the urban community.[7] It was a "major symbolic resource" for the religious
culture of late Middle Ages, "the site of a two-way transference of sacrality"
in which the body of Christ was God made man, and through operation of
faith and grace men and women could be made one with God. But resisting
what she sees as an idealist tendency to subsume theatrical meaning under a

single doctrinal formulation, Beckwith argues that Corpus Christi, the sacrament and the feast, was in practice available to a variety of factions and competing interests within the urban communities. The Corpus Christi cycles, therefore, could become complex, performative means of constructing *various* social meanings "through ritual knowledge and cultural enactment."

James, Travis, and Beckwith have developed increasingly useful and significant formulations of the relation between sacrament, feast, and drama. While that drama is not always tied to the specific occasion of Corpus Christi—the Chester plays, for example, were transferred to a three-day performance at Whitsuntide circa 1521—nevertheless the symbolic amplitude of the Eucharist, both expressive of social identity and a psychic access to the sacred, can be understood as complexly related to the mythic amplitude of the creation-to-doomsday dramatic narrative. But I want to argue that a larger reinterpretation of body and physicality stood behind both the impulse to drama and the new understanding of the eucharist in the early thirteenth century. As Caroline Walker Bynum has written, "wherever we turn in the later Middle Ages we seem to find the theme of body—and of body in all its aspects, pleasure as well as pain. . . . The piety of the mendicants, especially the Franciscans, was permeated by attention to the fact of body, both in intense union (through asceticism) with Christ's suffering and in a view of all creation as the traces and footprints of God."[8] The most extreme example she gives of this interest in the physical is also the most suggestive. Mechtild of Hackeborn, a late thirteenth-century mystic, had a vision in which she saw the celebrating priest in vestments covered with every blade and twig, every hair and scale, of the physical universe. "As she looked in surprise, she saw that 'the smallest details of creation are reflected in the holy Trinity by means of the humanity of Christ, because it is from the same earth that produced them that Christ drew his humanity.'"[9] Such a vision makes evident that the concern with humanity of Christ is not simply theoretical but intimately concerned with the detail of what it means to have a body, to be part of the physical world. Bynum suggests that the challenge posed by the Cathars in the twelfth and thirteenth centuries stimulated a need to assert the dignity of matter, of the physical, and in the case of the central doctrine of the incarnation, of the carnal human nature of Christ. Indeed, the formulation of the doctrine of transubstantiation by the Fourth Lateran Council in 1215, as well as the church's encouragement of miracles in which the host was perceived to turn into actual flesh, were a part of the general effort to counter the Cathar heresy. The eucharistic visions of Juliana of Liège were the initial impetus for the feast of Corpus Christi, but Hugh of St. Cher, the cardinal legate who helped her propagate the feast, did so in an explicit attempt to counter the dualism of the Cathars.[10]

Whether or not Catharism stimulated the more general assertion of the dignity of the phenomenal world and of human corporeality, it is evident that the Cathar heresy represents the obverse of this development and as such is intimately bound up with the altered understanding of the body and the humanity of Christ that spans the twelfth and thirteenth centuries. Like the

Manichaeism of the ancient world, Catharism viewed matter as the creation of an evil force and all participation in physical process as a denial of the benevolent God, who rules solely in and through spirit. As a Christian heresy, it denied the essential humanity of Christ and viewed it as mere appearance. What gave Catherism its force, clearly, is that it mimicked, and carried to an extreme degree, ascetic tendencies within Christianity itself. In its anticlerical and anti-institutional manifestations, it could claim to be purifying the ascetic and monastic practices of the medieval world and at the same time to be making them available to lay participants. (Indeed, one etymology ties Cathars to the Greek χαθαρός for "purified," and adherents of the sect claimed to be returning to the purity of the Apostolic church.) The Cathars attacked marriage and sexual intercourse, and the *perfecti,* those who had received the *consolamentum,* abstained from eating flesh because it was the result of sexual intercourse. In some cases, the *endura,* a fast that was to lead to death and hence to the liberation of spirit from body, was administered to believers who were ill or otherwise thought to be approaching death. If heresy can be understood as symptomatic of the deeper pressures of an age, the emergence of Catharism in the 1140s indicates an intellectual climate in which the question of physicality and the body is paramount.

I

The question of the "origins of medieval drama" is one that has exercised scholars for over a century.[11] But it is evident that no single account of "origins" can satisfy our sense of its complexity. Causality is always a multifaceted thing, as the scholastics knew, and this is especially true for a phenomenon like drama. The drama's beginnings in liturgical practice, for example, must be different in kind from causes in social or economic circumstance or in derivation from a rhetorical heritage. There is, in fact, room for a variety of potential explanations, and no single cause need be seen as bearing the entire explanatory weight. This said, it seems remarkable that the question of the origins of drama *as drama,* that is, as embodied representation, has been so little addressed in terms of the intellectual climate of the twelfth century. However one speculates on the prehistory of European drama, its actual beginnings must be seen as largely a twelfth-century phenomenon. The *Quem quaeritis* tropes of the Easter liturgy can be dated as early as the tenth century, but these passages must be described as "quasi-dramatic," representational only in a rudimentary sense, and it is not until the twelfth century that the tropes give way (if in fact they can be said to do so) to actual liturgical drama. This drama appears to have been the first fully-realized drama in Europe in some six centuries; except for popular forms of mime, the classical traditions of theater ended in the sixth century, and apart from architectural ruins and linguistic vestiges, virtually no survivals of the Roman theater as such penetrate into the medieval era.[12] Then in the period extending approximately from the first third of the twelfth century to the early thirteenth century there cluster the most extensive early examples of liturgical dramatic texts, the plays of Hilarius (fl. 1125), the Montecassino Passion (mid-twelfth century), the Tegernsee *Anti-Christ* (c. 1160), the Beauvais *Daniel* (c. 1180), the Beauvais *Peregrinus* (twelfth century), the Benediktbeuern Christmas and Passion plays (c. 1200), the plays in the Fleury collection (c. 1200), and the earliest vernacular plays—the Anglo-Norman *Jeu d'Adam* (mid-twelfth century) and *La Seinte Resureccion* (c. 1175), and the Castilian *Auto de los Reyes Magos* (mid-twelfth century).[13] It seems suggestive, at the least, that dramatic representation should arise at a time when the question of corporeality was so much at issue.

I propose that the profound shift of consciousness that occurs in the twelfth century, what has been called the "twelfth century renaissance," is itself bound up with the origins of dramatic representation. Two figures in particular can be taken as expressing significant elements of this shift of consciousness, especially as it relates to the question of corporeality and the new emphasis on the humanity of Christ. Hugh of St. Victor (1096–1141) is a central theorist both of the relation of body to spirit and of the incarnation. To his anthropology the succeeding century would owe the vindication of the bodily senses as conduits of knowledge and grace. His theoretical account of the incarnation of Christ elaborated its bodily character, in a sense anticipating the need of an intellectually articulated defense against Catharist dualism. Bernard of Clairvaux (1090?–1151), on the other hand, is not a theorist but the most influential voice of the century, the reformer who transformed the Christology of the high Middle Ages and turned it toward a deep emotional involvement with the humanity of God. His influence is strongly felt in the spirituality of the succeeding three centuries, perhaps particularly in that of the mendicant orders which would reorder the religious life of the West. Neither Hugh nor St. Bernard specifically mentions drama; in fact their lives very likely precede the flowering of monastic Latin drama. But the implications for drama, and indeed for representational art generally, can be clearly sensed in their writings.[14]

In his main theoretical work on the relation of body and spirit, *De Unione Corporis et Spiritus,* Hugh begins with a quotation from John 3:6 that seems to emphasize the distance between flesh and spirit: "What is born of the flesh is flesh, and what is born of the spirit is spirit." But the purpose of the treatise is rather to show the relation between them, to develop a rationale which will account for their relation in humankind. The initial connecting terms are *sensus* and *sensualitas*: "Corpus sensu ascendit, spiritus sensualitate descendit" [the body ascends by sense, the spirit descends by sensuality].[15] In describing the four elements, he sees an ascent toward a kind of quasi spirituality in the *vis ignea* by which vegetative and animal life is sustained; unlike earth, water, and air, only fire both moves and cannot be contained. Though properly corporeal rather than spiritual, the *vis ignea* is more subtle and "more spirit" (*magis spiritus*) and hence more closely approximates incorporeal matter. "Indeed," Hugh asserts, "insofar as it excites sense, it imitates the rational life, and insofar as it forms imagination, it imitates living wisdom." What this seems to mean is that the warmth which interacts with both sensitive life and rational life by creating sense and imagination is analogous to the powers of reason and contemplation, both of which enable humankind to rise above its limited state and move toward the divine.[16]

For Hugh vision appears to be the sensible power par excellence. He explains its operation by describing how sensible reality, taken from outside by means of the "radios visionis" (here conceived of as active powers of the eye), by the operation of nature is brought back (*retrahitur*) to the eyes where it is called vision. Then by the membranes of the eyes and the three humors, it is further purified and brought within to the cerebrum, becoming "imaginatio." Next, passing from the frontal section to the middle, it touches the substance of the rational soul and excites discernment (*discretionem*); it is thus so purified and rendered so subtle that it is joined without mediation (*immediate*) to spirit itself. Although body is raised to spirit and spirit is humbled to body, the one is not transmuted into the other. Nevertheless, it is clear that body and sense play an essential role in the creation of knowledge and in the ascent of the rational soul. As a whole the brief treatise is a vindication of the powers of the body in the human nexus of body and spirit. Vision in particular is privileged in Hugh's account; it appears to be a crucial power in the ascent to contemplation.

In the *De Sacramentis* Hugh develops a theoretical understanding of how God could take on a human body and the implications of this. It is the flesh, he insists, that is the medium through which Christ is associated with humanity (I.viii.7). He is concerned to combat a kind of docetism that would deny true suffering and pain, as well as affection, in the human flesh of Christ. Some have asserted that the flesh of Christ "took on indeed a likeness of suffering and pain, but endured no pain or suffering at all." But he asks how there was true compassion if there was not true suffering. Those who would deny that there was true suffering "according to the weakness of the flesh" would thereby deny the redemption, which was made through the suffering of Christ.[17] Hugh ponders the precise mechanism by which the Son took flesh, how the human mother was able to conceive from the spiritual nature of the Holy Spirit (II.i.9). In usual human conception the "substance of flesh" is transfused from the flesh of the man through coition and made one flesh with the flesh of the woman, so that the flesh of both is involved in the flesh of the child. But this cannot be the case for this conception since the Holy Spirit is not flesh. Hugh concludes that the substance of Christ's flesh came entirely from Mary through the transforming love and power of the Spirit. He argues further that the Word assumed human flesh and soul at the same time, taking on human nature in its entirety (II.i.9). Christ would not have been true man if he had assumed flesh alone or soul alone, because man is both flesh and soul: "He assumed man because He assumed human flesh and human soul." He insists that Christ truly died because the flesh of Christ died. God therefore died because the humanity of God died.

Hugh's precise attention to the interaction of body and spirit and the mechanism of incarnation argues a renewed interest in the fact of body. In neither treatise does he refer to Catharism; indeed his writing probably precedes its emergence as a specific heretical movement. But he seems in some ways to be dueling, *avant la lettre*, with this denial of body. Hugh's interpretation establishes the integrity of humanity's fleshly as well as its spiritual being. It is humanity's existence as *caro* that ties it to Christ, not its spiritual nature. Moreover, he sees the union of divine and human natures in the incarnation as analogous to the union of soul and body in the human person. It would seem a relatively short step from these positions to the enactment of Christ's physicality, of his actions while in the flesh, by means of other human bodies.

In the case of St. Bernard there is admittedly an element of paradox in asserting his role in formulating artistic embodiments of spiritual narrative. Bernard opposed ornamentation and the Romanesque representation of the early twelfth century, and he insisted on a pure simplicity for the monastic churches of the Cistercian order.[18] And yet his devotion to the humanity of Christ gave potent verbal expression to the impulse for representation, expression that itself frequently verges on the theatrical. The eloquence of his Latin sermons warmly conveys his sense that divine love, rather than logic or necessity, impelled the incarnation:

> He came in the flesh, to show Himself to people living in the flesh; and His humanity appeared that men might know His kindness. For how could he commend His kindness to me better than by taking my flesh—*my* flesh, not such as Adam had before he fell. What could mightily declare His mercy as this assumption of our misery?

> (*In Epiphania Domini* I, 1–4).

What so builds faith, strengthens hope, kindles charity, Bernard asks, as the humanity of God?[19] In a sermon on the Passion, he speaks of Christ's having embraced human toil and pain in his incarnation, and he exhorts the return of that embrace through acting and suffering for justice.[20] Bernard's major spiritual work is his eighty-six sermons on the Song of Songs. In the second of these he advances the interpretation of the kiss of the bridegroom as the divine assumption of human flesh: "The mouth which kisses signifies the Word who assumes human nature; the flesh which is assumed is the recipient of the kiss; the kiss, which is of both giver and receiver is the Person which is of both, the Mediator between God and man, the Man Christ Jesus."[21] The mystic kiss thereby becomes the intimate relation between the human and the divine that the incarnation expresses. It is through this that the mediator makes humanity able to accept the divine as part of itself. Bernard speaks of a human trust in the divine as coming of this shared flesh: "Then there can be no mistrust. For he is brother to my flesh. For I think that bone of my bone and flesh of my flesh cannot spurn me."[22] The fifth sermon is a kind of justification of body. Only through the body, he insists, does the ascent to the life of blessedness lie open to human beings. He quotes Romans 1:20: that through visible things are the invisible things of God understood. Those visible things come to humans only through the senses, and even angels have need of bodies to accomplish their tasks. "The spirit of man, which has its place between the highest and the lowest, has a need for a body for two reasons. Without it the soul cannot act for its own benefit, or do good to others." Though writing in a practical, hortative genre, Bernard's thought here seems close to Hugh's theoretical formulation of the relation of body and spirit. While one may not ordinarily think of Bernard of Clairvaux as a celebrant of the flesh in relation to spirit, in his meditations on the Song of Songs he returns time and again to this theme of the fleshly link between humanity and God in the incarnation. In sermon 20, after discussing the love of Christ in the spirit, he adds that devotion to the fleshly humanity of Christ is a stage toward this higher love, "as they rest in the shade who cannot yet bear the heat of the sun." They are nourished, he says, "by the sweetness of the flesh" while they are not yet able to perceive those things of the Spirit of God. "Indeed I judge this shadow of Christ to be his flesh, by which even Mary was overshadowed in order that by his coming the head and brightness of the Spirit would be tempered for her."[23] As he develops this theme, he interprets this "fleshly love" ("carnalem tamen dixerim hunc amorem") as an affective devotion to the humanity of Christ, the devotion of one "who step by step suffers with Christ suffering, is stung and easily moved at the memory of the glories which he bore and feeds on the sweetness of this devotion."[24] Such a person—one who is moved by such devotion to a life of holiness and to ardently pursue justice, truth, and humility—he believes, becomes in a certain sense superior to one given over to a simply contemplative meditation on spiritual love. In so developing this sense of "amor carnalis" Bernard seems to be anticipating the spirituality of St. Francis and the Franciscan movement, almost as if foreseeing the limitations of a purely monastic spirituality in relation to the mendicant spirituality of the succeeding century. Indeed, while convinced of the superiority of a meditative *amor spiritualis*, he seems nevertheless drawn by his own predilections toward such devotion to the corporeal humanity of Christ.

If this emphasis on the fleshly humanity of Christ in Bernard's devotional writing can be understood as a potential stimulus for the bodily enactment of that humanity, the rhetoric of his sermons becomes an equally powerful inducement to dramatic representation. As Bernard preaches on a scriptural narrative, he is frequently concerned to establish the presence of the narrative moment for his auditory, using the present tense and rendering the sacred event contemporary. In a Nativity sermon he imagines humanity present at the birth and creates a theatrical moment in the warmth of his rhetoric: "Why do you fear, O man? Why do you tremble before the face of the Lord when He comes? . . . Do not flee, do not fear. . . . Behold, he is an infant, and without voice. For the voice of one crying is more to be pitied than feared." Indeed, Bernard makes this presence explicit, insisting that he acknowledges *as his own* the time and place of the Nativity and *claims for himself* the poverty and watchings of the shepherds.[25] Even for carnal human beings, he insists, the Wisdom of God is now made openly clear, for the stable and manger call out to them, and the very body of the infant, the crying and tears of that body, speak directly to humanity.[26] Bernard savors the sense of drama in paradoxes and contradictions—the Word who is speechless ("infans"), the Child who chooses his own time to be born. In preaching on the Epiphany he again imagines the historical as the present moment: "*Today* the Magi came from the East. . . . *Today* they worship the child born of a virgin."[27] The commemoration of the Passion in Holy Week evokes for him a similar emotional engagement with its events.[28]

II

The Latin liturgical drama realizes this sense of the presence of the historical, turning it from rhetorical projection to physical enactment. What had been only implicit in the allegorical understanding of the Mass, moreover, became representationally explicit through bodily enactment by actors. At the same time this drama shows an intermittent thematic concern for the enfleshment of God in Christ. This is particularly the case with the Fleury plays. In the Resurrection play one of the three Marys bringing spices to the tomb says they do so to preserve the "blessed flesh" of Jesus ("ne putrescat in tumulo / caro beata").[29] Mary Magdalene, in the same play, speaks of the "well beloved body" ("corpus tam dilectum") that she thinks has been taken from the tomb. The Herod play (*Ordo ad Repraesentandum Herodum*), which was likely performed on the feast of the Epiphany, concludes with a celebration of what the incarnation means for humanity; the Magi sing that the Creator has taken a living body of the human race ("generis humani animatum corpus sumens") and has bestowed his godhead on humanity ("largitus est nobis suam deitatem"). The Fleury play on the conversion of St. Paul expresses the same understanding of incarnation that Hugh of St. Victor had elaborated. In preaching to the Jews, Paul asks why they deny that the Virgin Mary brought forth God and man in Christ; he asserts that Christ is both God and "fleshly man" (*homo carneus*), "deitatem a Patre retinens, / et a matre carnem suscipiens."[30] A similar concern is evident in the Beauvais *Peregrinus*. There Christ insists on his fleshly resurrection; his words go beyond the words of the gospel as he appeals to doubting Thomas: "Touch and understand that spirit does not have flesh and bones, as you see that I have. . . . Look now on the wounds of my body" ("Palpate and videte quia spiritus carnem and ossa non habet sicut me videtis habere . . . nunc vulnera conspice corporis.")[31]

But as with the "fleshly love" that St. Bernard saw coming from meditation on the humanity of Christ, several of these plays also make the incarnation the explicit source of human emotional engagement with the divine. In one of the Fleury St. Nicholas plays, *Filius Getron*, the mother of the abducted boy prays for his return by reminding God that he too had a son, whom he sent to earth. In the Benediktbeuern Passion Play the maternal emotions of Mary become the fulcrum of emotional response for the audience of the play: "Fleant materna viscera Mariae matris vulnera. / Materne doleo . . ."[32] Indeed, one characteristic of this drama is a seemingly exploratory fascination with the expression of emotion. In the otherwise stylized representation of the Slaughter of the Innocents in the Fleury manuscript, the lament of Rachel has an almost operatic character. She is led in by two comforters but in her lamentation refuses their consolation. That she is called "Virgo et Mater" makes evident her proleptic relationship to Mary and her sorrow. The *Suscitatio Lazari* of Hilarius which includes refrains in French, is centered on the expression of grief by Martha and Mary. The play appears to ratify this emotional expression in contrast with the frigid responses of the *consolatores* who argue the uselessness of grief. Strangely, the text of the play does not take up the possibilities inherent in the gospel's admission of Jesus' grief ("Et lacrymatus est Iesus"). But the Fleury play on the same subject does portray the grief of Jesus and has him responding to the emotions of Lazarus' sisters: "Iam me movet vestra miseria; / iam me movent vestra suspiria, vestre cure." In the Benediktbeuern Passion Play the lamentation of the Virgin at the foot of the cross is given highly emotive expression in both German and Latin. The vernacular passages in these plays may have been directed to a lay element in the audience, but it seems just as likely that they represent part of the exploratory representation of emotion.[33]

The first two decades of the thirteenth century represent an extraordinary turn in the character of European Christianity. The founding of the mendicant orders would have the effect of disseminating widely through the urban centers of Europe an affective piety based on a newly-defined conviction of the complete humanity of Christ. Through the Franciscans in particular—and the astonishing sense of theatricality inherent in the very character of their spirituality—this consciousness of the fleshly link between the human and the divine would stimulate visual and physical representation. Sarah Beckwith has written acutely of the way the Franciscan movement "was a decisive reorientation of the relations between sacred and profane," using "violently inverting tactics replacing health with sickness, embracing the leprous and the maimed, the high with the low."[34] She sees simultaneous strategies of "profanation and sacralization" in its intense focus on the torn and bleeding body of Christ, introducing "a complex language of identification whereby through the medium of Christ's body, identities are restored, transformed, revived, absorbed, submerged." His body becomes "the symbolic vehicle for an astonishing transference of sacrality." Indeed, Francis's own spirituality was bound up with an extraordinary apprehension of the power of representation, a theatricality intrinsic in his very sense of the way the God has interacted with humanity. While the worship of the shepherds and the Magi, for example, had been the subjects of Latin drama prior to Francis, no single event would do more to provoke the representational character of the incarnation than the *presepio* he established at Greccio in 1223. What St. Bernard had made a rhetorical invocation of the scene of the nativity became with Francis a visual tableau and the object of intense lay devotion. Thomas of Celano tells how the depiction established in the open air became so vivid that some spectators imagined they saw an actual child appear amid the saint's *mise en scène*.[35] The stigmata Francis experienced were yet another indication of the way identification with the physicality of the incarnate Christ would result in bodily reenactment of that physicality.[36] This sense of the transformative character of the body and the phenomenal world, as well as of the necessity of physical representation of Christ, is clearly one of the most potent legacies passed by Francis to his followers.

Franciscan revaluation of the physical world and of vernacular lay culture, in fact, stands between the twelfth-century drama—for the most part Latin, monastic, and liturgical—and the drama of the thirteenth and early fourteenth centuries, which was vernacular, urban, lay, and centered upon civic festivals. It is in the latter that the theme of the incarnation as the enfleshing of God becomes widely disseminated. In Italy, initially in Umbria, this development is centered on the Disciplinati, the lay confraternities whose devotions centered on the singing and enacting of *laude* and on the physical discipline of self-flagellation. The *Laus pro nativitate domini*, belonging to the repertory of the Disciplinati of Perugia, announces the theme of enfleshment in its opening lines:

Piacesse a Dio biato
spezzare glie Cieglie e 'n Terra descendesse,
nostra carne prendesse,
che lungo tempo l'avesse suspirato!

[The blessed God was pleased to break through the heavens and descend upon the earth and take our flesh, for which he had long yearned.][37]

The prophetic David addresses the high Majesty of God as it approaches human nature, "joining yourself to it" ("o alta Maestade, / a la umana natura oggie t'apressa; / congiognendote ad essa"). The divine yearning for human flesh suggests a sense of the incarnation characteristic of Franciscan auspices. The drama of the play consists in large measure in how the humanity of God is to be treated. When her child is born, Mary at first feels herself unworthy to touch him; Joseph wonders what to cover him with. But the deeper mystery consists in the abject poverty of the flesh into which the divine has descended. Mary remarks that the Infinite is enfleshed for human nature, but the parents have nothing with which to enwrap that flesh. The child can be covered only with the mother's veil, some rags, and later the shepherds' cloaks. The latter speak colloquially of the child as a "mamulin" and "zitello" and ask to touch him (pp. 54, 57). But the tenderness of their worship of the child is toughened by their insistence on the poverty of his coming and its connection with the poverty in the urban world. Never, they say, has a woman brought forth her child in such naked poverty, and hard indeed is the heart that would not turn in pity toward Mary:

Povertà cosí nuda
maio non provò donna che partorisse.
Bien ha la mente dura
che con piatà verso Maria non gisse. (p. 59)

They speak harshly to the proud and the avaricious who are satisfied only in gathering money and disdain their poor neighbor. The theme of incarnation in this nativity play is emphatically tied to its insistence on the need to treat all human flesh as accepted by, and tied to, the Godhead. The theme of incarnation generates both the realism of the play and its radical critique of social pride and avarice.

In the Florentine *sacre rappresentazioni* of the fifteenth century there is less overt insistence on the enfleshing of God as a specific theme, yet an equally strong sense of the need to incarnate biblical story within a specific civic, social, and economic milieu. *La rappresentatazione del Figliuol Prodigo* by Castellano Castellani, for example, through its colloquial language and contemporary setting, brings the story of the prodigal son directly into the city life of contemporary Florence. The dialogue of the Prodigal and his friends reproduces the language of Florentine youths in their raillery and quarreling. Clearly, the action of the play must similarly have represented the tussling of young men in the taverns and streets. The companions leading the Prodigal astray mock the friends trying to give him better counsel as members of various Florentine lay confraternities. The sumptuous meal the Prodigal orders up for his friends consists of Florentine dishes and wines. And the relationship of the Prodigal to his father and brother depends on a sense of filial piety and responsibility that have their meaning within the Florentine civic world. Closer to a morality play than a biblical representation, *The Prodigal Son* brings the parable into its contemporary setting with a judicious sense of purposeful anachronism.

La Rappresentazione di Abramo e Isacco of Feo Belcari, one of the earliest *sacre rappresentazioni* (played for the first time in 1449), does not gesture anachronistically toward the Florentine milieu, but it does employ a thoroughgoing naturalism of emotional response. There is not apparent in the text any attempt at symbolism or any attempt to foreshadow in a direct way the sacrifice of Christ. What matters is the emotional character of what Abraham must do and Isaac's reaction to it. In fact, Abraham will not carry out the sacrifice until he has disclosed it to Isaac and persuaded him of its necessity. The latter's reaction is not immediate acquiescence but a natural horror of death. He even reminds his father of the reaction his death will provoke in Sarah. But there is a human tenderness in Abraham's account of what Isaac has meant to him; he wants Isaac to understand how devastating to him is the duty that has been laid upon him. As in the Brome *Sacrifice of Isaac* (though with an even greater degree of psychological naturalism), Isaac's acceptance of the necessity of his death reconciles Abraham to his terrible charge. But the play increases the sense of emotional complexity by interpolating an extra-biblical scene of Sarah's distress and fear at the sudden disappearance of her husband and son. Though a servant rebukes her apprehension, what the audience knows is happening confirms her fear and extends to her as well the sense of potential suffering; she herself is vindicated in that fear when Isaac, rather than Abraham, tells her at the end what has almost occurred. The theme of "santa ubidienza" is thus played out against a very full sense of human emotional response. Such familial response is similarly elaborated in the Virgin's role in Castellani's *Rappresentazione della Cena e Passione*. There, in the extra-biblical scene of a visit by Jesus to his mother before the Last Supper, his revelation to her of his imminent death provokes an emotional storm of protest such as a Florentine widow might direct against an only son announcing his intention of going off to war.[38] The relation of Mother and Son in fact is the dramatic center of the play, and both their meeting on the road to Calvary and the scene of *pietà* at the end have an almost operatic intensity of emotive expressiveness. This play and Belcari's treatment of Abraham and Isaac clearly intend to naturalize the emotions they understand to inhere in the biblical narratives in terms the contemporary audience can readily accept. It is much less doctrinal understanding than emotional engagement that is the point of the plays' embodiment of the narratives.

Perhaps the most extraordinary of the *sacre rappresentazioni*, however, in its integration of biblical story into a social context and its elaboration of the human, "carnal" reality of Christ is the anonymous *Rappresentazione della conversione di Santa Maria Maddalena*. The first part of the play, quite loosely related to the gospel narratives, portrays Mary Magdalene before her conversion as a lively, self-indulgent woman who could easily be a wealthy young Florentine *borghese,* more interested in pleasure, music, and fine clothes than in spiritual matters. A fashionable *carpe diem* song sung to her celebrates a sense of *dolce vita* expressive of the upper-class contemporary world. When her sister Martha, converted by Jesus, urges Mary to accompany her to hear him preach, she begs off, laughing that she intends to enjoy life and save repentance for the end, calling Martha "ipocritona." Martha (identified by the play as the woman cured of the flux of blood) tells her sister of being miraculously healed, but Mary protests that since she is rich, noble, and beautiful, she has no need of miracles. Only when she hears how handsome and gracious Jesus is does she agree to see him, and only after elaborately dressing to convey her wealth and social rank—she says she does not want to appear "una befana" (an old hag) like her sister—does she actually go to hear him preach. The scene of conversion is also a scene of falling in love at first sight: the stage direction says that Mary initially does not attend to Jesus, but looks about her; Jesus, however, fixes her with his eyes as he speaks, and finally when she looks at him, her eyes meet his. His preaching is of repentance, and he directs to her (and to the audience) the parable of the talents: from those who are rich and well born, to whom everything in the world has been given, much will be demanded; those who place self before God and squander all in delight and pompous living will be judged severely. But this is succeeded by the parables of the lost sheep and the prodigal son, and the exhortations "O alma peccatrice, che farai?" and "Torna al pastore, o alma peccatrice," which seem directed expressly to the Magdalene. So too the final stanza of his sermon:

Alma, tu hai ferito molti cuori
stando in delizie, in pompe, e in van diletti:
tu hai fornicato con molti amadori,
e se' ripiena di molto difetti
e hai il tuo core ch'è pien di rancori:
ritorna a me, se brami ch'io t'aspetti,
perché con gli altri raddoppi il talento
acciò con gli altri in ciel viva contento.[39]

[Oh dear soul, you have wounded many hearts, living in pleasure, ostenta-
tion, and vain delights. You have committed fornication with many lovers.
You are filled with much guilt and you have a heart laden with rancor and
spite. Return to me, if you yearn for me to wait for you. For with the others
you will double the talent given you, and with those others live happily in
heaven.]

Clearly the words touch Mary, but it is evident that dramatically she is
struck as by a magnetic physical presence. After her tears and her washing of
Jesus' feet at the house of Simon the Pharisee, she tells Martha that she was
so inflamed with love of him that her heart was cleft with sweetness, her heart
so wounded with love that she can think of nothing but him:

> Allor m'infiammò tanto del suo amore
> che per dolcezza el cuor mi si fendea . . .
> tanto m'aveva il cor d'amor piagato
> ch'altro ch lui il mio cuor non pensava. (stanzas 110–11)

And indeed throughout the rest of the play she speaks of Jesus as of a lover.
As she longs for him to come to the dinner to which she, Martha, and Lazarus
have invited him, her yearning expresses itself in a language that suggests
mystic spirituality, but employs the terms of erotic love:

> Dolce speranza mia, or perché tardi?
> Vedi come per te, Giesù, languisco:
> chiamo, amor mio Giesù; tu non respondi,
> ché sol te chieggio, e sol te concupisco:
> Giesù, col tuo amore il mio cor ardi:
> tu m'hai ferito si ch'io me smarrisco.
> Quando sarà quel punto che tu venga
> acciò che la mia bocca a' piè ti tenga. (stanza 130)

[Oh my sweet hope, why are you waiting? See, my Jesus, how I languish for
you. I call to you, Jesus my love, but you do not respond. Only you I desire,
only you I long for. Jesus, my heart burns with love of you. You have
wounded me and I am lost. When will that moment come when you will be
here and I can press my lips to your feet?]

If the last couplet points to a humility that turns carnal love spiritual, we
should presume that the gesture will be enacted, that her lips will touch her
lover's feet. The mystic kiss that St. Bernard understood as the divine embrace
of human nature is here returned. The veil of erotic longing that conveys the
Magdalen's spiritual love materializes Bernard's symbolic interpretation of
the Song of Songs. If this use of a language redolent of erotic love seems
strangely daring in a mid-fifteenth century dramatic portrayal of Christ and the
Magdalen, it is important to recall that the physicality of Christ, and indeed
even his sexual identity as a human male, were an emphatic part of what Leo
Steinberg has called the theme of the "humanation" of Christ in the visual arts
from the mid-fourteenth to the early sixteenth centuries.[40] While not equivalent to the *ostentatio genitalium* that Steinberg finds most prominently and fre-

quently represented in paintings of the infant Christ, the language the Magdalen uses places a similar emphasis on Christ's identity as a male; his theatrical embodiment as the object of her love makes plain the fact that she has fallen in love with one who is man as well as God. The play capitalizes on the fact that human bodies are enacting her conversion and bases that conversion on a response that indicates her attraction to his physical presence, precisely to his "humanation." Significantly, there is no contradiction felt in the transposition of this attraction to spiritual conversion, spiritual love, the one signifying and expressing the other.[41]

III

In England the traditions of vernacular biblical theater that began in the latter part of the fourteenth century stimulated an attack on playing and theater on the very grounds that it is bodily play with what is spiritual. The *Tretise of Miraclis Pleyinge,* the most significant witness to dramatic activity at this time, is a Lollard work written between 1380 and 1425, probably before 1414, in the Central Midlands, an area that saw considerable Wycliffite activity.[42] While the extant texts of the cycles derive from later periods, it is known that the Corpus Christi plays of Coventry and York were already in existence. The accessibility to Coventry of the region where the *Tretise* was produced suggests that the writers may indeed have had this cycle in mind, but the *Tretise* shows a familiarity with a wide range of theatrical activity.[43] For the writers of both parts of the *Tretise,* the key difficulty with performance of religious pleys is that they induce familiarity with the works of God and blur distinctions between the sacred and the profane. Just as a servant should not take "in pley and bourde that his erthely lord takith in ernest, myche more we shulden not make oure pleye and bourde of tho miraclis and werkes that God so ernestfully wrought to us." The very act of performing means that men are using their own bodies and faculties to represent the deeds of God: miracle playing "reversith Crist" not only by *playing* what he *did* in earnest, but "in taking to miraclis of our fleyss, of oure lustis, and of oure five wittis that that God tooc to the bringing in of his bitter deth" (Davidson, pp. 93–94). Any playing is "of the lustis of the fleyssh and mirthe of the body," and one cannot effectively hear the voice of Christ and the voice of the flesh together (p. 96). The writer of the first part summarizes and responds to six defenses of miracle-playing, a fact that suggests that the innovation of vernacular theater had been specifically defended, perhaps even within Wycliffite circles. Interestingly, the final defense to which the *Tretise* responds is that theater is analogous to painting, and if the painting of God's miracles is allowed, why should not the "quick book" of performance be allowed in place of the "dead book" of painting? The Lollards, as I noted in the last chapter, did not generally favor visual art, but here there is a qualified acceptance of painting, as long as it is truthful, not too curious and concerned with "fedinge mennis wittis," and not an occasion of idolatry. But playing, the *Tretise* insists, is not equivalent to painting because it is "made more to deliten men bodily than to ben bokis to lewid men" (p. 104). The element of bodily portrayal becomes the sticking point: the use of human bodies to portray what God has done can only falsify and confuse. The writer of the second half of the *Tretise*, even more the rigorist, sees plays as empty signs, void of reality because they attempt to use bodily play to interpret the spirit, "pleyinge that is fleschely with the werkis of the spirit" (p. 107). In a striking anticipation of the Protestant antitheatricalists of the 1570s and 1580s, this second writer calls plays "maumetrie" (idolatry) and sees them as worse than the idolatry of the golden calf. He also reprehends those who "blasfemely . . . seyen that suche pleyinge doith more good than the word of God whanne it is prechid" (p. 112).

While the texts of the English cycle plays, dating from the latter half of the fifteenth to the early sixteenth centuries, strongly emphasize the physical body of Christ, the phrase "mirth of the body" scarcely describes that emphasis.[44] All the cycles include prolonged scenes of torture in the sequence of plays narrating the Passion, and all conclude those sequences with agonizingly detailed representations of the nailing of Jesus' body to the cross and the raising of the crucified body. Even Chester, otherwise the most conservative in representation, concludes with a Last Judgment spectacularly portraying Christ descending from heaven with blood still flowing from his wounds. The body of Christ is emphatically central to all the English cycles; violent torture and physical pain are the virtual meaning of the passion plays.[45] Understood in devotional terms contemporary with the cycles' construction, this emphasis had as its purpose the formation and structuring of an empathy with the suffering of Christ in the fullness of his humanity. The influential *Mirrour of the Blessed Lyf of Jesu Christ*, attributed to Bonaventure and translated by Nicholas Love in the first decade of the fifteenth century, identified as a devotional problem the misapprehension of the relation of the divine and human natures: "For there beth so many so blynded gostly by unresonable ymaginacioun of the myght of the godhede in Jesu / that they trowe not that any thing myghte be peynefull or sorwful to hym as to another comune man that hath only the kynd of man."[46] Against such understanding, the treatise insists that because Christ's purpose was to suffer the hardest and most painful death, his divine will was therefore evacuated in relation to the human. His human will was tripartite, the "wille of the flesche and the sensualite / and that grucched and dredde and wolde nought gladly suffre death" and the "wille of resoun," that was "obeissaunt and assentaunt," and "the wille of the godehede" (p. 219). Christ suffered and died "only after the kynde of man," entirely suspending "the myght of the godhede fro the infirmyte of the manhede" (p. 216). His bodily kind, moreover, was of such perfection, "of the clennest complexioun that ever was man or myghte be," that his suffering was the most intense, "the peynes in the body . . . the more sore and bittre and harder to suffre." The trajectory of the Passion therefore is from the healthy and vigorous body "of a faire yonge man of the age of xxiij yere" to the progressively beaten, bruised, lacerated, bloodied, and finally lifeless body that is taken down from the cross. The resurrected body that completes the trajectory in the cycles is not a return to the intact and unblemished body, but one that retains all the imprints of torture amid the return to life. This of course is one meaning of the spectacular bleeding Christ of Chester's Last Judgment.

Of the extant English cycles, York develops most strikingly this insistence on body, elaborating it into a thematic emphasis that is played out in its very theatricality, particularly in terms of the dramatic polarities of voice and body. Peter Womack's recent formulation of the effect of York's processional staging expresses brilliantly this relation of theatricality to theme: "The proliferation of imitation Christs, twenty-seven of them a dozen times each, preaching, blessing, suffering, judging, all day, on every corner, represents a total *permeation* of the town by the divine body whose originating oneness their very multiplicity denotes."[47] The insistence on body culminates most complexly in its representation of physical power and tortured powerlessness in the sequence of plays portraying the Passion. But it also stands at the opening of the play, preceding the plays centered on the actual incarnation and asserting this self-conscious interest in the theatrical body. In the first stanza of the creation play, God the Father, in defining his incomparable being, speaks of "my body in blys ay abydande."[48] In fact, of course, a body arrayed in visual splendor was playing God. When the angels are created, their reaction to that theatrical body is at immediate issue. What separates the good angels from the soon-to-be-fallen is their response, expressed in physical stance and gesture, toward God's body. While the first of the good angels turns immediately toward God, Lucifer turns away and begins to admire his own body ("O, what I am fetys and fayre and fygured full fytt! / The forme of all fayrehede apon me es feste" [p. 51].) His sin is manifested as a pride in his own physical being. A good angel, obviously still facing God, asks "to be fede with the fode of thi fayre face" (p. 51). This insistence on body and visual appearance, which might prove puzzling in modern performance and was certainly transgressive to Elizabethan churchmen, was precisely what the York playwright wished to evoke. Corporeality thus stands at the center of the first play of the cycle. But this particular thematics will be echoed time and again in the plays concerned with images of corrupt power in Herod and Pilate, who echo Satan in requiring physical homage and acknowledgment of their beauty.

That this emphasis on the body of Christ is part of a coherent understanding of the incarnation is indicated by the fourth play of the cycle. Expressed there is what may seem a surprising understanding of that doctrine in relation to humanity's fall. Instead of what may be termed the classic, and usual, understanding—that the incarnation was the divine response to the fall of Adam and Eve—the incarnation is here constructed as logically *prior to* the fall; it is made Satan's retrospective, revisionary justification for his own fall and the motivation for his desire to corrupt Adam and Eve. He says he perceived that God would take on the nature of some degree of his creation, and he was offended that it would not be that of the angels, but of humanity:

For woo my witte es in a were
That moffes me mykill in my mynde;
The Godhede that I sawe so cleere,
And parsayued that he shuld take kynde
Of a degree
That he had wrought, and I dedyned
That aungell kynde shuld it noght be:
And we wer faire and bright,
Therfore me thoght that he
The kynde of vs tane myght,
And therat dedeyned me.

> ("The Fall of Man," Beadle, *The York
> Plays*, pp. 64–65)

[For woe my wit is in misery, which moves me much in mind. I saw the Godhead so clear and understood that he should take on the nature of a part of
what he had created. I was offended that it should not be the angelic nature,
for we were fair and bright and therefore I thought he might have taken ours.
At this I was deeply offended.]

This understanding of the incarnation, a Franciscan interpretation deriving
from Duns Scotus and suggestive of Franciscan involvement in the cycle,
serves to make the doctrine emphatically positive.[49] Rather than God's responsive reaction to the sin of humankind, a kind of divine attempt to heal
humanity's self-inflicted wound, the incarnation was planned from the beginning, was not dependent on the Fall, and instead represented God's sponta-
neous acceptance of the full nature of his human creation. While it cannot be
assumed that this position controls the entire cycle, it is at least clear that it coheres with the general emphasis on body and physicality. If the "body" of God
the Father is to be understood as figural—and even this understanding may involve the fastidiousness of modern construction—the metaphor has a kind of
deep propriety to it, for the dramatic, *physical*, portrayal of God the Father
stands as analogous to what was planned for the Son and his relation to the
created world: like Son, like Father. It coheres moreover with the dramatic
medium itself, in which not only the Son but the Father is physically incarnated on the stage. In this York shares with the other cycles a lack of hesitation
about bodily portrayal of the Father; there is no supposition that a mere offstage voice would more appropriately render his nature.[50]

The comparative simplicity of the York pageants centered on the nativity
has nothing comparable to the emphasis on divine enfleshing in the Umbrian
lauda. But the figure of Joseph is made to convey something of the physical
effect of incarnation. While not the comic cuckold of the Wakefield cycle
or the fussy old dotard of the true Coventry plays, Joseph in York is similarly
old and physically feeble, in this expressive of the world before the incarnation. In the Flight into Egypt pageant, Joseph is portrayed as growing gradually stronger as he must comfort the uncomprehending Mary. Finally he takes
the child from her and in doing so feels a new physical strength come to him:

Such forse methynke I fele,
I may go where I schall.
Are was I wayke, nowe am I wight.
My lymes to welde ay at my wille.

This leads to the paradox at the end of the play: as they flee to Egypt to protect the child—though neither one has any idea where Egypt is—the child gives them strength and protection. Joseph remarks that he holds their help "here in myn arme" and believes that the child will keep them from fear and harm. This motif is repeated in the pageant of the child Christ among the Doctors. Joseph is bashful about speaking before a group of learned men and tells Mary she must go first and address them. She does, but as soon as Joseph catches sight of the child, his timidity appears to vanish; he says that the mere "sight of thee" has cured their sorrow and he is able to speak.

The plays centered on the Passion most fully exploit this concern with body, its physical presence and its pain. Elaine Scarry's discussion of the "materialization of God" in the New Testament and her contention of the centrality of the body not only in the scriptures themselves but in "the choices that are unconsciously and communally made about representations of Christ," are especially germane to the York Passion.[51] Scarry argues that the New Testament recasting of the biblical story in terms of the createdness and exile of God, his embodiment, "endow the interior facts of sentience, the facts of being alterable, creatable, woundable, with absolute authority":

> In turn to place sentience and authority together, to make sentience authoritative, is to place pain and power on the same side of the weapon, and so restructure the object itself. One of the peculiar characteristics of pain is that something which is its opposite, power, can reside in a different location yet come to be perceived as increasing or decreasing as pain itself increases or decreases. . . . The altered relation in the Christian scripture between the body of the believer and the object of belief subverts this severed relation between pain and power, assuring that sentience and authority reside at a single location and thus cannot be achieved at each other's expense. (pp. 218–19)

The issues of sentience and authority are never far from the surface of the nine plays, from the Agony in the Garden to the Death of Christ, that make up the York Passion. Where does power lie, play after play asks, and what does it mean that torture and pain are repeatedly inflicted on the one body where authority most resides? The audience's own sentience is tested throughout, for the potential for feeling pain is something shared with the body whose torture is being enacted before them. Over and over the audience is threatened with torture and punishment by the figures of authority, Pilate and Herod, unless they cease speaking and attend only to them. Such threats, entirely fictional in relation to the audience, are enacted on the figure whose suffering is bound up with the audience's salvation. If the threats are seen as comic, as at one level they are, the comedy rests on a knife edge when they are subsequently fulfilled in the prolonged scenes of torture that the audience witnesses. Pilate, Annas, and Caiaphas maneuver back and forth in the assertion and quest for authority, but paradoxically, the acceptance of the brutality and pain they inflict become its real source.

The pageant of the Agony and Betrayal enacts most explicitly the evacuation of the divine will in favor of (in Nicholas Love's words) "the wille of the flesche and the sensualite." Jesus repeatedly refers to the dread and fear he feels in his flesh ("My flesshe dyderis and daris for doute of my dede" [p. 234]; "My flesshe is full ferde And fayne wolde defende") and he asks the Father to pity his humanity ("Haue mynde of my manhed, my mode for to mende" [p. 237]). The repetitions of this motif in the text suggest a powerfully emotive soliloquy broken only by attempts to rouse the sleeping disciples. It is in fact the last major speech assigned to the role of Christ until he speaks from the cross. Language and speech are thus potently thematized in relation to physicality and the silent acceptance of physical torture. Though Christ appears in six of the intervening seven plays, he is all but speechless in three of them, completely speechless in one, and speaks only two stanzas each in the Road to Calvary and the Crucifixion. The speech assigned is almost entirely confined to what the Gospels report he said, and one stanza that is the exception to this (deriving in part from the Gospel of Nicodemus) suggests the specific significance of the curtailment of Christ's voice. In response to Pilate's question of how he replies to the charges brought against him by Annas and Caiaphas, Jesus replies:

> Euery man has a mouthe that made is on molde
> In wele and in woo to welde at his will,
> If he gouerne it gudly like as God wolde
> For his spirituale speche hym thar not to spill.
> And what gome so gouerne it ill,
> Full vnhendly and ill sall he happe;
> Of ilk tale thou talkis vs vntill
> Thou accounte sall, thou can not escappe.

> ("Christ before Pilate 2: The Judgment,"
> *York*, p. 301)

As the first and last utterance assigned to Jesus in this pageant in which he is judged and condemned, and his first speech since the complete silence he keeps in the appearance before Herod, it judges all the uses of the human voice that have surrounded the human body of God. His own "spirituale speche" emerges from silence in contrast with the mockery, falsity, laughter, and simple triviality that have assailed his silent presence in the preceding pageants. But it spills over as well onto the festive chatter of the audience that the threats of Pilate and Herod must counter at the beginning of each pageant and onto their laughter at the comic mockery. At the very least it makes clear the polarity of voice and body enacted in these pageants. "The devell haue the worde, lorde, he wolde telle vs," says one of the soldiers to Caiaphas after they have just attempted to beat Jesus into speech ("Christ before Annas and Caiaphas," *York*, p. 253).

His silence is maintained in the next pageant until Pilate asks Jesus if he is the Christ and God's son; then that silence becomes absolute in the bizarrely comic play of his appearance before Herod. A rhetorically violent Herod addresses Jesus in an absurd melange of English and court French, and when his courtiers have tried unsuccessfully to get him to kneel, Herod remarks punningly, "He knawes noght the course of a kyng" ("Christ before Herod," *York*, p. 275). The course—or corse, body—of a king is precisely what is at issue. Failing to elicit any response, Herod successively shrieks at him, threatens him with a sword, tries out Latin, then nonsense words, whispers, shouts again, then gets his three sons to bellow at him in unison. Still lacking any response, Herod and the court decide that Jesus is mad and dress him in white. The play's farcical character has as great a comic potential as any play in the cycle—where does real madness lie, it seems to query—and the audience's laughter may draw them into complicity with the cacophony of false speech. The dramatic significance appears to lie in the unbending and silent bodily presence of the one figure on the stage against whom the capering and jeering noise of the court is directed. Words and oral sound, whether bellowing noise or the responding laughter, become the equivalent of the blows of the torturer's fists in the previous play. As God's voice is silenced in the suffering of his manhood, surrounding human utterance becomes violent and absurd. The Crucifixion pageant modulates and extends this pattern somewhat in its depiction of four common soldiers measuring, pounding, re-measuring (for either they get the dimensions wrong or the wood of the cross keeps shifting shape to frustrate their efforts), and finally hauling and stretching Jesus' limbs to fit the bored holes—all the while talking and quarreling among themselves about the job as if they were familiar Yorkshire craftsmen repairing a door. Their conversation stands as a strikingly ordinary foil to the torture they are carrying out on the silent body of Christ. When the latter finally does emerge from his silence, it is to speak in an entirely different register, addressing the audience in the traditional language of the liturgical "reproaches" and praying forgiveness for the torturers. The combination of the utterly commonplace dialogue of the soldiers and the unutterable horror of their torture has long been felt as one of the cycle's most potent effects.

At the same time the figure of Christ seems, one might say, to increase in corporeal density in almost direct relation to his silence. In the first interview with Pilate (in the play of the Dream of Pilate's Wife), Pilate's beadle, previously so obsequious to his own master, suddenly and without warning goes down on his knees to worship the prisoner "with witte and with will." When Jesus is brought in a second time before Pilate, Pilate's soldiers cannot hold their standards upright, cannot keep them from in effect bowing in homage. Stronger soldiers are found, but again the bodily presence of Christ seems to cause unbearable weight in the standards. Similarly, even Pilate cannot prevent himself from rising in honor when the prisoner is brought back onto the stage. This motif culminates in the crucifixion when the four soldiers try to raise the cross but cannot for its apparent weight. They complain of bodily harm to themselves from their attempt and assume that the preternatural weight of the cross must come of some spell. "He weyes a wikkid weght,"

says one after they have finally heaved the cross into its mortice ("The Crucifixion," p. 320). Whatever the theological explanation for the wicked weight,
the immediate stage effect is to endow Christ's body with an apparent mas-
sivity, to make its physical density overwhelm the besetting activity of the soldiers. The effect, it would appear, of somatic agony and, paradoxically, of silence is to increase the weight of the body until it vastly exceeds its expected
physical dimension.

York, like the two other northern cycles, contains in its Passion sequence
three separate scenes of protracted physical torture (the East-Anglian *N-Town*
adds another scene of scourging by Herod). Jesus is first beaten by order of
Annas and Caiaphas, then scourged by Pilate, and finally nailed to the cross,
a scene that includes the elaborate stretching of his limbs with ropes. It is altogether clear from the texts that the scenes of torture were performed with
the utmost realism. No stylization, as has sometimes been done in twentieth-
century productions, was allowed to mitigate the pain and horror of the scenes.[52]
Verbal violence by the torturers accompanied the representation of physical violence and completed a sense of human power attempting utter dominance of the
human body of God. The text suggests that a grotesque poetry of torture corresponds dramatically to the intense physical activity of arms and bodies:

II Miles. Swyng to the swyre [neck] to swiftly he swete.

III Miles. Swete may this swayne for sweght of our swappes.

IV Miles. Russhe on this rebald and hym rathely rehete.

I Miles. Rehete hym I rede you with rowtes and rappes.

II Miles. For all oure noy this nygard he nappes.

III Miles. We sall wakken hym with wynde of oure whippes.

IV Miles. Now flynge to this flaterer with flappes.

I Miles. I sall hertely hitte on his hippes
          And haunch.

II Miles. Fra oure skelpes not scatheles he skyppes.

III Miles. Yitt hym lest not lyft vp his lippis
           And pray vs to haue pety on his paunch.

("Christ before Pilate 2: The Judgement," *York,* pp. 302–303)

Three more stanzas of equal verbal violence comprise the flagellation. Our contemporary saturation with images of physical brutality may tempt us to under-
estimate the effect of the spectacle, but it seems likely that the witnessing of the
torture of Christ's body was as potent a visual experience as late-medieval
culture could offer. Pain is notoriously resistant to mere verbal description[53]—
visual imaging is far more effective, as we know from the traditions of fifteenth-
and sixteenth-century painting—but vivid enactment with actual bodies must
have provided a near-overwhelming emotional experience. (Indeed, vivid enactment drawing forth intense emotional response was another reason the *Tretise of Miraclis Pleyinge* rejected theatrical representation; such emotion was
mistrusted as insincere.[54]) The sentience shared between each member of the

audience and the body of the actor enacting the suffering of torture is the pivotal element in this portrayal of dominance; though the brutality is presumed fictive, the body of the actor registers the pain consonant with its apparent force. (One wonders if there may also have been some frisson attendant on the fact that the actor's body was indeed at some risk in the process of being raised on a large wooden cross, to which he is helplessly bound, the same sort of frisson which rivets attention on the body of anyone performing a dangerous physical feat.) The bond rests on the imaginative acceptance, which may be almost involuntary, that the pain portrayed as felt by another body may be experienced by one's own body. That the body in question represents God's body and that this pain is understood as endured for humanity's sin are secondary imaginative elements, significant in the theological and devotional context but subsidiary to the immediate effect of shared bodily sentience.

Audiences were compelled to experience this effect through the prolonged scenes of suffering. The visible effects of the suffering continue even into the plays following the Passion. The texts make clear that the appearances of Christ's resurrected body did not elide the images of wounds and blood, the sense that the interior of his body is now made visible. Mary Magdalen addresses a body with open wounds:

A, blessid body that bale wolde beete,
Dere haste thou bought mankynne.
Thy woundes hath made thi body wete
With bloode that was the withinne.

> ("Christ's Appearance to Mary
> Magdalene," *York*, p. 358)

"Grathely gropes my woundes wete, / Al that here is," the disciples are instructed; "Felys me grathely euerilkone, / And se that I haue flessh and bone" ("The Incredulity of Thomas," *York,* p. 368). When Thomas appears, he is told,

"Beholde my woundis are bledand,
Here in my side putte in thi hande,/
And fele my woundis and vndirstande
That this is I"

> ("The Incredulity of Thomas,"
> *York,* p. 372)

What in the gospel narrative is required only of Thomas the play asks of all the disciples. The emphasis on the stage business of *each* of the disciples groping his wounds extends to all of them the need to approach Christ's body to inspect, touch, and enter into his wounds. This dramatic emphasis on the openness of Christ's body seems to press the play's audience toward the consciousness created by late-medieval meditative tradition that Sarah Beckwith has described in texts like *The Prickynge of Love* and in Richard Rolle's "Meditations on the Passion."[55] The permeability of Christ's body, its openness through its wounds, blurs the boundaries between the self and Christ and, through the stage mediation of the disciples, seems to invite the audience into Christ's body. This relation of bodies in the audience to the body of God is made thematically explicit in the play of "The Last Judgment," when Christ directs the audience to see into his wounds:

> Here may ye see my woundes wide,
> The whilke I tholed for youre mysdede.
> Thugh harte and heed, foote, hande and hide,
> Nought for my gilte, butt for youre nede.
> Beholdis both body, bak and side,
> How dere I bought youre brotherhede.
> Thes bittir paynes I wolde abide—
> To bye you blisse thus wolde I bleede.

("The Last Judgment," *York*, p. 412)

What the audience is to discover in this bodily interior is in some sense themselves. In the final play the sense of shared sentience is reversed: the audience learns that what it feels is also felt by the body of God. The good souls are told that Christ has felt his hunger and thirst satisfied by them, that they have clothed and housed his body; the damned are told that they have denied his body these necessities. The radical openness and woundedness of his body, continuing from the Passion to the final play of the cycle, becomes also metaphoric and expressive of the vulnerability of the corporate body of Christ in the communal world. Peter Travis has acutely linked the image of the wounded, bleeding body of Christ to the desolation of late-medieval English cities; that body may be perceived as "a dystopic image of the city in its most observable material condition—once, in the mythic past, glorious, and now impoverished, profoundly exhausted."[56] At the same time the image is speaking, literally, to each individual of the city, who will of course face that judgment. There is in the end, the wounded and bleeding Christ says, no distinction between the bodies of the city and his, between what may be done for bodies in York and what may done for his own body. The torture and suffering that open out and make visible the interior of his body must elicit a corresponding opening out of sentience within the urban space where the spectacle is played. Human bodies in York *are* his body.

If this is one of the meanings of the intense foregrounding of body in the York play, it is not something with which the Reformers could necessarily quarrel *as meaning*. But that foregrounding itself and its explicit connection with the sacramental Eucharist could not be acceptable in any form. Moreover, in the case of the Passion sequence at least, the very phenomenology of theater, the embodying of narrative, is implicated in this foregrounding of Christ's body. The intense emotion that the lurid scenes of torture and crucifixion are meant to evoke require bodily enactment. The Passion sequences of the cycle plays are only the most prolonged instances of concentration on the body and its suffering. At two other points the audiences witnessed the representation of physical violence and death; the pagents on the killing of Abel and the slaughter of the Innocents both produce an intense emotional reaction. Bodily suffering, torture, bloodshed, and violent death were essential elements in the cycles—and fully implicated in the theatrical medium. Though the elucidation of theological meaning was important, it was constructed through the impersonation of God's human body, its analogues and types, and could not be divorced from a vivid reenactment of its mutilation.

IV

It would be extraordinary if the 150-year tradition of vernacular biblical theater had left no trace on the vigorous theater that succeeded it. This is the theater Shakespeare saw in his boyhood; references and allusions in his plays testify to the impression it made on him. The final performance of the Coventry cycle, whose fame extended far beyond Warwickshire, occurred in 1579. Its disappearance except for two lively pageants—surely the single greatest loss in British theater history—deprives us of the most direct link between this tradition and Shakespeare. With the scholarly and theatrical revaluation of the mystery cycles in the last two decades, we are now closer to realizing the impact of what has traditionally been called "the medieval theater" on the early modern stage. But we are closer to acknowledging that there a *was* an impact than understanding exactly what that impact was. The glimpsing of continuities between the stagecraft and dramaturgy of the mystery cycles and the public theaters is an important beginning.[57] But what did it mean that audiences had been, within the memory of one generation, used to seeing the *fact* of body so prominently emphasized on stage, that they had witnessed God's body beaten, tortured, and graphically crucified, watched children grabbed from their mothers' arms and run through with swords? Claudius' reflection on his crime in *Hamlet*, that "It hath the primal eldest curse upon't, / A brother's murder," came of and evoked not so much the knowledge of a text but the recollection of the vivid representation of the murder of Abel. The very phenomenology of theater carried with it these connections, and in that phenomenology was the insistence on empathy, especially in the plays centered on Christ's Passion—that the audience was to *feel* the sufferings of his body and to acknowledge the connection between that body and their own. The relation is not a theological one, at least not one that can be spoken of in terms of "types" and secularized transpositions of sacred figures. The iconoclast attack on the traditional theater had severed any possibility of a theological linkage. It is rather a relation that rests at the level of body. I would suggest that it was the traditional biblical theater that in fact authorized the portrayal of violence and physical brutality on stage and gave it a moral valence. If the Elizabethan and Jacobean stage retained the possibility of being, to appropriate Artaud's famous phrase, "a theater of cruelty," this was a direct legacy of the late-medieval theater of cruelty; scenes of bloodshed, torture, and violent death follow from the scenes of torture and cruelty in the cycle plays. At an indeterminate distance behind the blinding of Gloucester in *Lear* stands the moment in the Wakefield play when a violent Caiaphas threatens to "out-thrist" Christ's eyes—and in fact Gloucester's torture frequently looks on stage startlingly like the stage image of the mocking and buffeting of Christ. In Shakespeare at least, bodies in pain, bodies that have suffered violence and death, achieve a kind of authority and power over those who have inflicted their suffering. In *Macbeth* Banquo's silent "ghost" is a body that carries its wounds, "twenty mortal murders" on its head, a body whose sway comes of the blood so appallingly covering its face and hair. As a figure of judgment, Banquo evokes the figure of the wounded and bloody Christ of the Doomsday pageant, the very image to which Macduff had referred in the scene when Duncan's gashed body was discovered: "Up, up, and see / The great doom's image" (*Macbeth* 2.3.74–75). Banquo's body achieves complete power over his murderer, reducing him to apparent madness before the court. The theatrical potency of this bloody body becomes a fulcrum in the play, linked imagistically with the living body of the "bloody child" shown by the witches. The bloody child is not a body in pain, for it is the prophetic image of Macduff, "untimely ripped" from his mother's womb, but spectators with memories reaching back to the cycles would perhaps inevitably have associated it with the murdered children of the Innocents' plays. Such an association is strangely, obliquely confirmed when Macbeth repeats Herod's crime in the killing of Macduff's children. The blood of these vulnerable and murdered bodies gathers to a kind of force in overturning the Herod-like tyranny of Macbeth. In *Othello* the momentary return of Desdemona's body from apparent death, in its evocation of pity and judgment, is another instance of the authority accorded suffering in Shakespeare's dramaturgy, suffering in this case suffused with a language that strangely insists on comparison with Christ. There are, surely, other thematic and moral links between these theaters—the jealousy of Joseph in the cycle plays and Shakespeare's frequent portrayal of groundless male jealousy is one[58]—but the central point of relation is one that rests on the implications of incarnation, that God and man share a body, a body that may be shown to suffer and die. When the enactment of a singular sacred body became transgressive, the new public theater that emerged in the last quarter of the sixteenth century can be understood as refracting that body into varieties of tragic experience. Not a process invoking theological linkage, there is nonetheless in the succession of these theaters a connection in the moral status of bodies that undeservedly suffer pain and death, whose suffering becomes authoritative in relation to those who have caused it. In Elaine Scarry's terms, this involves the imaginative making, or remaking, of the world. In the late-medieval world of the cycles, this remaking involved the projection of the suffering body of Christ into the social and political world and the demands on that world implied in the "Last Judgment" play. In the early-modern world of Elizabethan and Jacobean theater, this required the equally complex process of creating a sense of affect in secular tragedy, of awakening through tragedy the *seeing* and the *feeling* of which the blinded Gloucester speaks when he gives alms to the suffering poor Tom and curses the man "that will not see / Because he does not feel" (*Lear* 4.1. 68–69).

FOUR

The Textualization of God's Body

In view of the association between the origins and practice of dramatic embodiment and the incarnational aesthetic of medieval culture argued in the last chapter, the Reformation ambivalence about theater might seem virtually inevitable. In contexts in which theater was put to specifically religious uses, and especially in the representation of biblical narratives, this ambivalence necessarily mounted toward rejection. The Elizabethan suppression of the vernacular mystery cycles surely represents a decisive turn from the religious aesthetic that prevailed from the twelfth through the sixteenth century. But this was not a conclusion that sprang full blown from the mind of the Reformation. Paul Whitfield White has recently shown that in the first generation of the Reformation, English Protestants embraced the stage as a polemical weapon; as playwrights and performers, patrons and audience, they attacked the doctrines and practice of Catholicism and promoted even Calvinist theological positions.[1] Most of this polemical theater took the form of moral interludes, whose dramaturgy, based on late fifteenth- and early sixteenth-century models, was well suited to ideological usage. But there were also several significant attempts at biblical theater, generally through a melding of moral interlude with biblical narrative. There would remain the impulse (perhaps, viewed in hindsight, the *temptation*) to return to the Bible, the central subject for the vernacular stage in the previous century and a half—and, of course, the imaginative mainspring of Protestantism.

In addressing the issue of Protestantism and drama, one must begin by acknowledging a larger sense of "drama," that there is something inherently dramatic in the very character of the Reformation itself. Conversion from the traditional form of Christianity to its purified successor that every member of the first generation of the Reformation underwent was itself a powerfully dramatic psychological turn. Behind it lay the conversion narratives of St. Paul and St. Augustine, and every Christian who newly found himself a Protestant from the 1520s on must have been aware that his life had changed course in a way that recapitulated those earlier narratives. The sense of drama, or at least its potential, would continue in the convert's need, imposed or sought, to con-

front the authority of the old order. A classic text of the English Reformation
like John Foxe's *Acts and Monuments* reflects awareness of the dramatic character of the encounters it narrates; its success with readers comes of its ex-
ploitation, in dialogue and characterization, of the histrionic potential inherent in its narrative materials.[2] Moreover, at the center of Protestant worship
stands an essentially dramatic performance, the sermon. Clearly the successful
preacher of the sixteenth century, who held his auditory for the space of two or
more hours, had something of the skill and physical presence of an actor. In
his recent study of the reciprocal nature of the relation between the stage and
the pulpit, Bryan Crockett points out that the preacher in the sixteenth century
was understood to be playing a role, that of a prophet mediating the word of
God to the people: "Like Shakespeare's Prospero, the preacher quite literally
dons a robe and heightens his language for the prophetic performance."[3] Edmund Grindal, who as bishop of London and Archbishop of York had opposed
the stage, promoted the development of effective, actorly preaching; in fact,
his suspension as archbishop of Canterbury in 1579 came of his refusal of
Elizabeth's demand that he suppress the "prophesyings" that aimed to increase
the numbers of clergy who, rather than reading from the *Book of Homilies,*
would perform genuine sermons. The Reformation could not be inimical to
the sense of inner drama that conversion implied nor unaware of the theatricality of conflict. And in the latter half of the reign of Elizabeth, it became increasingly conscious of the need for the histrionic presentation of God's word
and of its own ideology.[4]

    While there is, then, nothing inherently antitheatrical about Protestantism,
and while the first generation of the Reformation, particularly John Bale,
would exploit its oppositional status in moral interludes, by the 1560s and
1570s this larger sense of the dramatic would increasingly collide with the
more specific sense of drama as a mode of representation. The preacher,
though he assumed a prophetic role and aimed at an actorly delivery, did not
portray another with his physical body. The sermon can be understood perhaps
as the quintessential form of Protestant drama, one in which a solitary figure
assumes the role of conveying and interpreting God's word. But its representational character is limited to this function. Beyond the sermon, the larger impulse to convey a dramatic sense of ideological and psychological change
stood in an uneasy tension with physical representation of the sacred. The
iconoclasm that brought an end to the cycle drama between 1565 and 1579 did
not mean that biblical subjects were thereafter forbidden on English stages.
But the new plays written under Protestant auspices, both before and after the
ending of the civic cycles, show an increasing anxiety and ambivalence about
representation. They illustrate as well, even in spite of some notable successes, the process leading to the ultimate rejection of the idea that the sacred
could be represented on stage, a rejection that replicates the rejection of visual
representation in painting and sculpture a generation earlier.

    The record of surviving plays in England drawn from biblical material
from the late 1530s to the end of the 1560s shows an initial attempt by Protestant writers to create a reformed drama, to harness the considerable energy ap-

parent in the religious drama of the fifteenth and early sixteenth centuries. Though that drama was Catholic in the ideological and cultural use to which it had been put, its potency was undeniable to the Reformers and the utility of its appeal to large urban audiences clearly evident. Indeed, that potency must have remained a strong memory even in the decades after the great civic cycles of York, Chester, Coventry, Wakefield, and Norwich were ended. Records of biblical drama are conspicuous by their absence in the 1580s, the decade immediately following the *coup de grâce* of the last civic cycles. A small handful of plays on biblical subjects emerged in the public theaters in the 1590s, then in a single year, 1602, seven biblical plays were written or performed by companies under Philip Henslowe's aegis. Of the plays of that decade, only two texts survive, Thomas Lodge and Robert Greene's *A Looking Glasse for London and England* (1594) and George Peele's *David and Bethsabe* (1599); of the nine other plays, only titles indicate their subject matter. *David and Bethsabe* can tell us something about what the representation of biblical narrative had become at end of the 1590s. But there is something strange about the silence that surrounds the bare titles of six of these plays that are recorded as associated with one of Henslowe's stages in 1602: "Judas," "Pontius Pilate," "Jephthah," "Tobias," "Samson," and "Joshua." Their titles indicate subject matter quite different from that of the earlier cycle drama; if, as seems likely from the other titles, "Judas" refers not to the betrayer but to the Jewish warrior of the Hasmodean wars, then the plays represent a mix of the historical and the erotic in their orientation. Even "Pontius Pilate" was more likely to have been drawn from apocryphal material than from the New Testament. As I shall suggest below, the concentration of these plays in the single year of the Lord Admiral's repertory may point to an ideological gesture aimed toward patronage or the building of a particular kind of audience. While it is perilous to argue from silence, the fact that none were published or left any trace beyond Henslowe's diary may indicate how little effect this last, brief crop of Protestant biblical plays achieved. Peele's *David and Bethsabe* may indeed have stimulated this brief fashion—and it must finally represent it.

Before tracing the transformation and attenuations of biblical drama in the Reformation, I want to underscore the momentous centrality of the forcible ending of the cycle drama in the second decade of Elizabeth's reign. It is in fact literally central to the narrative I want to establish, occurring at the midpoint between the first attempts to initiate an equivalent Protestant drama in the late 1530s and its last moment in the record of Henslowe's plays in 1602. The significance of the suppression of the traditional drama can scarcely be overestimated. Successively, the civic cycles of Norwich, York, Wakefield, Chester, and Coventry, a tradition of local theater extending back to the late fourteenth century, were ended. In York and Chester at least (the only cases where a record survives) the cycles were ended *against* the wishes of the municipal authorities and, presumably, against the desire and interests of a substantial part of the citizens. As a cultural phenomenon, this civic theater represents something entirely different from the professional theater which may seem to succeed it. Though of commercial importance to the towns and cities, it had never been directed to specifically commercial ends. While entertaining enough to draw audiences from the surrounding regions, it was not defined as entertainment. The festive elements of its annual performance were obviously an important part of its appeal, but its explicit purpose was not recreational but religious. It was not under aristocratic patronage, as the London theater would be, but resolutely bourgeois, the property of the craft guilds who owned the individual pageants and the town councils who oversaw their production. At Coventry and York performance was normally annual, at intervals of three or four years at Chester, absorbing the energies of the guilds for up to half of the year and providing a focus that was largely provincial. It was not, finally, separate from and inimical to the civic authorities (as the London theater would be) but patronized, indeed sponsored, by them as an expression of their city's identity and pride. While typically set within annual religious festivals, Corpus Christi or Whitsuntide, it shared as well in the characteristic blurring of the sacred and secular that festival implies.[5] For most people who saw it, it was the only theater they experienced in the year, for some, no doubt, the only theater they witnessed in their lives. Its loss was a local and regional loss, an impoverishment of the life of provincial centers.[6] In this, as in so many other elements of English Reformation culture, a centripetal force was at work, moving authority and control away from the regions and toward the capital. But—and this is perhaps strange—its disappearance had little direct consequence for the new London theater. The indirect consequence, especially in the self-definition of the London theater, is of course another matter.

I

In England the Reformation attempt to use biblical theater for its own ends begins with the potent figure of John Bale. Bale's life illustrates the dramatic personal history of the first generation of reformers. He was born in Suffolk in 1495 (at Cove, near Dunwich), was sent to the Carmelite house at Norwich at the age of 12, then to Jesus College, Cambridge in 1514.[7] After travel and study in the Low Countries and at Toulouse in the 1520s, he became the Carmelite prior first at Maldon (Suffolk) in 1530, then at Ipswich two years later. His conversion probably began about this time, when he came under the influence of Thomas Lord Wentworth, who was already a Protestant and a patron of reform. Bale became Carmelite prior at Doncaster in 1534, perhaps with the brief of preaching the royal supremacy in the north. By 1535 or 1536 his conversion was complete; at this time he left his order to become parish priest at Thorndon, also in Suffolk, and married. Much of Bale's life up to the time of his conversion was spent in East Anglia, and he must have been deeply imbued in that region's rich theatrical culture. We cannot know for sure of his direct participation in theatrical performance before his conversion, but two of the plays that he would later list as having composed, "On the Lord's Prayer" and "On the Seven Deadly Sins," sound pre-Reformation in theme: a third is an immensely long play, listed as extending to fourteen books on the life of John the Baptist, a significant figure in Carmelite tradition.[8] By the second half of the 1530s, Bale was clearly active in the creation of a Protestant religious theater. When in January 1537 he was imprisoned for heresy at Greenwich by the Bishop of London, the antiquary John Leland interceded with Cromwell for his release "because of the comedies he has brought forth" ("ob editas comedias"). It seems likely that from late 1536 until 1540 Bale led a traveling acting company under Cromwell's patronage that performed his own plays.[9] In September 1538 "Balle and his ffellowes" were given 40 shillings "for playing before my lorde" (Cromwell) and a payment of 30 shillings for the same activity, before the same lord, in January 1539. Other evidence points to a production of *King Johan* before the archbishop of Canterbury at Christmas, 1538. Together these details suggest that Bale was active in the construction of an early Protestant theater, one patronized by Cromwell and no doubt directed toward polemical ends. After Cromwell was executed in 1540, Bale fled with his family to the Continent. Four of his five surviving plays, including his three biblical plays, were printed by Dirik van der Straten at Wesel in 1547–1548. But the extent of Bale's theatrical activity very likely goes well beyond these published plays. Bale made four lists of plays he claimed to have written, encompassing in all some twenty-four plays, including the three whose titles suggest possible pre-conversion composition. Titles such as "On the Papist Sects," "On Critics," "On the Traditions of the Papists," "Against Corruptors of the Word of God," and "On the Impostures of Thomas Becket" indicate plays of a polemical Protestant character analogous to *King Johan*, which survives only in manuscript.

At the center of Bale's dramatic activity was the attempt to construct something like a reformed version of the cycle plays that he would have known in the East Anglian dramatic tradition, of which the plays now known as *N-Town* are the sole surviving example. Peter Womack has astutely suggested that in this dramatic activity we can see something like the reverse of Roland Barthe's famous "death of the author."[10] In Bale's revision of pre-Reformation biblical drama, there occurs the birth of the author as "[t]he iconoclastic playwright moves in on a pre-existing scene which belongs not to another playwright but to an institutional set of functions," the words of Scripture, a tradition of interpretation, and "the performance requirements of a customary social and devotional event." Bale may not wish or intend to be the author of his plays—he lists his role as "compiler" on the title pages—but he becomes one in the middle of an ideological struggle. A gap has opened up, Womack suggests, between God's word and its interpretation: "Into this gap comes the Prolocutor, arguing with the audience about the meaning of the play itself" (p. 8). In 1548 Bale returned to take up the living of Bishopstoke in Hampshire; he writes that he was reviled for rehearsing—or having performed—his *Three Laws*, a large, sprawling polemical morality play, in Hampshire in 1551. In 1552, preferred as bishop to the see of Ossory in Ireland, Bale records how he performed his surviving biblical plays *God's Promises, John Baptist's Preaching in the Wilderness,* and *The Temptation of our Lord*—at Kilkenny on August 22, 1553, at the proclamation of Queen Mary's accession. Other biblical plays Bale lists as having written, "Christ and the Twelve," "On Lazarus," "On the Council of Priests," "the Feast of Simon the Leper," "On the Supper and the Washing of Feet," "On the Passion," "On the Burial and Resurrection," suggest a "cycle," but one concentrated on the New Testament—and focused on the preaching and public career of Christ. What is conspicuously absent are plays on the A. nunciation, the Visitation, the Birth of Christ, the Shepherds, the Flight into Egypt, the Adoration of the Magi and the Slaughter of the Innocents. These plays would necessarily have featured the Virgin and the inarticulate infancy of Christ.[11] Equally significant is the fact that these are the plays that in the traditional drama celebrated incarnation itself and whose appeal was strongly affective rather than verbal or doctrinal. They centered particularly on the fact of Christ's human flesh and its shared vulnerability with that of general humanity. If, as seems evident, Bale did intend a replacement of the traditional cycle, then his cycle would have concentrated instead on an articulate and very talkative Christ, one who could be made to argue the polemical issues of reformed theology. In such a scheme *God's Promises* would stand first and would do duty as a truncated version of the substantial Old Testament portion of the medieval cycle. Seen in the light of the cycle plays, it is a "prophets play" like that which immediately preceded the Annunciation play in the East Anglian *N-Town* collection, but it includes Adam, Noah, Abraham, and Moses as well, and encompasses an idea of Old Testament justice to be completed by the mercy of the New.[12]

What is significant about Bale, in contrast to the Protestant playwrights who would follow him, is that the issue of representation as such does not appear to trouble him; he is not concerned to excise the body of God from the stage.[13] In *God's Promises*, after a prologue of theological exposition by "Baleus prolocutor," the drama proper begins with Pater Coelestis, who enters with an Adam who has already sinned. But what is left out of Bale's version is as significant as what is left in. Bale's Pater Coelestis defines his nature just as the God the Father does at the beginning of the traditional cycle plays. But Bale omits the narrative drama of Adam and Eve's temptation and sin and instead begins with God's accusation of Adam. This brings the play abruptly to its doctrinal center, the issue of justice and mercy. This happens without what Bale may consider the distraction of narrative. Though God is represented, it is Adam who becomes the interesting figure in the action. God speaks simply from a static position of injured justice; it is Adam who insists upon mercy. Pater Coelestis is content to condemn Adam until the latter reminds him he is made in his image and likeness and is therefore worth his mercy. The same pattern obtains with Noah and Abraham; the traditional narratives are omitted, and a dialogue is substituted in which the human figure must persuade God to grant mercy. It is not surprising that Bale should omit the non-scriptural quarreling between Noah and his wife of the traditional plays, but he ignores as well the biblical narrative of the sacrifice of Isaac, which had been the most emotionally potent Old Testament play of the cycles.

Bale's interest, clearly, is in discourse; he steers wide of the narrative elements that draw the audience toward emotional engagement and instead dramatizes purely verbal arguments about the issue of mercy and justice that can
be defined in terms of the six Old Testament figures brought on stage to dis-
pute with Pater Coelestis. Whatever dramatic interest the scenes have is centered solely on the two figures arguing the doctrinal question.[14] While Bale
does not shy away from bringing God forth on stage in visible dramatic form,
he is not interested in physically embodying the biblical narratives themselves. Instead, the play grows increasingly textual. Isaiah responds to Pater
Coelestis's accusation of idolatry by summarizing several chapters of the book
of Kings:

For that cause thu hast in two divided them—
In Samaria the one, the other in Hierusalem:
The kynge of Juda in Hierusalem ded dwell,
And in Samaria the kynge of Israel.
Ten of the twelve trybes bycame Samarytanes,
And the other two were Hierosolymytanes.
In both these cuntreyes accordynge to their doyinges
Thu permyttedest them to have most cruell kynges:
The first of Juda was wycked kynge Roboam;
Of Israel the first was that cruell Hieroboam;
Abia than folowed, and in the other Nadab,
Then Basa, then Hela, then Zambri, Joram and Achab;
Then Ochosias, then Athalia, then Joas.
On the other part was Joathan and Achas;
To rehearce them all that have done wrtechydlye
In the syght of the it were longe verelye.[15]

It were indeed, but not so long that it prevents John the Baptist from a similar
listing of kings and prophets in the next act. It is not simply that the play
grows didactic; even long speeches can be made dramatically effective. It is
rather that the didactic character seems to find its exclusive point in discursive
exposition and a summarizing of the biblical texts themselves. Even Bale's
earlier attempts to make the discourse between the human and divine emotionally persuasive become eventually swallowed up in textual learning.

The two New Testament plays that were evidently designed to follow
God's Promises, and evidently did follow it in the performance recorded at
Kilkenny, show Bale's competence in dramatizing scriptural confrontations.
Both *John Baptist's Preaching in the Wilderness* and *The Temptation of Our
Lord* are more effective theater because they are able to make dramatic capital
of verbal disputation, a trait that fuses the late medieval tradition with Refor-
mation predilection. In the Baptist play fidelity to the text of scripture requires
John to confront first the repentant sinners, "Turba vulgaris," "Publicanus,"
and "Miles Armatus," then the unrepentant Pharisee and Sadducee, to whom
he can assign papist sins. The same pattern emerges in the play on Christ's
Temptation by Satan in the wilderness; the play effectively dramatizes their
confrontation. Bale is not shy about expanding the gospel text; the speeches of

the two characters are fleshed out in rather the same way a sermon would elaborate the spare dialogue of the brief gospel narrative. In fact what seems to attract Bale is the way the confrontation of Christ and Satan is a conflict over *texts*. As in the gospel narrative, Satan quotes the psalm text in order to tempt Christ to throw himself from the pinnacle of the temple:

> Tush, scripture is with it, you can not fare amys,
> For it is written how God hath geven a charge
> Unto hys Angels that if you leape at large
> They shall receyve ye in their handes tenderly,
> Least ye dashe your fote agaynst a stone therby.[16]

Bale's Christ replies that Satan has "omytted foure wordes whych foloweth next, / As 'in all thy wayes', whych if you put out of syght, / Ye shall never take that place of scripture a ryght." The words that Satan had quoted, Christ concludes, "maketh for non outwarde workynge, / If ye marke the Psalme throughly from hys begynninge." But why had Satan not quoted the next verse? It was not part of his purpose, Satan replies, but Christ may quote it if he likes. Since the psalm speaks of subduing the cruel serpent and treading down the lion and the pestilent dragon, Christ does, of course, hold it up to his adversary, then concludes with the sixth chapter of Deuteronomy: "Thu shalt in no wyse tempt God presumptuously." The episode in the New Testament clearly appealed to Bale because it was a conflict over texts. He intensifies this, adding to Christ's textual learning; his victory is the victory of one who knows more scripture and can more readily vaunt it. If both of Bale's New Testament plays lack sustained dramatic action, it is not a serious fault because of their comparative brevity and Bale's skill in animating the play of ideas in them. Their concentration in following the biblical episodes also concentrates Bale's polemic. Both plays, as well as *God's Promises*, begin and end with his spokesman, "Baleus prolocutor," pointing up the messages they intend. As in all of Bale's drama, they aim at being a theater of words and texts.

His longer, non-biblical plays illustrate most obviously how the fifteenth-century dramatic tradition was mutating in his hands in response to Reformation pressures. Much of Bale's dramaturgy, insofar as we can infer it from his four surviving dramatic texts, implies continuity with the East Anglian drama from which he emerged. For example, his plays imply a close relation between the dramatic action and the audience, even demonstrated by the audience's occasional inclusion within the drama. At the beginning of *Johan Baptystes Preachynge* the audience is assigned the implied role of the crowd to which John preaches. A similar relationship is indicated at the beginning of *The Temptation* when Christ appears to speak directly to the audience: "Thynke not me to fast bycause I wolde yow to fast, / For than ye thynke wronge and have vayne judgement."[17] "Baleus prolocutor" insists at the beginning of both plays that the action is present to the audience. "*Now* shall Messias, which is our heavenly kynge, / Apere to the worlde in manhode evydent," he says at the opening of the play on the Baptist's preaching. "*Now* is he gone fourth into the desart place" defines the action of *The Temptation*. The second act of *Three Laws* begins in lively comic fashion reminiscent of the East Anglian *Mankind* with Naturae Lex speaking in sermon fashion, then being interrupted by Infidelitas coming onstage like a peddlar selling brooms and other "gauds" and tossing vulgar insults at the serious character.[18] After Infidelitas insults Naturae Lex off the stage, he conjures up Sodomismus and Idolatria, the former costumed like a monk and the latter like an old witch, and all three speak a good deal of comic nonsense together. *King Johan* similarly contains some lively comic material. In Act I Clergy goes through a list of religious orders, some invented, that reads like a comic patter song. At other points the capering, singing villains clearly make for good theater, and the poignancy of the plaints of Vidua Yngland would seem similarly effective on stage.[19] Even considering the difficulty of knowing how what we have of the play was staged, whether indeed it was one play or two (as the concluding note suggests), it is clear that in *King Johan*, as in *Three Laws*, Bale's polemical and discursive impulses sooner or later get the better of his dramatic ones. The multiplicity of characters representing various elements of Bale's argument with Rome—"Sedicyon," "Dissymulacion," "Usurped Powre," "Privat Welth," "Treason"—introduces complication upon complication into the unfolding of the play; Bale's interesting innovation of making each of these characters metamorphose into a historical figure only adds to the dramatic confusion. As agitprop, both plays trade a clear, straightforward polemical thrust for an argument that is willing to risk its effectiveness in an insistence on elaboration and repetition. The interest of *King Johan* is the argument that Bale is mounting about the nature of the struggle in the reign of King John between the monarchy and papal power in England. The argument, however, confounds dramatic movement in long and overly similar dialogues. Verbal elaboration appears finally to win an unequal victory over stage presence.

II

This "textualizing" of biblical theater appears in equally emphatic form in a resurrection play, *The Resurrection of Our Lord,* that is roughly contemporaneous with Bale's theatrical activity. The play is fragmentary and anonymous, surviving only in manuscript and with no indication of its provenance as theater.[20] But the play is clearly Protestant, and its modern editor plausibly suggests the probable period of its composition as 1530–1560. Indeed, Bale himself lists a play "de sepultura et resurrectione Christi," but there is no external or internal evidence to link this play with his. It seems possible that this Protestantized mystery play was designed to be performed in somewhat traditional fashion as an adjunct to a religious festival since its action is divided into a "first day's play" and a "second day's play." It is of course difficult to make definitive judgments on the theatrical character of so fragmentary a piece. But it is clear that it is concerned to stay rather strictly within what the

texts of the Gospels would warrant. It allows none of the characterization of
Pilate, Annas, and Caiaphas that were part of the complex development of
these figures in the cycle plays. The opening of the play is lost, but the dialogue between these characters that begins what we have of the play is simply
a rather flat reiteration of what the Gospels narrate of Christ's trial and death.

Paradoxically, this concern for staying within the play's scriptural warrant
is no more apparent than at the one point where it exceeds that warrant and in-
vents a non-scriptural scene. The *N-Town* play, like a Florentine Resurrection
play roughly contemporary with it, had included, without apology or comment, a scene of Jesus' post-Resurrection appearance to the Virgin, before he
appears to the three Marys or to the disciples. The warrant for the portrayal of
this non-scriptural appearance is the assumption, based on Franciscan sources
and tradition, that Jesus would have *had* to have appeared first to the sinless
mother who bore him.[21] This Protestant resurrection play of course makes no
such assumption. But it too exceeds the strict narrative of the Gospel by interpolating a scene in which Jesus appears to Peter after his appearance to
Mary Magdalene in the garden (told in John 20:11–18) and before his meeting
with the two disciples on the road to Emmaus (Luke 24:13–35). In the non-
scriptural scene Jesus absolves Peter of the guilt of his denial, but blames him
for not believing the women who first told him of the resurrection and for not
crediting Jesus' own prophecies of his dying and rising. But now he says he
comes to reconfirm Peter's faith and through him that of the other disciples.
Peter is then left to blame himself in soliloquy for his faithlessness and to mar-
vel at the mercy he has been shown. At Peter's exit "Appendix" then enters,
the figure who offers homiletic commentary on each scene. Even his bookish
name suggests a supplement to a text rather than a speaker about an enacted
event; in the traditional mysteries such commentators were termed "doctor,"
"prologue," or in Bale's usage "prolocutor." Appendix admits, "We nowe have
noe scripture, doth teache vs such appearance / as we have made of Christ (to
Peter) in this order." But both St. Luke's words and St. Paul's, he says, indicate that Christ appeared to Peter, though when, where, or in what words,
scripture does not indicate. Nevertheless, by "conference" of scriptural passages, Appendix conjectures that the appearance must have taken place after
Peter, having been told by the women of the empty tomb, had gone to see it
himself. At this point, then, Christ must have shown himself to Peter during
the latter's perplexity. The ordering of events, Appendix insists "ys kept
Dulye," though the rest must be attributed "vnto our invention."

It is not just the authorial reasoning behind the placement of the scene
that distinguishes the play from late-medieval precedent but the fact that the
reasoning must be spelled out in detail and interpolated in commentary between scenes of the play. The logic of the appearance of Christ to his mother
in *N-Town* is essentially affective; he *must* have appeared first to the mother
who has agonized over his death. The logic of the Tudor resurrection play,
however, is philological: the comparison of texts indicates that Christ appeared to Peter, even though the scene is not narrated in the gospels. Texts are
the authority. And like Brechtian alienation, though without its self-conscious

intentionality, the commentary of Appendix between the scenes breaks into the narrative representation to remind viewers that the scene is invented, though invented with good textual warrant and due consideration of historical circumstance and probability. Clearly we are in a world where texts matter *as* texts. But the triumph of this textualizing tendency in the play comes in the portrayal of the Road to Emmaus that follows. The words of Luke's gospel, "he expounded unto them in all the Scriptures the things concerning himself" (Luke 24:27), are lavishly elaborated into a 246-line speech of Jesus punctuated only by a couplet each from Luke and Cleopas. At this point the action of the play ceases altogether and it becomes the sermon that Cleopas recognizes it as being. The center of the play thus merges with its framework in the surrounding commentary of Appendix. Both press the play toward the sermon genre and efface its dramatic character.

III

The portrayal of Christ on the Protestant stage of the mid-sixteenth century presented increasing difficulty. While Bale's two New Testament dramas do not shrink from the necessity or challenge, the Resurrection play shows some of the strain involved. Admittedly, what should be the most tender and powerful moment of his resurrection portrayal, his appearance to Mary Magdalene, is missing from the manuscript. But the two surviving scenes portray him as elaborating theological dogma rather than entering into dramatic relation with either Peter or Luke and Cleopas. This tendency is most strikingly apparent in another mid-century Protestant play text drawn from the New Testament, Lewis Wager's *The Life and Repentaunce of Marie Magdalene*.[22] Significantly, this is the last surviving Protestant play that would attempt dramatic portrayal of Christ. Though the play was published in 1566, the mention of the king in the prologue indicates that the play was written and performed in Edward's reign. Its dramaturgy indicates that it was performed by a traveling professional company. A five-actor company (though the title page says four) could perform the play with the doubling specified in the text; the prologue mentions admission prices of one pence and half pence. Significantly, the prologue contains indications of mid-century antitheatrical sentiment; Wager refers to detractors of the play and of the actors' "facultie" and defends them by saying they have played far and wide and indeed have acted even in the university. The terms by which Wager defends the play suggest Protestant detractors rather than Catholic. He insists that the play extols virtue and teaches the praise of God, obedience to the king, and godly sentences; its critics are mistaken in their blame, he implies, for this play tends strongly toward good Protestant ends. Why the play might have raised criticism in this quarter is something I shall address below.

What is particularly interesting about the play as biblical drama is the way it attenuates the Gospel narrative in its overall structure. We might at first suspect that it represents a Protestant grafting of morality drama onto the biblical play, here the dramatization of Luke 7. The play begins in lively enough fashion with the byplay of the morality vices through the first half, suggestive indeed of Bale's dramaturgy or perhaps similarly connected with East Anglian traditions (especially if the university where it was played was Cambridge). Wager introduces some bawdry when the pre-repentant Mary insists to the four vices that there is no instrument she cannot "handle" as well as any gentlewoman; Infidelity says he has a "goodlie pipe" so big that her hand cannot grip it. A song then rounds off the scurrility. But Wager's portrayal of the vices represents something of a representational failure of nerve; he does not allow them a consistent portrayal, but has them step out of character to deliver straight moralizing, for example when Infidelity points out that the indulgence of parents is the plague of children. It appears finally that it is rather the biblical play that has been grafted onto the moral interlude. The Magdalene as a biblical figure emerges only in the final quarter of the play. Her traditional story is largely eliminated—nothing connected with Lazarus or Martha occurs, let alone any hint of the extra-biblical traditions that give an aura of romance to the fifteenth-century Mary Magdalene play in the Digby manuscript. Wager's Magdalene play confines itself entirely to Luke 7, with additions to Jesus' role from the gospel of John. Jesus does not even appear until two-thirds of the way through the play. When he does, he is very much the austere Jesus of the gospel of John; what is emphasized is his theological significance, not his human character or his relation with Mary. In fact, it is the Pauline theology of Romans, and *not* the story of the repentant Magdalene, that finally controls the action. Mary is not converted by her encounter with Jesus. Her conversion begins in the previous scene when she meets a figure called Law. In an allegory that follows Romans, "Law," aided by another personification called "Knowledge of Sin," convicts Mary, who becomes persuaded of her reprobation, then repents of her past life, and finally despairs of forgiveness by God. When Christ enters, he then supplies the reality of grace. Even the words of Jesus in Luke, that Mary is forgiven because she has loved much, are subject to considerable glossing and extenuation—and indeed contradicted. After the portrayal of the biblical episode, Mary returns with Justification, who is at pains to insist that in fact Mary was *not* forgiven because she loved, that is, because of her *works*, but because of her *faith*:

> It were a great errour for any man to beleve
> That your love dyd deserve that Christ shold forgeve
> Your synnes or trespasses, or any synne at all:
> For so to beleve is an errour fanaticall.[23]

By contradicting the gospel narrative that is its source, the play veers away from a dramatic portrayal of the encounter. In this it seems precisely opposite to the Florentine *Rappresentazione della conversione di Santa Maria Maddalena* discussed in the last chapter. The scheme becomes entirely theological, entirely Pauline. Its Mary Magdalene seems, finally, not so much the woman of the Gospel story as a morality figure beset by abstract explanation. The biblical figures, including Christ, are there to illustrate, and are finally controlled by, the theological schema. Narrative—and the affective dimensions of the narrative—are subsumed by theological explanation.

After Wager's *Life and Repentaunce of Marie Magdalene*, the only other known instance of an English vernacular drama written in the sixteenth century that *may have* portrayed Christ is Thomas Ashton's play (or plays) performed at Shrewsbury in the 1560s. Ashton was the humanist headmaster of the Shrewsbury School and had been a pupil of Martin Bucer at Cambridge. No texts survive of Ashton's play, and even the unique record of subject matter, "Mr Ashton's first playe vpon the passion of Christe," is subject to doubt.[24] After Bale's *God's Promises,* no vernacular drama written under Protestant auspices would bring God the Father onto the stage. The traditional mystery cycles, of course, would continue to portray both the Father and the Son into the 1560s and 1570s but on the evidence of surviving plays, Protestant dramatists drew back altogether from the theatrical portrayal of the divine, even the human divine, from the mid-1560s. It is tempting to speculate that the antitheatricalism hinted at in Wager's prologue may have been provoked by his presuming to put Christ on stage—and that the failure of the portrayal, its being hedged about with theological abstraction, derives from anxiety over the attempt. In any case, the rest of the biblical plays written in the vernacular after Wager's and Ashton's are all drawn from the Old Testament or the Apocrypha, and all eschew the portrayal of the divine. Taken as a group they show both the dramatic possibilities that the Reformation had opened for biblical theater and at the same time the disintegration of the very idea of such a theater. Bale's ambition to create a Protestant version of the mystery cycle had virtually no influence and did not survive his own attempt. Ironically, his desire to center a Protestant cycle on the New Testament would prove the least acceptable element of this redirection of biblical theater; after the 1560s no play texts would be drawn from the New Testament. While the surviving "biblical dramas" from the second half of the sixteenth century go in essentially different directions, each lays some claim to some element of the dramatic character of the Reformation. What links them, however, is a common wariness about the stage embodiment of God.

Closest in conception to Wager's insertion of the gospel story of Mary Magdalene into a morality context is *The Commody of the moste vertuous and Godlye Susanna*, written by the otherwise unknown Thomas Garter. Though published in 1578, the note that it was "never before this tyme Printed" implies some previous theatrical life; indeed, its style and verse, rhymed fourteeners punctuated by less regular verse among the vices, also give it away as written perhaps a decade earlier. In fact, a Stationer's Company entry of "the playe of susanna" early in 1569 by a printer whose widow would marry the play's eventual printer confirms its composition and performance in the 1560s.[25] Whatever the play's limitations as poetry, it is altogether a livelier piece of theater than Wager's *Repentaunce of Mary Magdalene*. Freed of the necessity of representing the divine, and indeed drawing his narrative from the Apocrypha rather than one of the canonical texts of Scripture, the playwright is able to use the morality tradition to good effect in representing a narrative that centers on moral, rather than purely theological, issues. The story of Susanna features lust and voyeurism as well as issues of legal judgment, the need to discern perjury and disentangle conflicting testimony, and the vindication of the falsely accused. The play's treatment of these legal themes suggests that its auspices might well have been the Inns of Court or a gathering of magistrates. Joachim, Susanna's husband, is portrayed as a magistrate who is painfully aware of, indeed almost overwhelmed by, the responsibility of just rule. The essentially Protestant stamp of the play rests in his character: in spite of his upright character, he feels keenly the weight of his own unworthiness and the need of God's grace. His sense of the frailty of human justice is born out by the plot, for Judex, the judge who presides over the trial of Susanna, accepts the testimony of the elders, who are also identified as judges, and Susanna is condemned. Daniel then appears as a kind of judicial deus ex machina, and in a second trial, as in the conclusion of the book of the Apocrypha, Susanna is vindicated, the elders condemned and—on stage—stoned to death.

The play's resemblance to Wager's Magdalene play lies in the fact that the biblical narrative is set into a morality structure. The play begins with Satan's appearance on stage and his comically abusive bantering with his "son," Ill Report. Their capering and preening and scatological joking, again, extends from the traditions of fifteenth-century popular drama. The versification of their speeches follows too from that tradition, for instead of the plodding fourteeners of the rest of the play, the Satan and the vices speak in shorter, less regular lines, frequently in skeltonics. The two elders, unnamed in the Apocrypha, are called Voluptas and Sensualitas, and they too enter into comic byplay with Ill Report before the play turns to the biblical narrative. The play then quite carefully follows that narrative, emphasizing Joachim's role of magistrate and judge as it enters the story of Susanna's false accusation by the lustful voyeurs. When the biblical narrative is brought to conclusion with the stoning of the elders, the play returns to the morality mode for the arrest and hanging of Ill Report, whose death gives satisfaction even to Satan. The final appearance of Joachim, Susanna, and her parents then points up the requisite moral lessons and offers prayers for the queen and her counsel. Like Wager's Magdalene play, the *Comedy of Susanna* has no specifically affective or devotional end in view; at the same time, it does not have that play's polemical aim, but it shares its general subordination of biblical narrative to the demands of the morality interlude. While stageworthy, the play lacks the affective engagement with its audience that had characterized the traditional biblical cycles that were, in this same decade, receiving their final performances.[26] If biblical drama remained a possibility for a reformed England in the 1560s, it had to skirt carefully the devotional role it had played in the previous century and a half. Like the saints, whose affective and intercessory powers had been withdrawn and who now were to be understood simply as moral exempla, biblical narratives were now limited to the teaching of good doctrine and a moral life.

IV

Still, the possibility for an effective reformed biblical drama that aspired to engage its audience, even while avoiding the representation of the sacred, can be encountered in two plays contemporaneous with Wager's *Mary Magdalene* and *Godlye Susanna*, one labeled a tragedy and the other a kind of domestic comedy. *A tragedie of Abrahams Sacrifice* must have originally been written within a year or two of Wager's Mary Magdalene play, and it was published in its English translation a year before the *Comedy of Susanna*. The French Reformer Théodore de Bèze brought out his *Abraham Sacrifiant* in 1550; as it appears to come of his conversion to a Calvinist Protestantism, it was very likely composed in the previous year.[27] Arthur Golding translated Bèze's French into English some twenty-five years later and published his version in 1577. In 1598 Bèze wrote to Jean Jacomot (who translated it into Latin) that the play had been performed, almost fifty years earlier, by students at the Academy of Lausanne and in France "with great applause."[28] The comedy is *Jacob and Esau*, light years beyond Bale and far more effective theater than either *Mary Magdalene* or *Godlye Susanna*. It was called "a new mery and wittie Comedie or Enterlude" in the second (and only complete surviving) edition of 1568, but it appears to have been first published a decade earlier. If *Abraham Sacrificing* indicates what might have been possible for serious, quasi-tragic drama, *Jacob and Esau* stands as a curiously unique example of what could be realized in a domestic comic mode.

In comparison with Wager's *Mary Magdalene, Godlye Susanna*, or *King Darius*, the play *Jacob and Esau* shows a conspicuous turn away from morality play devices; no personifications of virtues or vices appear on the stage, later to take on the roles of characters in the narrative. Rather, the mode is entirely naturalistic both in characterization and in dialogue. In fact, the play is as lively a work for the stage as survives from the 1550s and 1560s, and the resemblance of its verse to *Ralph Roister Doister* has led to its attribution to Nicholas Udall.[29] Witty, mischievous servants enter the narrative and serve to naturalize the biblical figures. Esau's servant Ragau complains about his master to the audience, faulting his meanness to himself and his carelessness of his neighbors' sleep in blowing his hunting horn and shouting for his dogs (who are present on stage). Mido, old Isaac's servant, mocks his master's blind groping and later enters laughing heartily at the famished greed with which Esau has devoured the pottage exchanged for the birthright. Perhaps the funniest moment in the play is the *lese majesté* when Jacob must don the goatskin sleeves, gloves, and collar and his coarse brother's "fragrant" cloak. His mother's servant Debora comments ironically on how smart the fastidious Jacob looks in this outlandish gear. In the scene following, as Isaac strokes the supposed Esau's hairy skin, he remarks his elder son "is rough of heare as any goate." And yet the play also seriously engages contemporary moral and psychological issues. Esau's crudity and heedless prodigality is contrasted interestingly with Jacob's sense of filial obligation, and the opposition between the two raises questions of nature and nurture. Two of Isaac's neighbors, wakened by Esau's predawn hunting din, discuss the old man's apparent disinclination to check his older son and inquire into a father's responsibility for a son's bad character. Jacob's imposture is made to seem all the starker and more problematic by the servant Mido's inability to lie about it. The play portrays, with considerable psychological plausibility, a family characterized by unaccountable differences in the personalities of its sons. The story of Jacob's acquisition of the birthright and the paternal blessing is told in a brisk and straightforward narrative that illustrates the mystery of God's ways evolving from human deception, jealousy, and weakness. While clearly Protestant in its suggestion that Jacob represents one of the elect and Esau is reprobate, this is actually touched upon fairly lightly and confined for the most part to the prologue and epilogue. Some scholars have suggested that Esau is to be identified with Catholicism while Jacob and Rebecca must be Protestant in their righteousness, but nothing in the play bears this out.[30] In fact a polemical dimension is conspicuous by its absence. In its humor and naturalism the play goes well beyond the allegorical and morality mode of other mid-century drama that endeavored to turn biblical theater to Protestant uses. It seems rather to anticipate the theater that would develop in the 1580s. But another way to see the play would be as a revival of, or throwback to, the traditions of popular biblical theater still surviving from the fifteenth-century cycles. The saucy servants, Ragau, Mido, Debora, and Abra, may look from one perspective like imitations of Roman drama, but the resemblance to the comic servants of the mysteries, best known now from Wakefield, is at least as strong.[31] When Abra is making up the supposed venison stew for Jacob to serve Isaac, she says she trusts to make such a savory broth as "God almighty selfe may wet his finger therein." It is a bold enough quip for a Protestant play, but entirely in keeping with the sensibility of the older drama.

The question, however, is not which tradition has the strongest claim to the play, but why so lively a transformation of biblical theater toward Protestant ideology was not more influential. Unlike Golding's translation of Bèze's *Abraham Sacrificing, Jacob and Esau* was certainly intended for the stage and, though its theatrical auspices are not known, it must have been played in the first decade of Elizabeth's reign. While light in doctrinal comment—and free of doctrinal polemic—the play certainly represents a turn toward Protestantism. At the play's conclusion the poet emphasizes that the story of Jacob and Esau illustrates the contrast between election and reprobation and the necessity of trust in God's word. By its choice of subject, it avoids the representation of God on the stage, a trait it shares with *Abraham Sacrificing* and *Godlye Susanna*. But together with these plays it comes to represent something more like the end of the initiative begun by Bale in the 1530s than the realization of its success.

As a text Bèze's *Abraham sacrificiant* had phenomenal success—ten editions in the sixteenth century; besides its English version, it was translated into Italian and twice into Latin. It is not known that Golding's translation was ever performed or indeed that he intended it for the stage. But the evidence would appear strongly to point away from any theatrical intention or fruition. Golding is not known to have had any connection with the theater or players, and nearly all of his literary output consists of translation from Latin and French. Most of his French translation is of Calvin's sermons and of other works by French Calvinists, and it would seem likely that he translated *Abraham Sacrifiant* more as an edifying work by one of their number than as a piece for the stage. Bèze's prologue directs the audience to imagine that they are not in Lausanne but somewhere far away; Golding does not localize the city name to an English place, as would seem necessary had the text been tied to performance.

Whether considered as a work of the mid-century French Protestant stage or as merely a potential text for the English stage of the late 1570s, *A tragedie of Abrahams Sacrifice* shows the serious intent of dramatizing Reformation experience through the Abraham and Isaac story. It does in fact what Bale wished to do, but with more balance and subtlety. It is consistent with the growing Reformation hesitance about physical portrayal of the sacred in that the figure of God nowhere appears in the play; instead it is an angel who accosts Abraham with the demand that he sacrifice his son. While the play does not achieve the intensity of emotional engagement with Abraham's dilemma portrayed in such fifteenth-century plays as the Brome *Abraham and Isaac* and Feo Belcari's Florentine *Rappresentatazione di Abramo e Isacco*, it does confront the stark sorrow of Abraham's dilemma that any portrayal of the text, whether visual or dramatic, must achieve. The play is larger in scope than the pageant on the subject in the traditional cycle plays and shows humanist imitation of Greek models in the shepherds' choruses and the stychomythia in the *débat* between Abraham and Sarah. That Satan appears in the cowl of a monk is a superficial indication of its Reformation provenance. More significant is its powerful expression of the sense of isolation of the self. Abraham speaks a long and moving soliloquy at the center of the play expressing the distance he feels from all social support and the pain of the necessity imposed on him of the destruction of all that buttresses his psyche; he is stripped of everything as he confronts what he must do, and the play portrays him cut off from family, friends, and reputation. Interestingly, it does not show the reknitting of his familial world at its close, the return of father and son to Sarah, that had characterized Feo Belcari's Florentine version. All the Calvinist Abraham can rely on is the word of God; as he asks Sarah earlier in the play: "Can ever God his word once sayd unsay?"[32] But Bèze does not project Abraham as a personal allegory of his own experience. Rather, the emphasis on psychic isolation, as well as the subsidiary themes of exile and escape from idolatry, make the biblical protagonist seem a proleptic representative of broader Reformation experience. The apparent theatrical stillbirth of the English version is striking. In spite of its psychological interests and potential for staging, there is no record that it was ever played on the English stage. If so potentially impressive a play by a well known reformer was not mounted, it might be suspected that the tide had decisively turned at this point against biblical representation.

V

Except for the publication of *Abraham Sacrificing* in 1577 and the reprinting that same year of *King Darius* (a decidedly archaic work at this date), there are no records of biblical plays in the two decades between *Jacob and Esau* (in the late 1560s) until around 1590, when Thomas Lodge and Robert Greene's *A Looking Glasse for London and England* appeared. This two-decade hiatus, in spite of the example of *Jacob and Esau* and the potential of Golding's translation of Bèze's play, suggests that the strong ideological current running against the portrayal of God on stage extended as well to the staging of biblical narratives generally. Anthony Munday clearly was speaking for more than himself when he declared in 1580 that "of all abuses this is most undecent and intollerable" that sacred matters should be profaned by actors, that "the reverend word of God, & histories of the Bible" should be set forth on the stage "by these blasphemous plaiers"[33] (Twenty-two years later Munday himself would collaborate with Thomas Dekker on a biblical play, "Jephtha," for Philip Henslowe.) The ten-year period between 1569 and 1579, which would see the final performances of the York, Chester, Wakefield, and Coventry cycles, coincide with a more general hostility to the theater on the part of radical Protestantism. The coalescence of this ideology perhaps suggests why the lively theatricality of *Jacob and Esau* had no successor. If this play and others written at the time represented an attempt to keep alive a tradition of representation that could remain consistent with reformed doctrine, the impulse of iconoclasm, now largely victorious in the practice and fabric of the English church, would seem to have collided with it decisively. Philip Stubbes was most likely referring to the recently closed cycle plays when he condemned "the bawdry, scurrility, wanton showes, and uncomely gestures" with which actors profaned the word of God, but the effect of such comment was to confirm the anxiety about the playing of any scriptural texts over the next decade.[34]

Some of the failure to achieve a reformed biblical theater was no doubt extrinsic. The suppression not only of the feast of Corpus Christi but also of the celebrations of patronal saints' days meant that the communal occasions for biblical and religious plays were gone. New occasions might perhaps be created, but whether these would sustain a complex activity like play production would be uncertain, and in any case the current was running against religious holidays. Except for Bale's performance of *God's Promises, John the Baptist's Preaching*, and *Temptation* at Kilkenny on the occasion of Mary's accession, none of the mid-century Protestant biblical plays carries any indication of the context of its production. Internal evidence might give a clue to a possible occasion for performance but on the whole what we are left with is the impression of orphaned plays standing uncertainly in texts that remain silent about where or by whom they were performed. And indeed whatever the occasion that might support the performance of a biblical play, it could not accord to the play the devotional role that had tied play to event in the recent past.

As with painting, the devotional character of the earlier drama indicated that its affective character was aimed in a primary way at engagement with its audience. In its counter tendency toward text, from Bale onward, reformed drama seems little concerned with an affective response and more interested in advancing discursive argument. Not all of it is as polemical as Bale's plays but, as we have seen, a number of the plays seem inclined to express their relation to texts and to engage in theological discourse. Frequently, as in the case of Wager's *Repentaunce of Mary Magdalen*, this tendency drains the play of theatrical vitality and raises the suspicion that the discursive ends were ill suited to the purposes and character of theater. Choosing Old Testament subjects or those drawn from the Apocrypha was one way of avoiding, or blurring, the devotional issue. Patriarchs and their families had not been a focus of devotion, so they could be portrayed with less anxiety about what their theatrical embodiment might mean. Such subjects could also accomplish more oblique portrayals of sacred history and at the same time offer ethical perspective in terms of a history whose truth was ratified by its biblical status. A play like *Jacob and Esau* seems at once freed of devotional demands and enabled to explore moral and psychological issues in ways not dissimilar from plays concerned with classical or English history. But this freedom came at the price of the strong affective engagement that had animated the biblical theater whose ends had been devotional. In the face of possible objection to biblical representation generally, a Protestant biblical theater would have nothing unique on which to stake its claim.

VI

Still, a "revival" in the use of biblical sources comes in the early 1590s, beginning with Thomas Lodge and Robert Greene's *A Looking Glasse for London and England*. The play may be the first written for the public theaters that dramatizes a biblical narrative, but it also represents the apex of Protestant attempts to achieve an effective and popular biblical theater.[35] The play adapts new Marlovian fashions—high-flown rhetoric, the spectacular corruption of an overreaching Ninevite court, flaunted sexual taboos, cheeky low-life characters, spectacular stage effects—to the demands of satire and a serious moral critique. Marlovian fascination with violated boundaries is apparent in the play's portrayal of the King of Nineveh's incestuous love for his sister. The fashionable Ninevite court, with its aureate language and with corruption centered on usurers and legal officials, is aimed squarely at contemporary London. The low-life characters are energetic and amusing; elements of Adam, the clown, will reappear in Falstaff a few years later.[36] When the devil comes to take the clown to hell, the latter bandies wit with him and eventually cudgels him off the stage. What sets the play off from previous attempts at a Protestant biblical theater is partly its scope and quality; as a full-scale production for the public stage, the play is more seriously engaged with the need to entertain a large audience. At the same time it seems aware, in at least a general way, of the mystery tradition. The fact that Rasni and his court can remind one of Herod and his pretensions from the cycle plays—and at the same time seem an adaptation of Tamburlaine and his rhetoric—suggests conscious understanding of the mystery tradition and an intention to fuse it with contemporary styles. The characters of the usury plot, as well as the low-life comic figures, appear to be contemporary Londoners, a sense that gives the play a doubleness of time scheme, both ancient Nineveh and London *now,* that had characterized the working of the traditional drama. The biblical dimension of the play is interestingly doubled. Oseas (Hosea) is brought on early in the play to sit above the action and insist upon its meaning for London. The Jonah story is the narrative backbone of the play, even though Jonah does not enter until well after the Marlovian beginning, and demonstrates the goal of moral conversion of an entire city; the success of the conversion of Nineveh is of course meant as a lesson for the corrupt city that is to find itself in the looking glass of the play. In proper Protestant fashion, Lodge and Greene's play avoids portraying the sacred on the stage. An angel, rather than God, calls Jonah to his prophetic role. Later a hand, presumably God's, appears from a cloud wielding a sword of vengeance, but even the divine voice is rendered by an angel. But some of the spectacular stage effects—the lightning that burns Remilia to a crisp, the sister and object of Rasni's incestuous love, the flame that consumes the filial-ingrate Radagon, Rasni's corrupt counselor—are portrayals of divine judgment. Jonah "is cast out of the Whales belly vppon the Stage." A snake comes on stage to devour the vine that shelters Jonah. While not a complex piece, *A Looking Glasse* was a lively and spectacular theatrical experience that melded a biblical narrative with the latest fashions and demands of the public theater. It did so, moreover, with serious satiric intent, a desire to engage its audience with some moral demands of the moment.

It seems possible that the success of Lodge and Greene's *Looking Glasse* led to other biblical plays being attempted in the public theaters. To judge simply by its title—no text survives—the "Abram and Lot" that Henslowe records in January 1594 (n.s.) very likely shared with it an interest in lurid eroticism and a satiric stance toward London.[37] A "Heaster and Ahasuerus" followed in June 1594, but the two performances that Henslowe lists were not commercial successes. The "Nebuchadnezzar" that the Lord Admiral's Men played between mid-December 1596, and March 1597, enjoyed more success; though again no text survives, the title suggests a theme in common with both "Heaster and Ahasuerus" and *A Looking Glasse,* that of overreaching tyranny countered and punished by divine judgment. While no indications of its earliest performance history survive, George Peele's *David and Bethsabe* was published in 1599 with the note that it "hath ben divers times plaied on the stage." This play too appears to have been in the repertoire of one of Henslowe's companies.[38] What all of these plays share is an origin in Old Testament texts that had not been part of the traditional cycles. None are tied by liturgical or typological associations to New Testament texts, and none would have required the portrayal of God on stage. On this basis one may suppose that the

"Judas," for which Henslowe paid William Borne and Samuel Rowley in December 1601, was based on the career of Judas Maccabeus from the Apocrypha.[39] On the other hand, Thomas Dekker was paid ten shillings in January 1602 (n.s.) to write a prologue and epilogue for an earlier play of "Pontius Pilate." An inventory of the Lord Admiral's Men for 1598 included "My Lord Caffes gercken, & his hoosse," which may refer to Caiaphas in a play about Pilate.[40] So it is just possible that "Judas" may have focused on Christ's betrayer, though it is hard to imagine that either play would have ventured the portrayal of Christ on the stage at this date. More likely is the supposition that the play ventured to portray a fictionalized Pontius Pilate after his encounter with Christ and/or the legends associated with him.

Peele's *David and Bethsabe* can perhaps indicate something of the nature of this last burst of biblical theater. Seen in relation to that tradition, the play is extraordinary in its conscious revisionism. If the earlier Elizabethan and mid-century plays represented an attenuation of the religious dimension of that theater, in Peele's play that dimension reaches the vanishing point. The very choice of subject matter points in this direction. The narrative of David's kingship in the Books of Samuel is exceptionally subtle in its portrayal of a flawed but attractive personality, who is at once the focus of divine election and chastisement and is at the same time enormously successful in his consolidation of the Israelite monarchy. The sense of divine agency in the biblical narrative is quite limited, implicit mainly in the outcome of political events and in the rare interventions of prophets like Nathan. The narrative in 2 Samuel is, then, far closer to history understood in political terms and far less overt in its theological dimension. Peele, moreover, chooses to begin his play with the event that shows David at his moral and spiritual nadir, the seduction (indeed, in the biblical narrative, the *rape*) of Bathsheba, the wife of Uriah the Hittite, and the latter's virtual murder. At the same time Peele seems intent on manipulating his narrative source to mitigate or even significantly alter the moral judgments implicit in the narrative.

To some degree this comes of his need to compact the narrative. He is intent on interweaving episodes and foreshortening the time-scale of the story, and in some cases this causes a blurring of moral focus. For example, as David exits with Bathsheba toward the presumed seduction, he instructs Cusay to send for her husband, Uriah. In 2 Samuel 11 David sends for Uriah only after Bathsheba has become pregnant in the hope that the couple's sexual intercourse will cover her pregnancy and hide his own guilt. Peele's anticipatory sending seems less motivated—or strangely cold-blooded in the circumstances. David mentions in an aside his plan to murder Uriah by placing him in the vanguard of the battle against the Ammonites, but the omission of Joab's cunning discovery of the plot renders it less prominent. The total effect of Peele's portrayal of David is a strangely cool balance between the lustful sinner and the repentant king; David never emerges as hero, nor is he allowed to work on the audience's sympathy. Naomi Pasachoff, who considers the portrayal in relation to sixteenth-century attitudes toward David, concludes that "Peele's play offers the most ambiguous treatment by a Tudor subject of the life of the Old Testament monarch."[41] What is perhaps most surprising, however, is the image of rebellion that emerges in Absalom. While he has little of the attractiveness of a Hotspur, neither is he the demonized or foolishly naive rebel that Elizabethan audiences might well have expected. More surprisingly, Peele has altered his biblical source to render Absalom more sympathetic. 2 Samuel 16 recounts that Absalom followed the counsel of Ahithophel to lie with David's concubines, the sexual takeover confirming the political. But instead of allowing his Absalom to compound rebellion with incest, Peele has him treat the concubines mercifully, refusing advice to slay them. They are instead an excuse to chastise David's incontinence, "liquor to his inchaste and lustful fire," Absalom calls them. Finally, the doctrine that rebellion is a sin uniquely worthy of damnation undergoes challenge at the conclusion of the play. David's sorrow over Absalom's death is, of course, entirely biblical. But Peele goes beyond this to have David eloquently envision Absalom's reception into heavenly bliss:

> Thy soule there plac'd in honour of the Saints
> Or angels clad with immortalitie,
> Shall reape a sevenfold grace, for all thy greefes.
> Thy eyes now no more eyes but shining stars,
> Shall decke the flaming heavens with novel lampes.
> There shalt thou tast the drinke of Seraphins
> And cheer thy feelings with archangels food.
> Thy day of rest, thy holy Sabboth day
> Shall be eternall, and the curtaine drawne,
> Thou shalt behold they soveraigne face to face.[42]

Are any other rebels, one wonders, accorded such a send-off on the sixteenth-century stage? As this passage indicates, Peele assigns David an aureate style consonant with his identity as a divine singer. This style is frequently interfused with irony, an irony that comes partly of the moral position of the speaker and partly, one comes to suspect, from the pure excess of its rhetoric. The closest analogue perhaps is the overreaching poetry of Jonson's Volpone or Sir Epicure Mammon. But this passage does not appear to be meant ironically and is virtually the last word on Absalom in the play; David's kingly authority seems to fix the idea that Absalom is not damned for his rebellion, but saved—because of his beauty and his father's love.

David and Bethsabe represents the final transformation of the Protestant biblical play into history play. Not only does it aim at a swift-paced telling of a historical narrative, but it shares with the other history plays of the 1590s a sense of wanting to impart that narrative in its own way, giving a sometimes revisionist sense of its central figures and occasionally bending the historical source to suit the interpretation being developed. Gone are the prayers and on-stage piety of the mid-century reformed biblical plays. God makes no appearance in the play, even as an offstage voice, and no angel conveys or interprets his will. David is not the kingly patriarch and singer of sacred song, but a flawed historical king, subject to incontinent (if poetic) lust and though repentant, guilty of murder and controlled both by advisers and the events that are the consequences of his sin. It is not a play with a discernable religious perspective or ideology. What I identified earlier as the textualizing of biblical plays is here transmuted into a preoccupation with aureate poetry, a poetry frequently ironic in its effects, and a concern with the historical ambiguities of kingship.

Strangely, between winter and fall of 1602, Philip Henslowe appears to have been involved in no fewer than six projects with biblical titles. Payment had been made for a play of "Judas" some two years before, but it seems not to have been completed, and in late December 1601, he paid Samuel Rowley and William Bird for its completion. The subject of the play was probably Judas Maccabeus and the heroic story drawn from the Apocrypha. Since cloth was bought for costumes in early January, the play was probably performed early in 1602. At the same time Thomas Dekker was paid for a prologue for a revival of "Pontius Pilate," which appears to have been played some years earlier. This was probably a pseudo-biblical play drawn on legendary material from Josephus and perhaps from the Gospel of Nicodemus as well. That May Anthony Munday and Thomas Dekker were paid for the book of "Jephtha Judge of Israel," and in May and June payments were made for costumes and properties, so the play was probably given that summer. Its title certainly indicates a tragedy that would center on the pathos of the father, victorious in battle, who unknowingly condemns his innocent daughter to death. Though from the canonical scriptures, the text in Judges has little in its narrative that could be made to bear doctrinal or moral significance. Simultaneously Henry Chettle was writing a "Tobias," which he completed in late June; it may also have been performed in the summer, though no further records survive. The text from the Apocrypha would have featured the exotic story of the lover who, advised by an angel, wins his bride by outwitting her demon suitor. In late July of this same year, Henslowe lent six pounds in earnest of a "Samson," drawn obviously from the folktale in Judges, and in late September Samuel Rowley was paid seven pounds in earnest of a "Joshua." Nothing more is known about either play. Finally in early October Henslowe paid fourteen pence "for poleyes & worckmanshipp for to hange absolome," which indicates a revival of *David and Bethsabe* as part of this apparent project of biblical plays. As Peele's play had been published three years earlier, it may well have set the fashion for this last spate of biblical plays. All of these plays were drawn from subjects in the Old Testament and the Apocrypha, and on the evidence of their subjects, several appear to have been centered on exotic or romantic subjects, more martial and erotic than religious in their orientation. If *David and Bethsabe* was the model for, or in any sense representative of, these lost plays, this would lend support to the inference that these final plays with biblical subjects were using their source almost exclusively as a quarry of narratives— and not to produce work of a markedly religious character. Still, the striking concentration of plays drawn from the Bible in this single year suggests that the source was not irrelevant, indeed that something was intended by it.

But what *was* intended by this burst of biblical playwrighting, and what can we make of it from the perspective I have been tracing of the erratic

Protestant attempt to harness the, by this time, two-hundred-year-old tradition of biblical theater? Unfortunately, what we don't know about it seems to out-weigh what we do know. To begin with, we do not even know if all these plays were in fact played on Henslowe's stages. The fourteen pence paid out for poles on which to hang Absolom suggests that a production of Peele's play did take place. Since payments were made for costumes and properties, "Judas" and "Jephthah" appear to have been produced. "Pontius Pilate" was appar-ently a revival, so its costumes and properties would already have been avail-able for a production. But the one fact we do know suggests that we should be cautious about even assuming that the other two plays made it to that point: *no more plays with biblical subjects were ever played on the English stage in the seventeenth century.* In fact, none appear to have been played until well into the twentieth century.[43] It is entirely possible that the last two plays were not finally allowed on the stages of the Admiral's Company and that the subse-quent absence of biblical plays followed from such an inhibition. Could one consequence of this final burst of biblical plays have been serious opposition to any playing of sacred texts, even texts drawn from the Apocrypha? In 1596 Thomas Lodge, who had of course collaborated with Robert Greene on the biblical *Looking Glasse* a few years earlier, commented in his satiric pamphlet *Wits Miserie, and the Worlds Madnesse*, "Againe in stage plaies to make vse of Hystoricall Scripture, I hold it with the Legists odious, and as the Councill of Trent did, *Sess.* § 4. *Fin.* I condemne it."[44] Had Lodge, after his conversion to Catholicism (which came about this time), come to regret his turning of a biblical text into a play? The Council of Trent had not actually condemned the use of scripture in plays, though it had reproved generally "profane usages" of a frivolous, scurrilous, or sacrilegious character.[45] That Lodge interpreted the decree in this way suggests that there was already some discussion about the issue of turning even Old Testament texts into theater, perhaps discussion that followed from his own and the other three biblical plays of the 1590s ("Abra-ham and Lot," "Hester and Ahasuerus," and "Nebuchadnezzar"). That Lodge links his own position with the Council of Trent suggests that he wishes to pit what he implies is a Catholic position against Protestant practice. But Protes-tant practice was scarcely unequivocal on this point, and Puritans would be at least as inclined to condemn the mounting of biblical plays. In fact in the fol-lowing year (1603), Henry Crosse in *Vertues Common-wealth* would ask, "Must the holy prophets and Patriarkes be set vpon a Stage, to be derided, hist, and laught at? or is it fit that the infirmities of holy men should be acted on a Stage, whereby others may be in harted to rush carelesly forward into vn-brideled libertie?"[46] His second question in particular suggests he may have Peele's *David and Bethsabe* in mind. By commissioning four new biblical plays and reviving both *David and Bethsabe* and "Pontius Pilate," Henslowe was taking both a position and a risk. Was he doing so in the hope of appealing to a new part of the London audience? Richard Helgerson has recently argued that differentiation between the Lord Chamberlain's Men, Shakespeare's com-pany, and those associated with Henslowe, the Lord Admiral's and the Earl of Worcester's Men, was precisely one of audience. Henslowe's companies cultivated citizen and artisan audiences and appealed to their interests and values, in contrast to the more aristocratic interests played to by the Chamberlain's Men.[47] The history that the Henslowe companies staged was popular history, and the heroes of that history were the commoners who were frequently the victims of royal or aristocratic power. How this differentiation worked in terms of religious interests is difficult, perhaps impossible, to say with precision.

But a possible answer may be found in another type of play that Henslowe's companies staged between 1599 and c. 1605, one that concerned Protestant and proto-Protestant martyrs and heroes. John Foxe's *Actes and Monuments* was a source quarried for narratives about these religious heroes, not all of them commoners, of course, but all figured as heroes tragically martyred or persecuted by royal and ecclesial tyranny.[48] *I Sir John Oldcastle* (1599) is one such play, collaborative in its authorship, offered as a specific response to the slur on the Lollard martyr that was felt to have been given in the character of Sir John Falstaff (né Oldcastle) in Shakespeare's *Henry IV, Parts 1 and 2*; a second part of the play (now lost) followed in 1600 and was apparently revived in 1602. Two plays on Lady Jane Gray (also lost) are recorded in 1602; these may have been incorporated into Dekker and Webster's *Famous History of Sir Thomas Wyat*, which played a couple of years later. Samuel Rowley's *When You See Me You Know Me*, tracing the beginnings of the Reformation in Henry VIII's reign, appeared in 1603. In 1605 Thomas Heywood's *If You Know Not Me You Know Nobody* extended the role of Protestant saint to Queen Elizabeth. Except for the anonymous *Thomas Lord Cromwell* of 1600, once attributed to Shakespeare and given by the Chamberlain's Men, all of these plays were given by Henslowe companies, the Admiral's Men, Worcester's Men and its successor company, Queen Anne's Men. A number of the same playwrights—Rowley, Dekker, Munday, and Chettle—are involved in both the biblical plays and these Foxian Protestant saint plays. The overlapping list of playwrights and the coinciding dates may suggest not two projects, but two parts to a single project undertaken by Henslowe's companies late in the reign of Elizabeth and early in James's. Indeed, Crosse turns immediately from his objection to the staging of prophets and patriarchs to an equally vehement denunciation of the staging of kings and "antient Fathers and Pastors of the Church" (sig. P3r).

If we can see such a relation between these Foxian hagiographical plays and the biblical plays of 1602, then what the Henslowe companies appear to have had in mind was the conciliation of moderate Puritan elements among London citizens and an attempt to entice into the theaters those groups that had previously shunned it. If the companies could put both Protestant and biblical heroes on stage once again, a part of London that had been disaffected from the theater might be drawn toward participation. To effect this with biblical texts would require caution and an avoidance of those parts of scripture that were either controversial or associated with the traditional drama of the Catholic past. And most of all, it would need to conform to the iconoclast imperatives that forbade any representation of God. To judge by their titles,

Henslowe's six biblical and quasi-biblical plays of 1602 would respond well
to these needs. Several titles, including the accomplishment of *David and
Bethsabe*, suggest an erotic or romantic appeal; others would have presented a
military heroism that could be linked to uncontroversial Protestant virtues.
None would trespass on doctrine or even on religious conviction to any significant extent.

But whatever did or did not play on the stages of the Rose and the Fortune
in 1602, the gamble that Henslowe and his companies took in accentuating
biblical plays in the public theaters clearly failed—and failed decisively. Either the audiences failed to materialize, or other factors, perhaps the actual
opposition suggested by the passage in Crosse's *Vertues Common-wealth*,
conspired to keep biblical plays, from this point, off the stages of London's
theaters altogether. It is possible that the very constituencies that Henslowe
may have hoped to attract to the theater themselves objected to what was projected, and that the whole enterprise in this way backfired.

                                        VII

The relationship of iconoclasm to Protestant biblical theater, then, is complex
in its unfolding, but ultimately decisive. If John Bale and the anonymous playwright of the Resurrection play attempted to bend the late-medieval traditions
of the cycle plays toward a Protestant ideology, they did so by emphasizing
textuality, by attempting to create a theater that insisted that texts must be at
the center of a reformed Christianity. Bale did not shy from portraying an embodied God, either God the Father or Christ, on his stage. But his Christ was
predominantly created of and for words, a preacher, and Bale's plays es-
chewed an affective engagement with their audience in favor of a largely discursive, polemical one. Gone altogether was the emphasis in the traditional
theater on Mary and on Christ's incarnate body. By mid-century the implications of iconoclasm for the theatrical representation of Christ were becoming
evident. Lewis Wager's *Repentaunce of Mary Magdalen* portrayed Christ, but
the tendency toward textualization is apparent in Christ's subordination to a
theological scheme that overrides any dramatic relation to Mary and her conversion. After Wager's *Repentaunce* no subsequent English Protestant play
would attempt the portrayal of Christ on stage. The relation between iconoclasm and the theatrical embodiment of God was sealed by the ending of the
playing of the traditional biblical cycles in the 1560s and 1570s. During this
time and in the decade following, playwrights hoped to evade the iconoclast
issue of portraying the divine by resorting to Old Testament and Apocryphal
texts and avoiding narratives traditionally linked by typology to the New Testament. But the complete receding of biblical plays from the mid 1570s until
the late 1580s and Lodge and Greene's *A Looking Glasse for London* suggests
a general anxiety about the stage portrayal of any biblical text. The appearance
of *A Looking Glasse for London* on the public stage may have challenged this

understanding, as it attempted to engage its audience in something of the way the traditional drama had done. But the only other extant text of a biblical play, Peele's *David and Bethsabe*, retreats from such involvement and presses biblical drama toward the history play. The status of biblical drama in the public theaters appears to have rested on the implicit stipulation that the plays would avoid any of the religious issues and sensibility that had earlier characterized them. Even this stipulation proved unstable, however, and the final result was that the English theater abandoned its two-century engagement with representation of the Bible, an abandonment precisely parallel to what occurred in the visual arts—and even more enduring in the culture. What had been lost, or abandoned, in the textualizing of the sacred on stage was that quasi-ritualistic character of the late-medieval theater described in the last chapter, that understanding of an affective bond between audience and stage action that was directed toward spiritual and moral transformation. The break with the festive context of the earlier theater was clearly significant in this regard, as was the changed audience-to-stage dynamic of the public theaters. But as we know from the effect of the Shakespearean stage, that impulse toward an affective bond, the desire to *move* spectators of the drama as well as to entertain them, was not lost. While no longer religious in an explicit or intentional way, that stage would, potentially at least, still claim the power to transfix and transform its participants. It would continue to lay claim to the seriousness of purpose that theater had maintained. But it would now do so amid the Reformation anxiety about its visual character and the more general attack on images of the previous half century.

FIVE

"Let the Audience Look to Their Eyes"

Jonson and Shakespeare

In itself the attack of the antitheatrical writers described in chapter 1 would not necessarily have influenced the self-understanding of the Elizabethan public theater. There is little evidence that the playwrights or theater entrepreneurs took direct notice of the tracts when they first appeared in the late 1570s and early 1580s. But these tracts were the tip of the iceberg of social discourse about the nature and place of the stage, something that is evident in the mechanism of licensing and control that developed from the 1570s onward, in the jurisdictional contention, until the reign of James, between civic authority in London and the crown, and in sermon literature.[1] Opposition to the stage was not merely a response to the novelty of the public theaters at their inception; it clearly persisted through the first four decades of the seventeenth century. Thomas Heywood responded to the antitheatrical discourse with *An Apology for Actors* in 1612, and in 1614 Ben Jonson caricatured the continuing Puritan opposition in Zeal-of-the-land Busy, who attacks the puppet theater in *Bartholomew Fair*. Heywood's *Apology* elicited a bitter *Refutation of the Apologie for Actors* by "I. G." in 1615. William Prynne's *Histrio-mastix* of 1633 was the compendious capstone of this discourse. And finally, in 1642, Parliament would close the theaters until the Restoration, definitively ending the theatrical tradition that began with the opening of the public theaters in the 1570s.[2] Moreover, as my account of Reformation iconoclasm has argued, this opposition was part of a larger cultural movement that could not but affect the development of something so dependent on the visual as drama. In the not-so-distant cultural past stood what came to be seen as the transgressive representation of Christ's physical body that had been central to the traditional religious stage. But a persistent anxiety about visual representation itself would impinge on the identity of the stage as it developed in the late sixteenth and early seventeenth centuries.

Any reader of Elizabethan texts is well aware how this anxiety about the visual is enacted in suspicion of linguistic ornament: phrases like "painted shows" or "painted eloquence," "colors of rhetoric," "fine polished words" and "filed phrases" convey an at best ambivalent, and frequently pejorative, sense of the appeal to the eye. The underlying tropological sense of these phrases reflects an unease about visual art itself, suggesting an identity with the forgery of cosmetics. Distrust of the visual, while by no means universal, is a persistent strain in humanist poetics. Ernest Gilman has described the ways in the which the *paragone* between the "sister arts" was crossed by the Reformation rejection of images:

> It is important to realize that 'iconoclasm' is something that can happen to texts and within texts written during this period, and that the most com-pelling texts often betray a consciousness of the image-debate that reflects on the process of their own composition. The scene of such writing is set at the crossroads where a lively tradition of image-making confronts a militantly logocentric theology armed not only with an overt hostility to "images" in worship but with a deep suspicion of the idolatrous potential of the fallen mind and its fallen language.[3]

Gilman suggests that Philip Sidney, with his strong ties to the left wing of the European Reformation, "virtually suppresses" what must have been the lasting impression made on him by the Venetian painters, particularly Titian, whose influence he sees stamped on the ekphrastic style of the *Arcadia* (p. 12). In Son-net 5 of *Astrophel and Stella* Sidney shows himself clearly aware of the terms of the iconoclast debate and of what should be the sincere Protestant response to the temptation of even figurative image worship:

> It is most true, that eyes are form'd to serve
> The inward light: and that the heavenly part
> Ought to be king, from whose rules who do swerve,
> Rebels to Nature strive for their owne smart.
> It is most true, what we call *Cupids* dart,
> An image is, which for our selves we carve;
> And fooles, adore in temple of our hart.[4]

But in spite of such clear consciousness of his own idolatry, Astrophel cannot evade the worship of Cupid's dart and of Stella's inward image. As Sidney's sonnet—and Gilman's argument—make evident, the sense of iconoclasm was not limited either to strictly religious contexts or to the use of literal painting and sculpture, but was comprehended as well in the imagistic powers of lan-guage and the potential of poetry to emulate pictorial experience. Even the pictorialism of a poet so dependent on the potency of the image as Spenser is deeply implicated in a suspicion of what appeals to the eye. Indeed, distrust of the visual is virtually the mainspring of the allegory of *The Faerie Queene*. There the word *seems* almost invariably leads to the apprehension of visual deception; only the poet's own morally charged language and close attention to what characters *say* enable a reader to negotiate this world where what *is* must be discovered beneath the deception of what *appears*. In such a poetics language is represented as the only reliable index of reality. The very name of

Archimago, source of deception in the poem, carries with it the iconoclast argument. This is not to deny the pictorialism or its significance, but to suggest that in each of these pieces vision is implicated in an ambivalent process that both informs and deceives the mind. Gilman speaks aptly of "the agonistic mode of its pictorialism" (p. 80). A reader of *The Faerie Queene* can never simply rest in what the poem represents as visually portrayed; images are always to be interrogated for the deception they potentially—and most frequently—convey.

By the 1590s England had been an iconoclast culture for nearly half a century. Not only had the largest part of its medieval heritage of painting and sculpture been swept away, but England remained self-isolated from contact with European developments in the visual arts. Its style of portraiture (virtually the only form of painting practiced) favored the flat iconic image dependent on color and line but lacking the modeling, chiaroscuro, and perspective that characterized contemporary mannerist painting on the continent. Lucy Gent, in her book on painting and poetry in England between 1560 and 1620, notes the visual illiteracy of the culture: "the eyes of all but a very small handful of Elizabethans were uncultivated, in the sense that they were uneducated in looking at pictures."[5] Unless they had traveled to the continent, Elizabethans could in fact have seen very few paintings, and those few mainly portraits. Even among those who professed an interest in painting, there was much imprecision in the understanding of the basic terminology of the art. When Richard Haydocke came to translate Giovanni Paolo Lomazzo's *Trattato dell'arte de la pittura* in 1598, he was puzzled by the term *desegno* (Gent, p. 9). Leonard Barkan has recently called attention to the paradox of the "enormous treasury" of pictorialism that appears in Elizabethan writing in the work of the Sidney and Spenser and in the erotic epyllia of the 1590s and yet the "astonishingly low" level of visual culture "by any European—and not only Italian—standards."[6] When Sidney defends the mimetic character of poetry in the *Apology for Poetry*, the principle competitors of the poet are the historian and the philosopher, not, Barkan notes, the painter or sculptor. The "other nature" which the poet creates can be understood to be dependent on an *absence*, the specific absence of "the lively pictorial culture out of which painterly claims get made." Barkan shrewdly understands Sidney as appropriating and then suppressing the visual artist "because he wants his poetry to make pictures but does not want the pictures to be real" (p. 337). The stimulus of Sidney's *Apology*, we recall, was the dedication to him of Gosson's attack on the stage, but the theater is the one poetic activity that Sidney cannot defend. Suggesting that the problem for Sidney is that theater "is truly and literally a speaking picture," Barkan proposes that "the theater *is* England's lively pictorial culture, the compensation, the *supplément* in the face of all the painting, sculpture, and art theory that was so famously alive in the European civilizations that Elizabethans dreamed about" (p. 338). Dream they no doubt did, but for the culture generally these dreams carried the persistent risk of idolatry. And it was not an anxiety that theater could evade.

Theater, of course, cannot afford to be mistrustful of what appeals to the eye. Every bit as much as what is said, its stock in trade is what is seen. While the Elizabethan and Jacobean stage may have been, in comparison with contemporary Italian or later English theater, relatively unadorned in scenery and painted effects, it was richly costumed and impressed its spectators by the physical energy of the actors. In his second attack on the stage (c. 1583), Gosson paid a backhanded tribute to its visual appeal, speaking of "the beautie of the houses," the rich costuming, and the "maskes, vauting, tumbling, dauncing of gigges, galiardes, morisces, hobbihorses" that brought pleasure to the spectators.[7] The sumptuous costumes in fact were, along with the playbooks, the major material resources of the theater companies. Peter Stallybrass has recently argued for the centrality of clothing to the theater, indeed the embeddedness of the latter in the circulation of clothing, in the pawning, renting, and the buying and selling of clothes.[8] Henslowe's well-known list of properties drawn up in 1598 categorizes costumes as cloaks, gowns, "antik sutes," jerkins and doublets, French hose, and "venetians" (hose and breeches). While emphasizing the value and frequently the use of the costumes, his brief descriptions also give a sense of the visual splendor they represented on stage.[9] A jerkin is described as "of blak velvett cut on sillver tinsell"; one "antik sute" is "a cote of crimosen velvet cutt in payns and embrydered in gould." One perspective on such descriptions is to see them lending support to Barkan's suggestion that theater itself was the "lively pictorial culture" otherwise so conspicuously absent in Elizabethan and Jacobean England. Another is to follow Glynne Wickham in seeing the immediate parentage of this color and richness in the ecclesiastical vestments that had been purged from Protestant worship. Wickham adduces two instances where it was literally the case that liturgical vestments found their way to the stage: in 1570 Holy Trinity Church, Chester, sold vestments "to make players garments," and at Chelmsford, Essex, the church wardens hired out complete wardrobes to actors from 1562 until the vestments were sold outright in 1574. John Coldewey notes that Maldon and Braintree, also in Essex, rented out vestments as costumes before they too sold off wardrobes in 1564 and 1579, respectively, and New Romney, Kent, bought "copes and vestures" to make players' costumes in 1560.[10] If such instances were one way that no longer needed ecclesiastical vestments were disposed of by church wardens, they lend an unexpected resonance to charges like those of Anthony Munday that the theater was the "chappel of Satan."[11] There is of course no need for us to make a choice between these two ways of seeing theatrical splendor as the return of the repressed, whether that repression was historical or imaginative. What is clear is that theater represented a site where, perhaps uniquely for a majority of Londoners, the unrestricted play of color and movement—of illusory images and visual beauty—was allowed.

I

For both Jonson and Shakespeare the issue of theatrical identity is crucial, and both enjoin the issue of eye and ear in the self-reflexive moments when their plays project an awareness of their own artificiality. Jonson is ever the more agonistic in his assertion of the nature and ends of theater—and at the same time paradoxically the more inclined to quarrel with the demands themselves of creating theatrical spectacle. Jonas Barish has described Jonson's always ambivalent, frequently hostile relationship to the stage for which he wrote, characterizing it, without exaggeration, as "a deeply rooted anti-theatricalism."[12] Something of Jonson's hostility came of his contentious temperament and the quarrels that were somehow necessary to the kind of artist he was and the kind of theater he wished to create. But that hostility was founded intellectually on his primary allegiance to humanist culture. Richard Helgerson has shown how large a part this allegiance played in Jonson's creation for himself of a laureate identity *against* his identity as a man of the theater.[13] Even when promoting or defending his stage works, as he does almost constantly in his prologues, dedications, inductions, and epilogues, Jonson seldom appears able to allow a play simply to be a play. Most frequently he insists on them as *poems*, as for example in his dedication of *Volpone* to the two universities, or when he dedicates the failed *Catiline* to the Earl of Pembroke, assuring him that posterity will honor him for countenancing "a legitimate *Poem*" in these "jig-given times." Mockery of the physical requirements of staging, predominantly the movement and visual effects required by an audience for whom a play was not a poem but a *show*, also pepper the prefatory explaining he found essential to his identity, not as a playwright, but as a "dramatic poet." Jonson's insistent hope that readers would find in his plays what mere spectators had missed reached its logical end when, in mid-career, he printed them in his *Works* of 1616, a gesture of self-presentation as characteristic of Jonson as it was innovative for the stage. After the theatrical failure of *The New Inn*, he bitterly dedicated the printing of the text of the play "To the reader." If his reader-patron can but construe the sense of the words, Jonson insists, he is better off than the "hundred fastidious impertinents" who saw the play but never made it out. Erasmus' insistence on the higher truth of the verbal, printed edition of Christ finds a significant counterpart in Jonson's valuation of the printed texts of his plays against their theatrical incarnations.[14]

If costume was the most impressive hold over the eyes of London theatergoers, it is telling how frequently Jonson throws back the charge of fashion-mongering and display at his audiences. He dedicates *Cynthia's Revels* to the court, where it had been played, saying "In thee the whole kingdom dresseth itself, and is ambitious to use thee as her glass." But "Beware," he immediately adds: "It is not powdering, perfuming, and every day smelling of the tailor, that converteth to a beautiful object." In the comic induction to the play, one of the child players parodies the hypercritical playgoer who would find fault in the play and the company. But another of the children counters with the poet's charge that some of the audience have no more learning than of the price of satin and velvet, know nothing but "the wearing of a neat suit." Jonson blamed the failure of *The New Inn* on an audience that came simply to see and be seen, "to make a general muster of themselves" in their fashionable clothes. And in his comedies, of course, satire of costume is a staple. On the one hand his tricksters and hucksters manipulate costume, and his gulls and dupes, on the other, are seduced by their own attempts to create a self through expensive and fashionable dress. For Jonson costume represents not the necessary external means of portraying self or theatrical character, but an *alternative* to language and its ability to convey the mind.

Jonson's quarrel with Inigo Jones can be understood at one level as centering on the losing battle that the word waged with the multiplicity of arts appealing to the eye in the court masque. Intensified by this quarrel, Jonson's cross-grained dislike of the theatrical seems to have increased rather than decreased in the latter part of his writing for the stage. If the Puritans would have worshippers avoid the idolatry of the visual to attend wholly to the word of Scripture, Jonson wished them to evade the seduction of spectacle to attend to his words. The prologue to *The Staple of News* not only distinguishes between the poet and those who perform his words on stage, but seems indeed to yearn for a blind audience:

> For your own sakes, not his, he bade me say,
> Would you were come to hear, not see a play.
> Though we his actors must provide for those
> Who are our guests here in the way of shows,
> The maker hath not so. He'd have you wise
> Much rather by your ears than by your eyes.[15]

This comes but as an extreme version of what Jonson in one way or another seems always to have wanted: near exclusive attention to the verbal element of the mixed art that theater is. In the play itself this is tied to the falsity that the display of costume represents. Pennyboy Junior, naively believing in the adage *vestis virum facit*, puts on the fine clothes that represent his majority and supposed heirship, which will be tested and found wanting in the course of the play. His still-living father, Pennyboy Canter, who is disguised even from the audience by a beggar's cloak, embodies Jonsonian judgment about money and character. In this way Jonson tricks also his audience's eyes and dares them to be wise solely by their ears. He enforces, but doesn't give away, this ploy by his induction, which brings on four London matrons, self-admittedly "come to see and to be seen," who sit on the stage and comment on the action between the acts. In their first commentary Tattle, says she cannot abide "that nasty fellow, the beggar." If he had been a fashionable court beggar, "a beggar in velvet, as they say," she could have put up with him. When Canter unmasks (or uncloaks) himself in the fourth act, the women are outraged at this spoiling of what they had taken to be the fun of the play. For Jonson, of course, they represent precisely the wrong, ocular rather than auricular, way to experience a play.

With his brilliant stage caricatures of the Puritans, Jonson met the opponents of the theater head-on. In *The Alchemist* the "faithful brethren" Ananias and Tribulation are forced to listen to Subtle's list of insults that accuse them of hypocrisy, including railing against plays "to please the alderman / Whose daily custard you devour."[16] Jonson skewers Puritan language by appropriating the discourse of idolatry to questions of fashion and costume: whether "matrons of the holy assembly" may have "that idol starch about their linen" (3.2.82—the words are Subtle's, but Ananias immediately concurs, "it is indeed an idol") or Ananias's immediate apprehension of zeal against Surely's Spanish slops: "They are profane, / Lewd, superstitious, and idolatrous breeches" (4.7.48–49). *Bartholomew Fair* is the highwater mark of Jonson's quarrel with the Puritans as he ridicules their concern with idolatry in Zeal-of-the-Land Busy's iconoclastic attack first on hobby-horses and gingerbread men, then on the puppet theater (only to be confuted in his disputation with a puppet!).[17] Again, it is Busy's language that so comically caricatures Puritan sermon rhetoric:

> I will remove Dagon there, I say, that idol, that heathenish idol, that remains, as I may say, a beam, a very beam, not a beam of the sun, nor a beam of the moon, nor a beam of a balance, neither a house-beam nor a weaver's beam, but a beam in the eye, in the eye of the brethren; a very great beam, an exceeding great beam; such as are your stage-players, rhymers, and morris dancers, who have walked hand in hand in contempt of the brethren and the cause, and been borne out by instruments of no mean countenance.
> (5.5.4–12)

Busy's punning is as comically lame as that afforded Littlewit, but stands in fact at no great distance from the language of controversy. Leatherhead, the puppeteer, protests to Busy that he has the Master of the Revels' hand for his performance. "The Master of the rebels' hand for it thou hast—Satan's!" exclaims Busy (5.5.16). But the use of puppets to stand for actors is Jonson's most brilliant comic stroke, producing as it does the wonderful effect of the Puritan preacher arguing the issue of idolatry with a talking idol. When Busy trots out the accusation against actors that they have no calling, the puppet Dionysus says that his calling is to be an idol, a calling made lawful by Busy himself, who calls him that and whose own calling is "of the spirit." But the best of it is that it enables Jonson to provide a comic rebuttal of the centerpiece of the controversy: that the cross-dressing of actors violated the Deuteronomic prohibition of males dressing as women, "for the male among you putteth on the apparel of the female, and the female of the male," Busy says. Leatherhead's Dionysus "takes up his garment" to prove that the puppets "have neither male nor female amongst us" (5.5.93), parodying a text of St. Paul in the bargain (Galatians 3:28). Moreover, puppets, like Puritans, speak "by inspiration" and have nothing to do with learning. Busy must admit he is confuted by this, is converted to theater, and becomes a beholder of the puppet play. Jonson's idol-actor has bested the iconoclast at his own game.[18]

Jonson is constantly concerned with the nature and status of his plays, but his theatrical self-reflexivity, unlike Shakespeare's, is confined mainly to the prologues and inductions that argue for his particular kind of theater. Except in polemical contexts, as in *The Poetaster*, Jonson rarely seems to address the question of theater from within, and even in that play the issue is not so much theatricality itself as the status and calling of the poet. *Bartholomew Fair* is the exception, unique in its self-reflexive address of the issue of theater itself. All of Busy's obsession with "vanity of the eye," especially as he attempts to control the eyes of the Littlewit family, serves to draw attention to the gaudy visuality of the fair—and hence of the play itself. While the concluding puppet play-within-the-play is designed in large part to satirize Puritan antitheatricalism, it is for Jonson a rare moment of self-conscious exploration of the materials of playwrighting. Wonderfully, the subject matter of the puppet show itself can even be understood as self-parody of Jonson's own playwrighting: a classicizing story, Marlowe's *Hero and Leander*, is given a resolutely, if comic, London local habitation and name. Leatherhead says he has asked Littlewit to take pains "to reduce it to more familiar strains for our people," and the latter says he has only "made it a little easy and modern for the times" (5.3.108–111). We are not expected to admire Littlewit's decidedly downmarket accomplishment, but this idea of Englishing the classical tradition becomes oddly amusing as it plays over Jonson's own career. Various individual elements of the larger play similarly suggest a self-reflexive character. At the end of the induction, the scrivener calls attention to the "special decorum" of playing the play at the Hope, "the place being as dirty as Smithfield, and as stinking every whit." This was, of course, because it was also used for bearbaiting. The *genius loci* of Jonson's play, then, becomes Ursula, the immense pig woman whose name renders her a bear who is baited by two of the killjoys of the fair, Quarlous and Winwife. Justice Overdo, with his classical allusions (particularly his fondness for "my Horace") and his desire to correct social enormities, looks very like a self-caricature of Jonson the satirist. And yet there seems nothing programmatic about the self-reflexivity. Overdo also looks curiously like Shakespeare's Prospero, especially in the final scene where he assembles all the supposed malefactors and prepares to render judgment.[19]

What is finally striking about all the self-reflexivity of *Bartholomew Fair* is that it is so different from the Shakespearean variety; while it calls attention to the art of the play, it does not in the least want to celebrate that art or theater in general. The fair itself is the main imaginative site on which reflection on the nature of theatrical art is centered and condensed. As an event that is at once festive and entertaining, socially inclusive in its mingling of high and low and thoroughly commercial, the fair provides an apt metaphor both for the operation and experience of theater and for the imaginative material out of which it is made. But in Jonson's portrayal, theater is hardly flattered by the comparison. The gaudiness, the tawdriness even, of the fair with its gingerbread and hobbyhorse vendors, its pickpockets, its pig booth and puppet show, evokes at best a qualified, provisional sort of tolerance. Only the simpleminded or foolish in the play are allowed to be wholehearted partisans of fair and puppet show. The main partisan (and eponymous champion) of the fair— and chief enthusiast for its puppet theater—is Bartholomew Cokes. While Cokes may be appealing in his childish enthusiasm, he is also thoroughly foolish. He reminds us in some ways of Shakespeare's Bottom, but in relation to Bottom his imagination is passive and omnivorously accepting. He is unable to handle the complexity of the fair and loses purses, cloak, hat, and sword to the pickpocket. Similarly, Littlewit lives up to his name in his contribution to the imaginative life of the fair. The simple and undiscriminating nature of the two are the audience's way into the world of Smithfield, but they can offer no positive account of it. At the same time the play does not allow any admiration for the opponents of the fair, Busy and Overdo, or Wasp, Quarlous, and Win-wife, who seem rigidly incapable of festive enjoyment. In this the play seems suspended in its judgment of the theater world, endorsing wholeheartedly neither critics nor proponents, willing to portray imaginative festivity but unable to accept a positive account of it.

In performance the most telling—and most theatrical—moment comes at the very end, when Overdo's attempts at judgment are interrupted by Mistress Overdo, who, having overdone, suddenly awakens, is sick, and vomits into Ursula's pan. She has had too much of the fair and spews it forth. This is the anagnorisis of the play: Overdo is silenced and now recognizes both his wife and his own manifold errors. In this moment of grotesque physicality, the claims of the body are utterly decisive, and another sort of oral response overcomes Justice Overdo's mistaken attempts at verbal discrimination of what the fair has been. Instead it is left to Quarlous, one of the fair's least enthusiastic participants, to explain the true nature of things. He reminds Overdo of his first name, "You are but Adam, flesh and blood," and invites him to invite them all to a supper that, in good Horatian fashion, will "drown the memory of all enormity" in the biggest bowl he has. Overdo does invite them and in so doing does seem to conclude the play with a sense of festive acceptance of common human frailty. Perhaps also the claims of a flesh-and-blood audience could be understood as comprised in this concluding acceptance. From such a perspective Mistress Overdo's vomiting may be read as purgative. But coming after the use she has just had for Ursula's biggest pan, this hope for drowning the memory of enormity in the household's biggest bowl may seem less than enticing. On stage Mistress Overdo's vomiting is more shocking than purgative to an audience. As the anagnorisis of a comedy, it is a brilliantly visual stage coup, a manifest *theatrical* enormity. But it is also decidedly alienating, one that leaves its spectators with, so to speak, a sour taste in the mouth. The vomiting has been brought on by, and seems a response to, the fair, and as the fair has been the play (and is indeed its eponym), the vomiting also seems to express a strange revulsion with the whole enterprise of putting bodies on stage. *Bartholomew Fair* strikes me as in many ways Jonson's most complex and brilliant comedy, but also the one most revelatory of his own conflictedness. As his most self-reflexive play, it gathers up all his ambivalence and doubt about spectacle and about the theatrical enterprise itself. Zeal-of-the-Land Busy is the play's most vigorously drawn character, the central vehicle of its satire, but in creating a milieu in which Busy may appear absurd, Jonson seems half to concede the Puritan argument. Laura Levine, moreover, argues tellingly that the puppets and the puppet show, drained as they are of any sense of sexuality, express the lack of any positive erotic experience in the play itself, that in this "Jonson acknowledges an uneasy analogy between his own sterility and the antitheatricalists he so viciously attacks."[20] Theater is of course not only puppet shows, pig booths, hobby-horses, gingerbread men, pickpockets, and madmen, but insofar as it can be fittingly imaged by these things, Jonson seems to suggest that Mistress Overdo's response is perfectly understandable, perhaps indeed the proper one. *Bartholomew Fair* would not appear in Jonson's *Works* of 1616; did he fear he had revealed too much about theater—or too much of his own sense of the enormity of theater?[21]

For all the vigor of his satire of the Puritans, and his hatred of what he took to be the hypocrisy of the sectarians, a part of Jonson remained as convinced as they that sight and the physicality of theatrical spectacle distracted the mind from the truth that was to be found most emphatically in language. Occasionally he even falls into their style and tone. Asper, the satirist "of an ingenious and free spirit" in the induction to *Everyman Out of His Humour*, is told by Cordatus not to lose his purpose, which cannot but be acceptable to those who see "how the poor innocent word is rack'd and tortured." Capitalize "word" and the sentence might well have come from a Puritan controversialist concerned with Catholic or Anglican interpretation of Scripture. In the induction to *Bartholomew Fair* the bookholder, with Shakespeare in mind, says that Jonson is loath to violate the canons of realism like those who beget Tales and Tempests and such, "let the *concupiscence* of jigs and dances reign as strong as it will amongst you" (my emphasis). The single word puts the whole issue in quasi-religious terms that any sectarian could endorse. Jonson's anxiety about spectacle points emphatically to the problem of definition that humanism and the Reformation created for theater. While his greatest stage creations are masters of deceiving the eye, characters for whom the costume change is as essential as breathing, he is never able to rest easy in this power of the stage.[22]

II

Without Jonson's primary allegiance to humanist values, Shakespeare could assert the equal claim of the eye in the epistemology of theater. One of his obvious differences from Jonson is that throughout his career he was far less anxious about the status of theater in relation to humanist canons of literary definition. In the self-reflexive moments in his plays, moments when the character or status of theater emerges thematically, he can insist in a positive way on the identity of theater as a visual art. But this difference is not an unproblematic assertion of that identity, nor is it consistent over the two decades in which he was writing for the theater. Still less does it come of a simple disregard of the position of Reformation iconoclasm.[23] Like Jonson, Shakespeare was touched by the pervasive anxiety about the visual and understood clearly that he was a maker of images as well as of words. Hamlet, in speaking of "The Mousetrap," calls it "the image of a murder done in Vienna." If a play could be an *image* to an avid theater-goer like the prince, then the stage would indeed be subject to many of the same apprehensions that surrounded the visual in an iconoclast culture.

Significantly, terms like "idol," "idolatrous," or "idolatry" bear no single or unambiguous valuation in Shakespeare's dramatic and non-dramatic texts. Lovers can enthusiastically embrace the charge of idolatry. Juliet urges Romeo to "swear by thy gracious self, which is the god of my idolatry" (2.2.114). And Helena, in *All's Well that Ends Well*, can muse that it was "pretty, though a plague" to see Bertram every hour and draw his portrait in her "heart's table." "But now he's gone, and my idolatrous fancy / Must sanctify his relics" (1.1.100). Similarly, Hamlet seems innocently to have addressed Ophelia as "my soul's idol" in the letter Polonius reads to the king (2.2.109). These usages may suggest a kind of moral neutrality in the "idolatry" of the lover, even Helena's collation of "idolatrous fancy" with "relics." But the Venus who addresses the unresponsive Adonis is clearly well versed in Protestant polemic:

> Fie, lifeless picture, cold and senseless stone,
> Well-painted idol, image dull and dead,
> Statue contenting but the eye alone . . .
>
> (*Venus and Adonis*, 211–13)[24]

And in *Twelfth Night* Antonio, confronting the perplexity of a Sebastian who disclaims knowledge of him (in reality the disguised Viola), says with bitterness that he rescued him from the jaws of death,

> "Reliev'd him with such sanctity of love,
> And to his image, which methought did promise
> Most venerable worth, did I devotion. . . .
> But, O, how vile an idol proves this god!"
>
> *Twelfth Night* (3.4.361–65)

"Image" covers a much wider range of meaning, of course, but two usages in the early history plays indicate a similar doubleness of attitude in the way the term reflects theological debate. In *Henry VI, Part 2*, Queen Margaret speaks contemptuously of the king's piety in relation to chivalry: "His study is his tilt yard, and his loves / Are brazen images of canonized saints" (1.3.59–60). More complexly, King Edward in *Richard III* refers to a drunken murderer defacing "The precious image of our dear Redeemer" (2.1.124), the term here referring to a violent death of one created in the *image* of God, but carrying as well the sense of sacrilege at the destruction of a crucifix or painting. This use of *image* to refer to humanity created in the divine image, and by extension the image of the parent reproduced in the child, significantly extends the sense of an artistic representation. Angelo, in *Measure for Measure* speaks of illicit procreation as a coinage of "heaven's image / In stamps that are forbid" (2.4.45–46). Falstaff jokingly redefines the relation between representation and what is represented; in playing possum to escape death, he has not counterfeited: "To die is to counterfeit, for he is but the counterfeit of a man who hath not the life of a man," while a living man is no counterfeit, "but the true and perfect image of life indeed" (*Henry IV, Part 1*, 5.4.115–19). In *Henry IV, Part 2*, the dying king says that Hal is "the noble image of my youth" (4.4.55), a usage that is paralleled in *Winter's Tale* when Leontes says to Florizel that his "father's image is so hit in you" that he could call him brother and imagine some prank the two of them had just played (5.1.127). Thus, while an image is frequently a painted or sculpted image, it is also the living human body—and as such, the dramatist's own medium. If lovers fall into idolatry, it is an idolatry of an image that lives and moves upon the stage. In this, Shakespeare responds suggestively to the antitheatricalist charge of the idolatry of the stage.

This positive familiarity with the discourse of iconoclasm—and its implications for the "idolatry" of the theater—is clearly on display in an early comedy. In *Two Gentlemen of Verona*, Proteus, after first seeing Silvia, asks Valentine, "Was this the idol that you worship so?" "Even she; and is she not a heavenly saint?" responds Valentine, countering Proteus' construction of his love as idolatrous with his own iconodulia. Proteus, still the precisian, protests the terms by which Valentine defines his "saint"; she is, he allows, "an earthly paragon," but he will not flatter by calling her "divine" (2.4.144–47). Proteus remembers Valentine's earlier mockery of his being in love, and the two of them indulge in a boyish debate over the worth of their mistresses. But Valentine's eloquent praise of Silvia has the ironic effect of inflaming Proteus, and having refused to allow Valentine's "idolatry," Proteus rejects Julia and falls into his own idolatrous love of Silvia. His love for Julia, he says, is now "thaw'd, / Which like a waxen image 'gainst a fire, / Bears no impression of the thing it was" (2.4.200–202). The iconoclastic trope he uses here becomes itself ironic when a consequence of his infidelity in love is that he himself soon falls into a literal idolatry. Finding Silvia deaf to his entreaty, he begs her picture of her:

> To that I'll speak, to that I'll sigh and weep;
> For since the substance of your perfect self
> Is else devoted, I am but a shadow;
> And to your shadow will I make true love. (4.2.122–25)

"I am very loath to be your idol, sir," she replies, but believing that his falsity in love makes it fitting that he should "worship shadows and adore false shapes," she agrees to send him her painted image. Clearly falsity in love is being analogized to a falsity in religion characterized by worship of an image. But the "idolatry" of the lovers in their true devotion to one another is left strangely untainted by the analogy. When Julia, "shadowed" as a man, must carry Silvia's picture to Proteus, she addresses herself:

> Come, shadow, come, and take this shadow up,
> For 'tis thy rival. O thou senseless form,
> Thou shalt be worshipp'd, kiss'd, lov'd, and ador'd;
> And were there sense in his idolatry,
> My substance should be statue in thy stead.

> I'll use thee kindly for thy mistress' sake,
> That us'd me so; or else, by Jove I vow,
> I should have scratch'd out your unseeing eyes
> To make my master out of love with thee. (4.4.197–205)

Julia is tempted to an iconoclastic act, like the scratching out of the faces of the saints on a rood screen, an iconoclasm that might cure her lover's idolatry. But she also admits a "true" idolatry, a *sensible* idolatry that would worship herself, her own bodily "substance," not merely the image of her rival. In this sense, the actors themselves would become the substantial images. The implications of this for such theatrical images are left undeveloped in the comedy, but they will be close to the heart of later Shakespearean self-reflexive play with the question of how theater is to define itself, how it might become a sensible idolatry such as Julia projects.

III

Closely related to this direct involvement with the discourse of iconoclasm is the epistemological issue of the relative importance of ear and eye in human knowing. Is it human speech, or is it what can be seen in the face and the carriage of the body that most accurately conveys the person, that best expresses moral character? Among the comedies of the 1590s, *Much Ado About Nothing* most programmatically addresses the cultural anxiety over the faculties of perception.[25] It does so, moreover, in a way that develops a curiously Jonsonian perspective on the relation of eye and ear. The dictum of Erasmus' Folly that speech is "the least deceptive mirror of the human mind," would seem an apposite statement of the play's interest in perception and the representation of self.[26] Don John, the villain, says, "I am not of many words" (1.1.157), and in context this becomes vaguely menacing. Beatrice says he is "too like an image and says nothing" (2.1.8). Where the epistemology of eye and ear is most fully worked out is in the contrast between the two sets of lovers. Claudio and Hero are also not of many words, at least to one another. We understand that Claudio's love comes entirely through the eye, for Hero says not a word after the returned soldiers enter. He seems so unsure in his estimation of her that he has to ask Benedick's opinion, who replies pointedly, "Would you buy her, that you inquire after her?" (1.1.180). Claudio's interest in Hero does in part lie in her value as commodity, for he later asks Don Pedro if Leonato has any son; Don Pedro understands him and replies, "No child but Hero; she's his only heir" (1.1.295). Claudio does not even woo Hero himself, and from this fact comes his initial, unfounded jealousy. The visual masking in this scene seems expressive of what has also been a verbal masking. Believing himself deceived by Don Pedro, Claudio concludes that "all hearts in love [should] use their own tongues: / Let every eye negotiate for itself / And trust no agent" (2.1.177–79). But when Hero is won for him, he discovers that he has nothing to say to her; Beatrice's encouragement to him becomes theatrically reflexive:

"Speak, count, 'tis your cue" (2.1.305). He does speak, but the words seem formulaic, even reminiscent of Don John's "I am not of many words": "Silence is the perfectest herald of joy; I were but little happy if I could say how much! Lady, as you are mine, I am yours. I give myself for you, and dote upon the exchange" (2.1.306–309). This also the only thing he has thus far said to her in the play.

This tongue-tied and eye-dependent love of Claudio for Hero achieves the significance I am suggesting it has mainly through contrast with the insistently verbal relationship of Beatrice and Benedick. The audience has heard them speaking together since the first scene of the play; language is very much the root of their mutual knowledge, language that never expresses love, but in its agonistic character suggests two competitive personalities more alike than either will acknowledge. We are never sure when they fall in love—have they been in love before? are they in some sense in love all along? These are questions that require decision on the part of the actors who play the roles. What is thematically significant is that the scenes in which they individually decide they are in love occur through hearing—their overhearing—and not through sight. In this business the play manages a delicate sense of difference. The beguiling of their ears may *seem* like the beguiling of the eyes in Don Pedro's wooing of Hero for Claudio. Yet what is overheard, while a fiction, is in some sense true, a truth proved in the fact that each assents so readily to an apparent change of mind. The ear, though formally deceived, nevertheless picks an essential reality from the apparent deception. The important fact would appear to be that it all occurs in language, the medium in which the two have each known the other from the beginning.

If Claudio falls in love by sight, he falls out of love just as quickly when the dumbshow played by Margaret and Borachio practices on his sight. "Out on thee, seeming!" he exclaims in response to her question whether she ever seemed other than modest to him. "Is this the Prince? is this the Prince's brother? / Is this face Hero's? Are our eyes our own?" (4.1.70–71). This last, of course, is a better question than he knows. Can the epistemology of the eye give a genuine sense of human interiority? Or is it limited, like the apparel that Borachio, in his drunken conversation with Conrade, mocks as "fashion": "Thou knowest that the fashion of a doublet, or a hat, or a cloak, is nothing to a man" (3.3.117–19). While Claudio is deluded by a dress and a cloak, even Dogberry and the watch, comically confused as they are in their language, somehow penetrate the villainy practiced on Hero. When Leonato confronts the villains, he naively asks, "Let me see his eyes, / That, when I note another man like him, / I may avoid him" (5.1.259–61). But Borachio cannot be so distinguished, and Leonato must acknowledge that "a pair of honorable men"—to all *appearance*—have had a hand in the *apparent* death of his daughter.

At the end of the play Benedick says to Leonato, "Your niece regards me with an eye of favor," and that he "with an eye of love" requites her. Of course these eyes are also ears, and what Benedick has "seen" of Beatrice's favor, what she has "seen" of his love, has been in fact heard. The Claudio/Hero plot has received a somewhat schematic resolution: to expiate his sin Claudio, who has misjudged by his dependence on appearance, must surrender sight and agree to marry Leonato's veiled "niece," who is of course Hero. An audience must accept this as a fitting cure and punishment of an over-dependence on the visual. The truer alternative is understood to rest in the witty lovers, whose words better mirror their minds. As if to underscore this, their written words are produced, Benedick's "halting sonnet of his own pure brain" written to Beatrice and one of Beatrice's "containing her affection unto Benedick" (5.4.87, 90). As I suggested above, the thematics of the play thus represents agreement with a humanist position on sight and language such as Jonson could endorse. Significantly, what is not developed are the implications of the antivisual thematics toward theater itself. If Claudio's outraged question, "Are our eyes our own?" were meant to turn reflexively onto the question of theater itself, the answer would in a sense be, no, our eyes are not our own; we deliver them up to the players and see as they want us to see. Theater is a practice on the eyes of the audience as well as upon ears, and *appearance* is as crucial as what is said and heard. The schematic resolution of the Claudio/Hero plot, through a sacrifice of sight to compensate for exclusive reliance on sight, is nearly always problematic in performance; seldom can it carry a persuasive sense of psychological resolution. But equally, the thematic insistence on the falsity of appearance sorts uneasily with the phenomenology of theater. The audience is aware of the falsity of Claudio's seeing, but the schematic division of sight and hearing, image and word, between the two plots separates what is the unified *epistemé* of theater. As we perceive and accept the thematic meaning, we are likely to remain less persuaded that it comments adequately on its theatrical medium, or indeed is conveyed persuasively by it. This separation expresses an anxiety about sight and vision similar to what one sees constantly on display in *The Faerie Queene*, an anxiety all the more significant in its coming from a poet who is also a practitioner of visual art.

IV

But in his most theatrically self-reflexive play from the 1590s, Shakespeare insists in a positive way on the identity of the stage as a visual as well as a verbal art. *Midsummer Night's Dream*, in the lovers' plot, appears to express the debility of sight in a way similar to what is conveyed in the Hero/Claudio plot of *Much Ado*. Puck's control of the lovers' eyes becomes an obvious analogue to the playwright's power over his characters—and as well over the eyes of his audience. Through the anointing and re-anointing of eyes, we sense our own need to comply with the processes by which theater practices on the faculty of sight. Because of the stylized characterization of the lovers, we are able to take them as theatrical counters, pieces to be moved about the board at will, and the pleasure an audience takes in this process is thus disconnected from the apprehension of pain such falling in and out of love would normally entail.

In this process sight becomes the essential component of the game. The lovers' language, comically formulaic as it is, is simply an expression of what their eyes are imperfectly seeing in the present moment. Even Titania's poetry must serve her eyes' delusion.

The issue of sight, especially in its relation to theater itself, is wonderfully expressed in what seems the subplot, but is really the imaginative heart of the play, the mechanicals' staging of *Pyramus and Thisbe*. While much of its humor remains impervious to analysis, we may sense that some part of it comes of their imperfectly literate status. This much they share with their imaginative neighbors, Dogberry and the watch in *Much Ado*. Clearly Peter Quince, as Prologue, is tripped up by the punctuation of a written text. In subject and rhetoric the mechanicals' play may be seen to parody humanist concerns by handing them over to ill-suited scholars; in this it resembles the more explicitly humanist parody of *Love's Labor's Lost*, where those who have, as Moth says, "been at a great feast of languages and stol'n the scraps" stage a masque of the nine worthies. But the wonder of Bottom and the mechanicals goes far beyond merely parodic intentions. Concern for vision, in every sense of the word, is the basis for the deep comedy of the mechanicals' plot, and Bottom impresses, and indeed achieves his imaginative centrality, by his ability to give himself up to vision. "Let the audience look to their eyes," he says with the logic that distinguishes him. He means, of course, the tears he expects them to shed in response to the tears *he* will shed in playing Pyramus, but looking to one's eyes strikes the characteristic Bottom note. Though a childlike eagerness to enter into the role-playing—he would play Pyramus, Thisbe, *and* the lion if he could—distinguishes Bottom from his fellows, he is also as anxious about appearance and disguise as the most antitheatrical Puritan. But his anxiety is more fundamental, closer to the real concerns that theater must always raise. He worries that Pyramus' violent suicide will be too much for the ladies of the audience. He seconds Snout's similar fear about the lion. But he has solutions to these problems, solutions that go to the heart of the phenomenology of theater: verbally, let a prologue tell that Pyramus is really Bottom the Weaver and that his suicide is feigned; visually, let just enough of Snug's face show through the lion's neck, and if that's not enough, let Snug also reassure the ladies in words. Bottom's imagination bounds between the extremes of realism and allegory: real moonlight from a casement window can solve the issue of time and setting, but the brilliant stroke of a personified Wall with plaster and roughcast overcomes the tricky problem of an unwieldy stage property. However comic it all is, Bottom's nervousness about disguise appears justified when he enters "translated" by Puck, and his fellows flee in terror. This is just the sort of thing playing can lead to; theater is such a "translation."

When Bottom exclaims on his fairy vision, we may properly take the synesthesia of his words as a judgment of the relative importance of the various senses to the theatrical experience: "The eye of man hath not heard, the ear of man hath not seen, man's hand is not able to taste, his tongue to conceive, nor his heart to report, what my dream was" (4.1.211–14).[27] Such a deformation of a text of St. Paul (1 Corinthians 2:9–10) would have an easily calculated effect on the Puritan antitheatricalists. But Bottom's "most rare vision" is a theatrical epiphany that expresses the undifferentiated sensual appeal of theater. With unassailable logic, his "o altitudo" concludes that the ballad of the dream will be called Bottom's Dream "because it hath no bottom." His synesthesia extends into the performance of *Pyramus and Thisbe*: "I see a voice: now will I to the chink, / To spy an I can hear my Thisbe's face." "Tongue, lose thy light; / Moon, Take thy flight," he exclaims as Pyramus dies. And finally he gives the audience a choice: "Will it please you to see the epilogue, or to hear a Bergomask dance between two of our company?" To object to Bottom's verbs would be to align oneself with the lame inability of the court to enter into theatrical play and, more importantly, to misunderstand the way they define precisely the phenomenon of theater. Theseus' reply to Hippolyta's apprehensions about the mechanicals' staging implicitly undercuts the pretensions of humanist verbal culture. He has, he says, "picked a welcome" from the dumbshows that even "great clerks" have made when, shivering and pale, they

> Make periods in the midst of sentences,
> Throttle their practic'd accent in their fears,
> And in conclusion dumbly have broke off,
> Not paying me a welcome.

From such embarrassed silence he has nevertheless "read" as much as from "the rattling tongue / Of saucy and audacious eloquence" (5.1.96–103). In such cases the eye can hear more than the ear. What is perhaps most extraordinary about *Midsummer Night's Dream,* in relation to Jonson's defenses of the stage, is the modesty of its claims for the essence of theater: the best in this kind are but shadows, and the worst no worse if imagination mend them. Again, the trope is visual, though Bottom would no doubt insist that the shadows are to be *heard*.

V

Hamlet, the highwater mark of Shakespearean self-reflexivity, poses the question of the visual character of theater as part of its thorough-going interrogation of the nature of theatrical mimesis. Robert Weimann has suggested that "the figure of Hamlet is itself so cast into multiple functions of mimesis that what the 'character' throughout reveals is some profound crisis in representativity."[28] From the very beginning the prince seems to protest against the reality of theatrical appearance. When Gertrude asks why his consciousness of mortality, expressed in his mourning for his father, seems so particular with him, he replies, "Seems, madam? nay, it is. I know not 'seems'" (1.2.76). He details all the elements of his actual stage presence—costume, breath, tears, "the dejected havior of the visage"—that denote the "forms, moods, shapes of grief," but protests that while these may be the visual signs "that a man might play," with him these are coterminous with his inward state, with his essential reality: "I have that within which passes show; / These are but the trappings and the suits of woe" (1.2.81–86). It is a strange moment. The central figure of the play, at this initial point, calls insistent attention to the visual theatricality of "show" while insisting that it is all extrinsic, mere trappings, to himself.[29] We have no doubt that this is true of life, where the self is only imperfectly expressed by externals, and as audience we are surely willing to extend this understanding silently to the figure acting a part before us. But instead of allowing the understanding to remain implicit, the figure insists on the distinction—and insists in a language that emphatically points to the very things without which theater cannot delineate character. This is the initial moment in which we see what Weimann describes as "the rupture in Hamlet himself, between what is shown and what is meant." If Hamlet were entirely "in character," entirely representational, he could insist on his inward sorrow without calling attention to the theatrical means by which he—at once character *and* actor—is defining sorrow in visual, histrionic terms.

But it is basic to the play that the theatrical metaphor becomes so completely identified with Hamlet's consciousness—and ultimately with the audience's—that the play can be said to have meaning only in terms of that metaphor. Shakespeare takes the strange risk of identifying the action and setting of the play with the theater itself. "Hamlet"—and again it is a puzzle whether we mean the character or the actor playing him, or both—seems to refer to the stage directly when he points down to it and calls the ghost "this fellow in the cellerage" (1.5.151). He likewise gestures to the physical features of the Globe when he directs Rosencrantz and Guildenstern's attention to "this goodly frame, the earth . . . this most excellent canopy the air, look you, this brave o'erhanging firmament, this majestical roof fretted with golden fire" (2.2.298–301). "Frame," "canopy," "o'erhanging," and "roof" hover between the metaphorical, as they refer to the cosmos, and the entirely literal, as they refer to the theater itself. Within a few moments in this scene, the representation of the Danish court is suspended as Rosencrantz and Guildenstern bring "Hamlet," evidently an avid London theater-goer exiled to—where, Denmark?—up to date on the latest gossip in the wars between the adult and children's companies. "Do the boys carry it away?" he asks. "Ay, that they do, my lord—Hercules and his load too," Rosencrantz replies, identifying the very icon of the theater in which the actors are playing. It is a risk, obviously, because such attention obtrudes on the representational fiction and distracts, at least potentially, from its acceptance. And yet Shakespeare seems intent on identifying his medium, theater in all its physicality and visual character, with what the play itself is coming to be and mean.

The double epistemology of theater is implied, I suggest, in the double performance of *The Murder of Gonzago*, first as a dumbshow, then with language. By the time of *Hamlet*, as Andrew Gurr notes, dumbshows were clearly archaic,[30] and the verse of *The Murder* is also old-fashioned and stilted. It is a very different sort of play from the neoclassical piece on Dido and Aeneas that pleases Hamlet: "never acted, or if it was, not above once . . . 'twas caviary to the general" (2.2.434–37). Hamlet, moreover, clearly finds the dramaturgy of *The Murder of Gonzago* embarrassing. "'Tis a knavish piece of work, but what of that?" (3.2.240). His commentary on the play, which ends up forcing the very question he wants the play to answer, puts him in the line of superior observers to staged plays-within-plays, not only Theseus' court in *Midsummer Night's Dream* but the ill-befitting mockery of the gentles of the Masque of the Nine Worthies in *Love's Labor's Lost*. The audience to *Hamlet* remains uncertain whether it was the play that caused Claudius to call for light and leave or Hamlet's pointed remarks. While Hamlet is elated at what he takes as the king's reaction to his "Mousetrap," Horatio's words suggest a more guarded reaction. Hamlet asks if he perceived Claudius' reaction "Upon the talk of poisoning?" But was the talk that of Lucianus, the stage murderer, or of Hamlet? My concern is not so much with the possible answers to this vexed question as with the nature of the "knavish piece of work" that Hamlet has chosen, "the image of a murder done in Vienna," to work upon the king—and, just as much, upon his mother. Does the doubling in its modes of representation, first the entirely visual dumbshow, then the theatrical completion when language is added, suggest a kind of progression in the character of the physical personifying that theater is? In experimental modes the theater seems frequently to insist on the primacy of the visual and the physical.[31] The stylization of each version, mimed and spoken, works to focus attention on them as complementary modes of representation. The words *show* and *tell* dominate the brief dialogue of Hamlet and Ophelia between the dumbshow and the "prologue," which in fact is too brief to tell much of anything. If, as Hamlet says, "the players cannot keep counsel; they'll tell all," it is finally he who does not keep counsel, but *tells* all. If he does not allow this image of a murder to work upon Claudius so that he may *show* his guilt to Horatio, the reason comes of his mistrust of mere seeming.

As has been frequently enough noted, Hamlet is obsessed with mere seeming. There is something paralyzing, though fascinating, about his intense consciousness of the distinction between what seems and what is. It is, of course, a consciousness very much at odds with the acceptance of theater itself. The play shows Hamlet finally able to achieve revenge only when he can embrace his role as a role and become, in both senses, an actor. In a larger sense this means that theater itself, including appearance, all the *seems* of costume, gesture, "havior of the visage," spectacle itself, must be accepted. The realizing of the metaphor that pervades *Hamlet* includes the building itself, the "goodly frame" whose cellerage, stage, tiring house, and canopy comprise the world. The literal redundancy of Fortinbras' final command, "Bear Hamlet like a soldier to the stage," is but a final example of the identification of *seems* and *is* that permeates the central metaphor of the play. The exploration of that metaphor in the self-reflexiveness of *Hamlet* points to the necessity of accepting the visual and the physical in the phenomenology of theater. But the play does not arrive at such a position easily, and as Huston Diehl argues, the intense anxiety about spectacle centered in Hamlet's own consciousness figures an awareness of the concern over word and image that had become central to Protestantism.[32]

An exploration of the image in many ways complementary with the exploration of theatricality in *Hamlet* occurs in *Troilus and Cressida*, a play composed, it seems likely, within a year or so. Together the two plays suggest a strikingly different sense of the relation of image and word from that projected in *Much Ado*. Perhaps no play of Shakespeare more insistently thematizes the issue of vision, and what is *seen* as a stage image, than *Troilus and Cressida*. Though we cannot know what exactly *was* seen on Shakespeare's stage, the text of the play insists on the need to surmise how the elements of spectacle interact with the verbal script. Barbara Hodgdon has recently considered, and critiqued, the way half a dozen twentieth-century productions have employed spectacle to construct gender relations and in particular to develop various versions of Cressida in terms of the male gaze.[33] Her analysis suggests how absolutely crucial visual interpretation is to what this play comes to mean. In a number of scenes the text appears to leave strikingly open what a theatrical audience is to see. And yet this much seems clear: the play intends generally to open an ironic gap between the literary tradition that conveys the heroic reputations of the Greek and Trojan warriors and what is laid before the spectators' eyes and ears. Achilles, Ajax, Ulysses, and even Hector are not whom we have taken them to be. The play's intentions toward Cressida are at once more complex and less determinate. She is in a sense confirmed as the faithless mistress of Troilus, just as Pandarus is confirmed as a pandar. While she is not the tragically beset heroine of Chaucer, a level of uncertainty remains for the reader of the text as to what motivates her—what, finally, she is.

Such indeterminacy is, of course, opportunity for theatrical performance. The least that can be said is that the play is iconoclastic in a figurative sense; the heroes deriving from the Homeric tradition are subjected to a thorough debunking. But this figurative iconoclasm is accomplished by visual representation on stage, the visual representation moreover deconstructing the heroism of the classical world and asserting a revisionist "truth" about figures who have been the *verbal* icons of humanist poetic tradition. So the figurative iconoclasm that abrades verbal tradition must rest on the visual construction of theatrical spectacle. Thersites' corrosive wit stands for a figuratively iconoclast position throughout the play, railing as he does on the Greek warriors, particularly Ajax, Achilles, and Patroclus, and reducing the argument of the Trojan war itself to "a whore and a cuckold, a goodly quarrel to draw emulous factions and bleed to death upon" (2.3.72–74). He calls Achilles "thou picture of what thou seemest, and idol of idiot-worshippers" (5.1.6–7). But the discourse of idolatry and iconoclasm enters through other characters as well. Most prominent is the reply of Hector to Troilus in the debate over whether to continue the war or return Helen to Menalaus. In response to Hector's argument that Helen is not worth the Trojan lives that her keeping costs, Troilus asks rhetorically, "What's aught but as 'tis valued?" Hector counters,

> But value dwells not in particular will. . . .
>   'Tis mad idolatry
> To make the service greater than the god,
> And the will dotes that is attributive
> To what infectiously itself affects,
> Without some image of th' affected merit. (2.2.53-60)

In this formulation Helen becomes an idol, a vacant image, and the war itself "mad idolatry" of her. In the playlet that Ulysses and Nestor stage for the sake of spurring Ajax's pride, Nestor asks why Achilles should "be worshiped, / Of that we hold an idol more than he?" (2.3.188–89). Ajax is the more valued idol of their little fiction.

But the moment of theatrical self-reflexiveness in the Greek council (Act 1, scene 3), when Ulysses imagines—and presumably mimics—Patroclus playing Agamemnon and Nestor, most complexly draws into question the whole endeavor of stage representation of the Trojan war and the nature of the stage characters. The moment is unique in Shakespeare: a character imagining an offstage character playing the very characters who are present on stage with him. Its self-reflexive audacity is like the moment when Cleopatra imagines future "quick comedians" staging her court and "some squeaking Cleopatra boy my greatness / I' th' posture of a whore" (*Antony and Cleopatra* 5.2.220–21). Ulysses supposes that Patroclus will play them in mockery: "With ridiculous and silly action / (Which, slanderer, he imitation calls) / He pageants us." He imagines Patroclus "a strutting player, whose conceit / Lies in his hamstring," pounding the stage with his pompous stride in imitation of Agamemnon, or acting Nestor's characteristic gestures and the coughing and palsied shaking of his old age. Ulysses' mimicry of Patroclus' mimicry itself mocks Agamemnon and Nestor, mocks the actors playing them, and implicitly mocks the very theatrical activity of which they are all a part. Like the moments of theatrical reflexivity in *Midsummer Night's Dream* and *Hamlet*, this one is superficially iconoclastic of the stage image, but seems in its effect paradoxically to extol the activity it has seemed to mock. The iconoclastic impulse calls attention to the mode of representation, challenging its acceptance.

Vision, and the stage image, are problematized as early as the second scene of the play, in which Cressida and Pandarus view the Trojan heroes as they pass across the stage returning from battle. On the assumption that simply the sight of him will cause her to fall in love, Pandarus wants Cressida to see Troilus. But meanwhile he offers a verbal commentary, a kind of gloss, on the representation of each of the heroes. These glosses, directed as they are to the icons of classical tradition, are thin in the extreme: "That's Aeneas; is not that a brave man? He's one of the flowers of Troy, I can tell you." Of Hector he can only exclaim, "That's Hector, that, that, look you, that; there's a fellow!" and concludes with the verbal tautology, "Look how he looks" (1.2.186–86, 199–201). What does the audience meanwhile see? Do they all—Aeneas, Antenor, Hector, Paris ("Is't not a gallant man too, is't not?"), Helenus, Troilus—look pretty much alike? Or are they differentiated simply by costume and armor? Whatever their theatrical guise, one imagines that disparity between what is seen and Pandarus' scarcely differentiated enthusiasm is the point of it all, especially since Cressida is intent on a mild mockery of that enthusiasm. She pretends not to recognize Troilus, and teases Pandarus by asking "What sneaking fellow comes yonder?" (1.2.226). Chafed by her apparent indifference, Pandarus asks, "have you any discretion, have you any eyes? do you know what a man is?" (1.2.225–52). He fondly imagines that all Troilus' abstract qualities, whatever they may be, can be viewed as he parades past.

What appears increasingly significant, however, is that the tableaux on which the play insists have a kind of stubborn reality of their own, independent of any attempts to fix them verbally. Thersites, who has just been beaten by Ajax, insists that Achilles look upon Ajax. "So I do," replies Achilles. "Nay, but regard him well," Thersites insists, and again, after Achilles protests he does, "But yet you look not well upon him; for whosomever you take him to be, he is Ajax" (2.1.60–64). We know this is Ajax, as does Achilles, but Thersites' point is that this, *this* is Ajax in all his mute silence and gross physicality. He is not words or mind, but a simple bodily presence; to be Ajax is simply to be seen to stand there and menace Thersites. In the final-act scene in which both Thersites on the one hand and Troilus and Ulysses on the other view the assignation between Cressida and Diomed, vision becomes doubly thematized. Thersites appears to derive a voyeuristic, almost sexual, pleasure from Cressida's apparently reluctant, but at the same time resolved, wooing of Diomed. Troilus views the same thing, but with such pain that Ulysses can scarcely contain him. What does the eye see? Cressida protests that she sees with a double eye, one still looking on Troilus, but "with my heart the other eye doth see" Diomed. "Minds sway'd by eyes are full of turpitude," she concludes sadly (5.2.108, 112). Troilus will not be swayed by what his eyes, and those of Ulysses and the audience, have obviously seen. There is a "credence" in his heart and "An esperance so obstinately strong / That doth invert th' attest of eyes and ears" (5.2.121–22). Against Ulysses' protest, he denies that Cressida has been present. "Will 'a swagger himself out on's own eyes?" Thersites asks (5.2.136). But Troilus is not deluded, except perhaps by an idealism so powerful that he can retain his faith in a Cressida that transcends what he has just seen. Consequently, he concludes, "This is, and is not, Cressid!" (5.2.146). If, in Thersites' formulation, Ajax is simply what is seen, Cressida has become a double reality. On the one hand she is the truth of Troilus' faith in her, what in fact his faith has made her, a now invisible Cressida. And she is what has just been seen and heard on stage, the theatrical presence that perpetuates what she has become in cultural fame.

This represents, we might say, a passive sense of the eye's power. Even Troilus must finally accept what his eyes have seen. But the play also implies an active, indeed deconstructive, power in the visual. At one significant moment vision becomes an aggressive faculty. When Hector and Achilles view one another during the truce, Hector merely looks upon his rival, but Achilles insists on a prolonged, searching gaze, not giving over until he has "quoted joint by joint" the body he means to destroy. "Why dost thou so oppress me

with thine eye?" Hector angrily asks. Breaking in as it does upon the formality
and chivalric courtesies of the previous exchanges between Greeks and Tro-
jans, Achilles' visual oppression has the effect of making evident the mortal
aggression that really underlies this meeting of enemies. What the eye sees it
may in a sense destroy. For the audience the climactic scene of the play accomplishes something very like this. What the stage represents in the killing
of Hector unravels entirely the heroic tradition of the Trojan war. Achilles instructs his Myrmidons to keep themselves fresh in the battle, then when he has
found Hector, to surround him and "In fellest manner execute your arms"
(5.7.6). If an audience is not certain exactly what this means, it soon sees.
Finding Hector unarmed, weary from battle, and asking Achilles to forego the
advantage he now has, Achilles nevertheless orders his men to strike. They do,
and Hector falls, not in single combat with Achilles, but unarmed, surrounded
by a superior force, slaughtered by Achilles' henchmen. Achilles instructs his
men to cry out, "Achilles hath the mighty Hector slain," whence, the play implies, comes the Homeric tradition. What the audience has seen contravenes
that tradition altogether. What actors and the stage represent overturns decisively the humanist poetic tradition and replaces it with an image of blood-
thirsty and ignoble brutality. What is seen is not necessarily more authoritative
than what the ear has received, but the "truth" of the Trojan war must now live
imaginatively, if it is to live, in much the same status as Cressida's "truth" to
Troilus, a matter of pure faith contradicted by what the eye has seen. The playwright has oppressed the tradition by the gaze that has been fastened on it—
and perhaps has deluded the eye of the audience. What the problematizing of
vision in *Troilus and Cressida* accomplishes is a literal *revision* of the Troy
story, iconoclasm, we might say, by visual image.

VI

Confidence in what is seen—extending even to what to Jonson's eye were im-
permissibly spectacular effects—characterizes Shakespeare's dramaturgy in
the latter part of his career. It is not that he sets eye against ear in specific reaction to Jonson. But he is able to employ masque-like scenes and extraordinary
stage effects with none of Jonson's anxiety about theatrical essence. This becomes especially true of the romances, those plays Jonson mocks allusively in
the induction to *Bartholomew Fair*. Referring obviously to *The Winter's Tale*
and *The Tempest*, Jonson brings in the bookholder to speak for the playwright
of this play:

> If there be never a servant-monster i' the Fair, who can help it? he says; nor a
> nest of antics? He is loth to make nature afraid in his plays, like those that
> beget Tales, Tempests, and such like drolleries, to mix his head with other
> men's heels, let the concupiscence of jigs and dances reign as strong as it will
> amongst you. . . . [34]

He might also have adduced the penultimate scene of *Cymbeline*, where by means of elaborate stage machinery Jupiter "descends in thunder and lightning, sitting upon an eagle" (5.4.93). Any number of scenes from the romances might illustrate Shakespeare's confidence in the visual and in the kind of spectacular effects disdained by Jonson. But the scene that involves the greatest dramatic risk is also the one that most emphatically represents the linkage between iconoclasm, images, and theatricality I have been pursuing. The final scene of *The Winter's Tale*, the transformation of a seeming statue into a living, breathing woman, one whom the audience as well as the characters have thought sixteen years dead, is a theatrical stroke of unparalleled boldness.[35]

We have learned to understand the scene, and indeed the play itself, as involving a high degree of self-reflexiveness on Shakespeare's part. The reason for this, I would suggest, lies in the extraordinary nature of its claims, that the fantasy it constructs, its transformations of romance into something like myth, are in some sense true. Such psychic redemption, such regeneration as Leontes undergoes in his sixteen-year repentance, the play seems to insist, can happen. The gravest of injuries, those Leontes inflicted on the innocent Hermione, can, through the cooperation of human design and will with the restorative properties of nature and its processes of growth and rebirth, be finally healed. To make such claims requires an art that is at once supremely confident and humble, but also entirely self-conscious. Graham Holderness has incisively suggested that the play's work of undoing Leontes' diseased imagination requires an art that is aware of itself as an imaginative construction. "If a work of art does not contain within itself that internal distantiation which enables the reader or spectator to deconstruct its compelling construction of the real, then it can only operate, like Leontes' jealous fantasy, to naturalize the products of imagination and to confuse them systematically with reality." To oppose such fantasy that confuses its construction with reality demands a countering fantasy that is willing to explore and to lay bare its own fonts and techniques. A play like *The Winter's Tale* is "imagination caught in the act of judging itself, creating images of the real and simultaneously questioning both its own reality and the reality to which it alludes."[36] The play's self-awareness of its own artfulness, and its witty play with that awareness, are necessary elements of the claim it lays to present an alternative to the single-minded fantasy that had consumed Leontes.

Preceding the scene of Hermione's revelation in the seeming statue is one that carries to a self-reflexive extreme the rhetoric of the eye as the faculty of emotive response. It is a scene of pure narration that paradoxically—and seemingly perversely—only recounts the recognition that the audience had presumed it would witness, the discovery of Perdita's identity and her return to Leontes. The reason for this perversity, of course, lies in the astonishment that is accomplished in the following scene in the return of Hermione, a recognition that is entirely unexpected. But without knowing what is to come, the audience is subjected, through the scene's strange play with visual and verbal perspective, to a kind of mockery that can only be described as baroque. At first it seems momentarily possible we will hear nothing at all: First Gentleman tells Autolocus that everyone was commanded out of the chamber after the truth about Perdita was conveyed by the old shepherd. First Gentleman can make only "a broken delivery of the business." But what he tells us is that Leontes and Camillo "seem'd almost, with staring on one another, to tear the cases of their eyes. There was speech in their dumbness, language in their very gesture" (5.2.13–14). The speech and language that were eloquent dumbness and articulate gesture are, to our regret as spectators, rendered as mere report, speech that cannot really convey the "notable passion of wonder" that we would hope for in the enacted scene. The teasing continues even after Second Gentleman comes on and delivers, baldly, the full revelation: "Nothing but bonfires. The oracle is fulfilled, the king's daughter is found." If the news is "so like an old tale" that its truth is suspect, then the circumstances are so full that what you hear, "you'll swear you see." But the scene itself has been entirely repressed. Where is it? Has it occurred or not? Did *anyone* see it? Is it really only to be imagined, imaged, by *hearers* of what happened? "Did you see the meeting of the two kings?" asks Third Gentleman. When Second Gentleman replies, "No," Third taunts him—and the audience—even further: "Then have you lost a sight which was to be seen, cannot be spoken of"(5.2.42–43). But spoken of is all it can or will be, and spoken of in such a way that the extremes of joy seem to have composed it simply into a melodrama: casting up of eyes, holding up of hands, exclamations, extremes of happiness producing tears, Paulina, implausibly or comically, having "one eye declin'd for the loss of her husband, another elevated that the oracle was fulfill'd" (5.2.74–75). What is wonderful for the participants can only be disappointment for the audience. "I never heard of such another encounter," Third Gentleman says, "which lames report to follow it, and undoes description to do it" (5.2.56–58). The rhetoric of the narrating eye becomes most extreme when he tells of Perdita's reaction to her mother's death: "One of the prettiest touches of all, and that which angled for mine eyes (caught the water but not the fish)" (5.2.82–83). Perdita's own eyes, he fain would say, did "bleed tears; for I am sure my heart wept blood." We cannot help but be struck by the extremity of the tropes here, moving as they do from the coyness of "angled for mine eyes" to the hyperbolic transference of eyes bleeding tears and hearts weeping blood. In being denied the scene it expects, the eye is nevertheless—or perhaps for this reason—figured in the most extreme, indeed bizarre, terms. But why, we would wonder if the scene gave us leisure to do so, has the playwright in fact given up on the eye that his rhetoric extolls in such extreme fashion?

The answer comes, of course, in the scene that follows, one that on the contrary appears to construct visual wonder as the truest image of what theater can be. The supposed sculptor of Hermione's statue, Julio Romano, is spoken of as the heroic maker of images, one "who, had he himself eternity and could put breath into his work, would beguile Nature of her custom, so perfectly he is her ape" (5.2.97–99). Inevitably we associate the playwright with this, with the addition that the playwright can in fact put breath into his work through the living bodies that are the medium of his "sculpture." Early in the scene the issue of idolatry is raised explicitly. Leontes' first words when he sees the "statue" play over the question of its identity in relation to the woman he assumes it represents: "Chide me, dear stone, that I may say indeed / Thou art Hermione; or rather thou art she / In thy not chiding" (5.3.24–26). His reaction, and particularly that of Perdita, raise what we can understand as the worst fears of the iconoclasts, *that a stone might so affect onlookers as to draw them to veneration.* "There's magic in thy majesty," he asserts of the statue, which has "conjured" his evils to remembrance and drawn him to renewed shame. Perdita's response is worship itself: "And give me leave, / And do not say 'tis superstition that / I kneel, and then implore her blessing" (5.3. 42–44). Worse, she addresses the statue as if it could respond, as if it were identical with the original: "Lady, / Dear queen that ended when I but began, / Give me that hand of yours to kiss." Leontes becomes rapt into an attitude of apparent adoration, for he too wishes to kiss the statue. What becomes most significant theatrically is the way the scene comes to insist on faith in what is seen. As spectators, the audience is at one with Leontes in its ignorance of the statue's reality; his increasing wonder is also ours. As Paulina intensifies the mystery about the statue, she insists on the necessity of Leontes' faith, but in speaking to the court, she evokes the audience's faith as well:

> It is requir'd
> You do awake your faith. Then, all stand still.
> On; those that think it is unlawful business
> I am about, let them depart.

> (*The Winter's Tale* 5.3.94–97)

Leontes' response to her is a command both to the court and to the audience: "Proceed; / No foot shall stir." As theatrical performance testifies, the faith and complicity of the audience are also at stake; if anyone indeed made a move to leave, one senses, the scene itself could not proceed. Though Paulina's words direct Hermione's movements, in a primary way an audience is required to accept, and is affected by, what is seen. Music, as well as Paulina's words, are the accompaniment and intensification of the visual moment. The effect on the spectators would appear quite precisely analogous to religious experience in that an act of faith is required for the enactment of the seeming miracle. In its quasi-religious enactment, the scene realizes the worst fears also of the antitheatricalists, for it presses an audience into idolatry as it assents with Leontes to whatever reality the apparent statue may mysteriously possess. Insofar as their desires coalesce with those of the characters on stage, the viewers become complicit in worship of the statue and thus agents in whatever it is that brings about the statue's incarnation into full theatrical life. If the scene for the moment fully associates theatricality with idolatry, Shakespeare does not counter, but embraces the charge.

The dramatist does possess the advantage of breath over the sculptor, breath that in the next moment issues in blessing over Perdita. T. G. Bishop has best described the position of the audience in that moment: "As our excitement becomes the 'subject' of the final scene, even as it prepares to end itself and leave us to ourselves, so the space 'between' stage and audience becomes the site of the scene's imaginative activity, in which the whole community may 'participate.;" And when Hermione prays, "You gods, look down / And from your sacred vials pour your graces / Upon my daughter's head!" there is a sense, he suggests, in which the audience are "at once co-petitioners and the powers to whom the petition is being addressed."[37] Such a moment of identification between audience and theatrical spectacle makes the association of the scene with idolatry all the more charged. As Perdita had asked for the statue's blessing, so the "statue," now incarnated as the mother herself, gives that blessing. The audience has assisted at the invocation of the statue and its evocation to warm-blooded life, and now, with the woman who was the statue, it seems to pray and confer blessing on the daughter whose discovery has precipitated the "return" to life.

It is no accident that criticism has frequently responded to this scene with frankly religious terminology. We are aware of the distinction between drama and religious ritual, but the play's own symbolic terms and the demands it makes upon its audience appear to blur the boundary. Louis Montrose in particular calls attention to the ways Shakespeare brings religious rites and magic into his plays to explore "the affinities between the theatrical playing space, the ecclesiastical sacred space, and the charmed circle":

> It is precisely by means of the boldest theatricality that the climax of *The Winter's Tale* is transformed into a rite of communion. The audience on the stage and audience in the theatre are atoned by the great creating nature of Shakespeare's art—an art fully realized only when it is incarnated by human players. If we take the attackers and defenders of the theatre at their word, and if we credit our own experience as playgoers, we may be willing to consider the possibility that a Jacobean audience could experience as intense an emotional and intellectual satisfaction from a performance of *The Winter's Tale* as from a divine service.[38]

Though the play is secular, the figural terms here combine to suggest displaced religious ritual. The combination of the final scene's frankness as spectacle, its rich emotive appeal, and our sense that ultimate human concerns are being addressed by its overcoming of tragedy and death conveys a powerful sense of transcending significance. It is surely for this reason that the words *rite* and *ritual* figure continually in critical discussions, even though the scene neither enacts a ritual properly speaking nor even portrays one. The words, however, seem the only ones available to us to describe our sense of the physical conveying the spiritual, of outward signs effecting inner transformations. The playwright incarnates characters who themselves enact and incarnate a Nature instinct with redemptive possibility. And the audience is bound intimately into the process by which a statue responds to prayer and desire, comes alive, and confers blessing on a world that had seemed lost to tragedy.

VII

In both Shakespeare and Jonson the iconoclasm of Reformation culture and its attendant antitheatricalism stimulate an intense need for reflection on the nature of the visual image, especially on the visual character of their art. For Shakespeare reflection on the nature of spectacle becomes, increasingly in his career, a necessary concomitant of the creation of spectacle. No longer innocent, the eye is implicated in the "idolatry" of theater, and its way of knowing, consequently, must be as self-conscious and reflective as the epistemology of the word. In the plays considered here, the visual becomes identified with the phenomenology itself of theater, and in the self-reflective moments that assert the nature of theater, visual and corporeal experience are constituted as the very center of theatricality. One may argue, as Huston Diehl does, that the power that Shakespeare attributes to theatrical representation resides primarily in language, in the words that "interpret and enliven" the visual images.[39] Understandable though such a judgment is, given the medium through which the plays have been transmitted and through which they are experienced outside the theater, it is sharply qualified by the metadrama itself, the reflection within the plays on the nature of theatricality, where the visual and the corporeal emerge as no less vital, no less significant, in the complex phenomenology of theater. By contrast, Jonson's dramaturgy and the self-consciousness about spectacle and word evident both in prefatory material and in the plays themselves show him more than half in agreement with Reformation anxiety about the image. His rejection of spectacle, and the romance plotting he associates with the investment in spectacle, suggest, in Barish's words, "a distrust of theatricality, even as he satirizes Puritan anti-theatricalism in figures like Zeal-of-the-Land Busy."[40]

While a play like *Much Ado* or elements of Hamlet's consciousness may momentarily align Shakespeare with this Jonsonian anxiety about the non-verbal elements of theater and with the coerciveness of the image, it is clear that a broader, more complex sense of the role of the eye is at play in the full range of his theater. It emerges in the insistent metadrama that is such a striking feature of his dramaturgy, evident not only in the plays-within-plays, but also in the almost habitual way language within the plays figures theatricality and playing. I have focused on a number of plays where this metadrama turns on the role of the eye and the visual elements of theater, but of course it is pervasive within the plays, almost a tic, one might say, of Shakespeare's dramaturgy. This self-reflexive sense, I want to conclude, is itself a response to the larger interrogation of the image that comes of the Reformation, an interrogation that, as it spilled over into the antitheatricalism of Puritanism, necessitated an intense self-consciousness about what theater is. Not all theater, of course, requires of itself such a self-accounting. But the fact that Shakespeare returns again and again to such metadramatic reflection registers the continuing demands of self-definition imposed on the Elizabethan and Jacobean theater and its practitioners.

While the contrasting ideological demands of the Reformation and the

Catholic Reform impel the need for this self-definition, drama itself appears for
the most part to evade clear identification with either side. Though Jonson is
known to have allied himself with Catholicism between 1598 and 1610, his theater cannot be said to express this alliance. His explicit quarrels are with the sectarians, and yet his humanist aesthetic on the issue of image and word shows
him more than half in agreement with them. Shakespeare's religious affiliations
remain more mysterious. On the evidence of his plays it would surely be hard to
align him with Puritanism or a radical Protestantism, yet his intense self-consciousness about the relation of image and word suggest a mind fully engaged
by the challenge such a perspective posed. If the conclusion of *The Winter's
Tale* might strike one as "Catholic" in its aesthetics, Hamlet's own consciousness might well seem "Protestant" in its intense suspicion of visual appearance.
To note this is not to argue for a Shakespearean transcendence of religious ide-
ologies, but rather to acknowledge a certain indeterminacy in the way his consciousness expresses itself in terms of explicit meanings—rather the way I suggested in chapter 1 that the Puritan antitheatricalism of the 1570s and 1580s was
replicated by the contemporary antitheatricalism of Borromeo's Catholic Reform in Milan. While a complex use of images would characterize Catholicism
in the seventeenth century and concentration on preaching and scripture would
define Protestantism, drama, and the way it was used in the Elizabethan and Jacobean periods, cannot be said to be defined by either.

What is remarkable about Shakespeare's self-reflexive characterizations
of theater is their willingness to enlist the image in the endeavor of definition.
I have argued that the metadrama of his plays represents a response to iconoclasm, and it is significant that the defenses of theatricality implicit in those
metatheatrical moments at the same time encompass various forms of skepticism about representation. There is never an uncomplicated devotion to the
word or to the image in isolation. But frequently, particularly in plays such as
Troilus and Cressida and *Antony and Cleopatra,* the image, while itself engaged in skeptical projects of redefinition, carries the burden of knowledge.
The theatrical image is made a way of knowing. If Othello's doubts can seem,
properly but only temporarily, to melt before the physical appearance of
Desdemona—"Look where she comes. / If she be false, o then heaven mocks
itself! / I'll not believe't" (3.3.277–78)—the moment recurs in various ways in
the late plays. Visual understanding can achieve its own legitimate status and
trust from the audience in relation to other possible understandings, including
the competing skepticism of verbal constructions. The statue scene in *The
Winter's Tale* is simply the most demanding and explicit of the frequent assertions of the eye's claim in the late plays. The affirmation of spectacle is thus
more than an allowance of the visual character of theater. It is a legitimation of
a way of knowing asserted against humanist claims for an exclusive, or near
exclusive, truth in language. To Jonson this could only seem naive, an expression of trust in the faculty of perception most easily deceived. But the fullness
of theater rests also on what is taken in by the eye, and its very ground is impersonation by living, breathing human bodies. In such assertion of the eye
and the body, Shakespeare the poet acknowledges himself a visual artist.

Notes

Abbreviations

EETS   Early English Text Society
ELH   *ELH: A Journal of English Literary History*
ELR   *English Literary Renaisiance*
JMEMS   *Lournal of Medieval and Early Modern Studies*
JWCI   *Journal of the Warburg and Courtald Institute*
MLQ   *Modern Language Quarterly*
PL   J. P. Migne, *Patrologia Latina*
REED   Records of Early English Drama

Introduction

1. M. R. James, *The Sculptures in the Lady Chapel at Ely* (London: D. Nutt, 1895), reproduces photographs of all the damaged sculptural reliefs and statuary and provides commentary, much of it necessarily conjectural, on their subject matter.

2. John Phillips, *The Reformation of Images: Destruction of Art in England, 1535–1660* (Berkeley: University of California Press, 1973); Phyllis Mack Crew, *Calvinist Preaching and Iconoclasm in the Netherlands, 1544–1566* (Cambridge: Cambridge University Press, 1978); Carl C. Christensen, *Art and the Reformation in Germany* (Athens: Ohio University Press, 1979); Carlos M. N. Eire, *War Against the Idols: The Reformation of Worship from Erasmus to Calvin* (Cambridge: Cambridge University Press, 1986); Ernest Gilman, *Iconoclasm and Poetry in the English Reformation: Down Went Dagon* (Chicago: University of Chicago Press, 1986); Margaret Aston, *England's Iconoclasts*, vol. 1: *Laws against Images* (Oxford: Clarendon, 1988); Eamon Duffy, *The Stripping of the Altars: Traditional Religion in England, 1400–1580* (New Haven: Yale University Press, 1992).

3. Frederic Jameson, *Signatures of the Visible* (New York: Routledge, 1990), p. 1. Jameson suggests that *writing* about film releases him from the spell cast by the visual: "I find I have no desire to see again a film about which I have written well" (p. 4).

4. W. J. T. Mitchell, *Iconology: Image, Text, Ideology* (Chicago: University of Chicago Press, 1986), p. 43.

5. E. H. Gombrich, *Art and Illusion* (Princeton, N.J.: Princeton University Press, 1956), p. 9.

6. See especially Roderick P. Hart, *Seducing America: How Television Charms*

American Voters (New York: Oxford University Press, 1994). Rather startlingly for my argument, Hart concludes his analysis of the corrupting influence of television on political life by recommending a return to explicitly Puritan values, including their suspicion of visuality. Probably the most extreme attack on television has been Jerry Mander's *Four Arguments for the Elimination of Television* (New York: William Morrow, 1978), especially his third argument (pp. 157–260), which concludes: "Our thinking processes can't save us. To the degree that we are thinking as we watch television, a minute degree at most, the images pass right through anyway. They enter our brains. They remain permanently. We cannot tell, for sure, which images are ours and which came from distant places. Imagination and reality have merged. We have lost control of our images. We have lost control of our minds" (p. 260).

7. The Internet addresses of these sites are, or were, http://demog.berkeley.edu/ ~bandy/antinetscape.html, http://world.std.com/~adamg/manifesto.html, and http:// www.abs.net/~mikebat/ode-to-lynx.html.

8. Jacques Ellul, *The Humiliation of the Word*, trans. Joyce Main Hanks (Grand Rapids, Mich.: Eerdmans, 1985). Though the subject of his attack is universal in Western society, the context of his quarrel seems specifically French. In his critique of Ellul, Martin Jay suggests that Ellul's hostility toward the visual, as well as his argument itself, is far less unusual than he implies ("The Rise of Hermeneutics and the Crisis of Ocularcentrism," in *The Rhetoric of Interpretation and the Interpretation of Rhetoric*, ed. Paul Hernadi [Durham, N.C.: Duke University Press, 1989], pp. 55–74). Jay finds "a remarkably pervasive and increasingly vocal hostility to visual primacy in France ever since the time of Bergson. Whether in the philosophy of a Sartre or a Lyotard, the film criticism of a Metz or a Baudry, the feminism of a Irigary or a Kofman, the theology of a Levinas or a Jabès, the literary criticism of a Bataille or a Blanchot, the literature of a Robbe-Grillet or a Bonnefoy, one can find a deep-seated distrust of the privileging of sight" (pp. 56–57). On the reaction to ocularcentrism in modern French culture, see Jay's recent larger study, *Downcast Eyes: The Denigration of Vision in Twentieth-Century French Thought* (Berkeley: University of California Press, 1993).

9. Ellul, *The Humiliation of the Word*: on sight, pp. 5–12; on hearing, pp. 13–26; on writing, pp. 42–47.

10. Ibid., pp. 79–80. For a contrasting sense of the significance of the incarnation, see Karl Rahner, *The Foundations of Christian Belief*, trans. William V. Dych (New York: Seabury, 1978), "On the relationship between human transcendence and hypostatic union," pp. 198–203. The most theologically sophisticated consideration of the relation between visual representation and Christian tradition that I've encontered is that of Aidan Nichols, *The Art of God Incarnate: Theology and Image in Christian Tradition* (New York: Paulist Press, 1980).

11. Margaret R. Miles, *Image as Insight: Visual Understanding in Western Christianity and Secular Culture* (Boston: Beacon, 1985); her second and final chapters in particular argue for a hermeneutic of images in response to the hegemony of language and language users in the interpretation of culture. An acute recent study of the role of the image in contemporary American religious culture is David Morgan's *Visual Piety: A History and Theory of Popular Religious Images* (Berkeley: University of California Press, 1998), which centers on the role of popular religious images, in particular those of Warner Sallman. Morgan finds that among evangelical Protestants, in spite of a minimal suspicion deriving from the historical tradition, the image has become an important element of twentieth-century religious devotion, frequently displayed in domestic settings and linking generational religious experience.

12. David Freedberg, *The Power of Images: Studies in the History and Theory of Response* (Chicago: University of Chicago Press, 1989).

13. Ibid., pp. 192–245.

14. At several points Freedberg takes issue, in particular with Nelson Goodman, over this issue; Goodman implies that representation is more than a matter of conventions and choices (pp. 59, 201, 427); see Goodman, *The Languages of Art: An Approach to a Theory of Symbols* (Indianapolis, Ind.: Bobbs-Merrill, 1968), pp. 34–39.

15. On the logical problem of the image, see in particular Jean Wirth, "Théorie et practique de l'image sainte à la veille de la réforme," *Bibliothèque d'Humanisme et Renaissance* 48 (1986): 319–58. In discussing the theoretical conundrum that the image presented for late-medieval philosophy, Wirth proposes Austin's idea of performative language, seeing performative signs in the sacramentals of the medieval world. "The efficacy of the sign depends upon an institutional context, on respect for the rules of the game."

16. In his analysis of the way television creates a cult of personality in politics, Hart notes the way the small screen concentrates on close-ups of faces, giving the impression of communicating intimacy (*Seducing America*, p. 38).

17. Significantly, each of these passages in turn depends upon a key text of the aniconic heritage in the Hebrew Scriptures; the climax of the Priestly account of creation with which Genesis begins states that God created humanity "in the image and likeness of God." Aidan Nichols points out that the word for image, *tselem,* is the word used of sculpting and painting (*Art of God Incarnate*, p. 17).

18. Elaine Scarry, *The Body in Pain: The Making and Unmaking of the World* (New York: Oxford University Press, 1985), p. 216.

Chapter 1

1. Phillip Stubbes, *The Anatomie of Abuses* (London, 1583), sig. [L.vi].

2. Stephen Gosson, *Playes Confuted in five Actions* (London, 1582?), sig. [B.8ᵛ]. Gosson drew his comparison from Tertullian's early third-century attack on the stage, *De Spectaculis*, 13.

3. Ben Jonson, *Bartholomew Fair* (1614), ed. Eugene M. Waith (New Haven: Yale University Press, 1963), p. 178 (V.v).

4. William Prynne, *Histrio-Mastix, the players scourge, or, actors tragoedie* (London, 1633; reprint, New York: Garland, 1973), p. 80.

5. *The Geneva Bible* (1560; facsimile, Madison: University of Wisconsin Press, 1969), p. 33.

6. John Rainolds, *Th'overthrow of Stage-playes* (London, 1599), p. 161.

7. John Northbrooke, *Spiritus est vicarius Christi in terra: A Treatise wherein Dicing, Daunding, Vaine playes or Enterludes . . . are reproved* (London, 1577?); Anthony Munday, *A second and third blast of retrait from plaies and Theaters* (London, 1580); William Rankins, *A Mirrour of Monsters* (London, 1587); Henry Cross, *Vertues Commonwealth* (London, 1603).

8. Northbrooke, *Spiritus est vicarius Christi*, p. 58.

9. Jonas Barish, *The Antitheatrical Prejudice* (Berkeley: University of California Press, 1981), p. 66.

10. On medieval attitudes toward drama, see in particular Rosemary Woolf, *The English Mystery Plays* (Berkeley: University of California Press, 1972), pp. 77–101, and Karl Young, *The Drama of the Medieval Church* (Oxford: Clarendon, 1933),

vol. 2:411–21. The two most significant medieval precursors of the *Tretise of Miraclis Pleyinge* are the chapter "De spectaculis theatricis in ecclesia Dei exhibitis" in Gerhoh of Reichersberg's *De Invesigatione Antichristi* (1161), given in Appendix C of Young, and Gerhoh's contemporary, Herrad of Landsberg, Abbess of Hohenburg (Young, vol. 2:412–14). For further discussion of the *Tretise of Miraclis Pleyinge,* see below, chapter 3.

11. Barish, *The Antitheatrical Prejudice*, pp. 80–131. Barish is concerned primarily with what connects the outbreaks of Western antitheatricalism. He sees it as "too widespread, too resistant to changes of place and time to be ascribed entirely, or even mainly, to social, political, or economic factors" (pp. 116–17). Such recurrent prejudice against playing rests on the Stoic ideal of stasis in the personality and "belongs to a conservative ethical emphasis in which the key terms are those of order, stability, constancy, and integrity." From such an emphasis, theater may seem deeply threatening in its basic premise that men may play different selves and that we may be spectators at an event in which a fiction is given the reality of performance. Rather than dealing with a centered, stable self, we assist at a process in which a true self has been cast off, even if temporarily, in favor of a fictive self. Although antitheatricalism in sixteenth- and seventeenth-century England was linked with a social movement, Puritanism, that represented radical challenge to the social order rather than conservatism, Barish's argument appears valid for Renaissance antitheatricalism in particular, for the Stoic ideal of a self resistant to change—perhaps in therapeutic reaction to the actual psychic change generated by the Reformation—had a powerful hold on the period. See William Bouwsma, "The Two Faces of Humanism: Stoicism and Augustinianism in Renaissance Thought," in *Itinerarium Italicum: The Profile of the Italian Renaissance in the Mirror of its European Transformation*, ed. Heiko A. Oberman and Thomas A. Brady, Jr. (Leiden: E. J. Brill, 1975), pp. 3–60.

12. On the social and political dimensions of the antitheatrical tracts, see Jean E. Howard, *The Stage and Social Struggle in Early Modern England* (London: Routledge, 1994). Through a "symptomatic reading" of the tracts, Howard puts them at the center of an acute analysis of social fears and preoccupations for which, in the understanding of the polemicists, the emergence of theater was an "instructive synecdoche" (p. 23). Howard reads the antitheatricalists as a discursive site where the anxiety about social change was both created and managed in various awkward and self-contradictory ways. This allows her to read theater as itself complexly implicated in the various discourses of social definition.

13. Iconoclasm in England was first given monograph-length treatment by John Phillips, *The Reformation of Images.* More recently it has been at the center of two studies of poetry in the period, Ernest B. Gilman's *Iconoclasm and Poetry* and Kenneth Gross's *Spenserian Poetics: Idolatry, Iconoclasm, and Magic* (Ithaca, N.Y.: Cornell University Press, 1985). James R. Siemon's pioneering study considers iconoclasm as a context for Shakespeare's dramatic poetry in a way that moves between literal and figurative senses of the term and centers on the image as a rhetorical element of the linguistic structure, *Shakespearean Iconoclasm* (Berkeley: University of California Press, 1985). The most recent full-length historical study of iconoclasm in England is that of Margaret Aston, *England's Iconoclasts.* See also Eamon Duffy, *The Stripping of the Altars,* on the religious context of iconoclasm in the period.

14. On the issue of cross-dressing, see Howard, *The Stage and Social Struggle*, pp. 93–128; Laura Levine, *Men in Women's Clothing: Anti-Theatricality and Effeminization, 1579–1642* (Cambridge: Cambridge University Press, 1994). Stephen Orgel acutely describes the writers' fear of a "universal effeminization" in theatrical practice

in *Impersonations: The Performance of Gender in Shakespeare's England* (Cambridge: Cambridge University Press, 1997). It is only the characterization of them as "pathological" (p. 35) that seems to me questionable, for the writers' perspective, even on sexuality and gender, is consistent with the dominant moral and religious culture. In fact, it is the very normality of their discourse that makes them so useful in gauging the position of theater. See also Orgel's earlier treatment of the issue in "Nobody's Perfect: Or Why Did the English Stage Take Boys for Women?" *The South Atlantic Quarterly* 88 (Winter 1989): 7–29.

15. Munday, *A second and third blast*, pp. 89, 92.

16. Jonathan V. Crewe explores the way William Rankins's 1587 attack on theater as montrous is reflected in the culturally montrous protagonists of Marlowe's *Tamburlaine* and *The Jew of Malta*, "The Theatre of the Idols: Marlowe, Rankins, and Theatrical Images," *Theatre Journal* 36 (1984): 321–33.

17. Prynne, *Histrio-Mastix*, pp. 34, 58–59.

18. Tertullian, *De Spectaculis*. On the context and influence of Tertullian's treatise, see Norman Davis, "Spectacula Christiana: A Roman Christian Template for Medieval Drama," *Medieval English Theatre* 9 (1987): 125–52. On Tertullian's antitheatricalism see also Barish, *The Antitheatrical Prejudice*, pp. 44–51.

19. Gosson, *Playes Confuted*, sig. E.i.

20. Munday, *A second and third blast*, pp. 95–96.

21. Gosson, *Playes Confuted*, sig. E.i.

22. Bert O. States, *Great Reckonings in Little Rooms: On the Phenomenology of Theater* (Berkeley: University of California Press, 1985), pp. 3–4; States quotes Heidegger's essay "The Origin of the Work of Art," in *Poetry, Language, Thought*, trans. Albert Hofstadter (New York: Harper and Row, 1975), p. 43. Exploring theater from a theological perpective, Max Harris similarly notes: "Though the human body may generate arbitrary sign systems of gesture, movement and expression, the body on stage is not, like the word 'corpus' or a particular confriguration of paint, an artribtrary signifer of human being. . . . Whatever may be true of other art forms, therefore, the theatre is irredeemably fleshy, incapable of loosing its link entirely with the world of flesh and blood in which we live" (*Theatre and Incarnation* [Basingstoke: Macmillan, 1990], p. 37). Though concerned with the relation of theater to Christian understanding generally, Harris is particularly well grounded in medieval manifestations of theatrical incarnation.

23. The final performance of the York Corpus Christi cycle was in 1569; in 1575 preparations were made for playing the cycle again the following year, but they were not be carried out. The Paternoster play was given at York for the final time in 1572. At Chester, the cycle, which had been transferred from Corpus Christi to Whitsuntide around 1521, was given in 1561, 1567, 1568, 1572, and the final performance in 1575. With interruptions because of plague in 1564 and 1575, Coventry produced its cycle continuously until the last performance in 1579. It is not known when the final performance of the Wakefield cycle took place; it is clear that there were plans afoot to perform it at Whitsuntide of 1576, when Matthew Hutton, the dean of York, issued an order prohibiting its performance. See *York*, REED, ed. Alexandra F. Johnston and Margaret Rogerson (Toronto: University of Toronto Press, 1979), vol. 1:355–58, 377–79; *Chester*, REED, ed. Lawrence M. Clopper (Toronto: University of Toronto Press, 1979), pp. liv, 104–105, 109–117; R. M. Lumiansky and David Mills, *The Chester Mystery Cycle: Essays and Documents* (Chapel Hill, N.C.: University of North Carolina Press, 1983), pp. 176–202; *Coventry*, REED, ed. R. W. Ingram (Toronto: University of Toronto Press, 1981), pp. xix–xxi. See also Nelson, *The Medieval En-*

glish Stage: Corpus Christi Pageants and Plays (Chicago: University of Chicago Press, 1974), pp. 57–65, 85, 162–65, and Howard C. Gardiner, *Mysteries' End: An Investigation of the Last Days of the Medieval Religious Stage* (New Haven: Yale University Press, 1946), pp. 65–93.

24. Gardiner first made the case that the medieval mystery cycles did not die by an evolutionary process in which things medieval inevitably yielded to things renaissance, but were a casualty of the Reformation desire to eliminate the vestiges of Catholicism (*Mysteries' End*). While the causes of the disappearance of the mysteries are more complex and multifaceted than Gardiner allowed, some version of his thesis is accepted as explaining the comparatively sudden disappearance of a number of cycles, particularly in the north. The main modification necessary in Gardiner's original thesis is skepticism about whether in fact there existed a single policy toward the traditional drama on the part of the central government; most likely this depended on the theological orientation and energy of the individual bishops as well as the local conditions within the city and its governing bodies. For a critique of the "suppression theory" see Bing D. Bills, "The 'Suppression Theory' and the English Corpus Christi Play: a Re-examination," *Theater Journal* 32 (1980): 157–68. But see also Alexandra F. Johnston, "Cycle Drama in the Sixteenth Century: Texts and Contexts," in *Early Drama to 1600*, Acta, vol. 13, The Center for Medieval and Early Renaissance Studies, ed. Albert H. Tricomi, (Binghamton: State University of New York, 1987), pp. 1–15.

25. See in particular Paul Whitfield White, *Theatre and Reformation: Protestantism, Patronage, and Playing in Tudor England* (Cambridge: Cambridge University Press, 1993; see also E. K. Chambers, *The Elizabethan Stage*, 4 vols. (Oxford: Clarendon, 1923), vol. 1:240–42; Gardiner, pp. 51–59; For further discussion of this theater, see below, chapter 4.

26. Martin Bucer, *De Regno Christi*, in *Melancthon and Bucer*, ed. and trans. Wilhelm Pauck, Library of Christian Classics (Philadelphia: Westminster, 1969), pp. 349–52.

27. Peter Meredith, "John Clerke's Hand in the York Register," *Leeds Studies in English* 12 (1981): 245–71. Meredith notes that in most cases Clerke's annotations give "a tantalising glimpse of the prevalence of revision with no indication of its extent or significance" (p. 257). Clerke's work, he concludes, was "part of a continuing process of city control and not the result of a sudden ecclesiastical interest" (p. 265).

28. Besides the newly registered Fullers' "Adam and Eve in the Garden" and the Masons and the Labourers' "Purification," six other plays had undergone significant recasting, but their new versions were not included in the register. The beginning of the Spicers' "Annunciation and Visitation" is annotated by John Clerke, "this matter is newly mayde wherof we haue no coppy"; the note could refer to the Doctor's twelve-stanza prologue or to the whole play. The Vintners' "Wedding at Cana" is represented only by its opening line and nine blank pages where the new play should have been entered in the register. Similarly, the Ironmongers' "Jesus in the House of Simon the Leper" appears only as the guild name and the notation in Clerke's hand, "This matter lakkes, videlicet: Jesus, et Symon leprosus rogans eum vt manducaret cum eo, duo discipuli, Maria Magdelena lavans pedes Jesu lacrimis et capillis suis tergens," followed by nine blank pages. The Cappers' "The Woman Taken in Adultery and the Raising of Lazarus" has two missing leaves and the notations by Clerke that at least part of what was in the register did not accord with what was played and that new material had been added. Clerke noted that the Girdlers' "Slaughter of the Innocents" "agryth not with the Coucher [i.e., the register] in no poynt," and he supplies the current opening verse. Each leaf of the Barkers' "Baptism" is marked "De novo facto" and annotated at the end, "This matter is newly mayd and devysed, wherof we haue no coppy regys-

tered." In addition, city records indicate that the conclusion of the Tilethatchers' "Nativity" was missing (and blank pages supplied for it in the register), and apparently substantial bits had been added to the Chandlers' "Shepherds." See especially *The York Play: A Facsimile of British Library MS Additional 35290*, introduction by Richard Beadle and Peter Meredith (Leeds: University of Leeds School of English, 1983), xxi–xxii, and the facsimile pages of the individual pageants. Clerke's annotations can also be read in the textual notes of *The York Plays,* ed. Richard Beadle (London: Edward Arnold, 1982). For the city record of the pageants still to be registered in 1567, see *York*, REED, vol. 1:351.

29. *York*, REED, vol. 1:291–92.

30. Exactly which play was being given by the Sledmen in the mid-sixteenth century is not clear in the manuscript because of confusion in the ascription of play XXXIX, Christ's Appearance to Mary Magdalene, which was, or had been, the Winedrawers' pageant. Peter Meredith suggests that perhaps the Sledmen had taken over both pageants, that both pageants were then assigned, temporarily as it happened, to the Weavers ("John Clerke's Hand," pp. 260–61).

31. For this succession of events, see *York*, REED, vol. 1:295, 297–98, 303, 307, 310, 322, 323, 327, 331–32, 340–44, 355.

32. *The York Plays*, pp. 230–31.

33. On that theological strain see Horton Davies, *Worship and Theology in England from Cranmer to Hooker, 1534–1603* (Princeton: Princeton University Press, 1970), pp. 165–226.

34. *York*, REED, vol. 1:353–54. On Matthew Hutton's career, see *Dictionary of National Biography*, ed. Leslie Stephen and Sidney Lee (New York: Macmillan; London: Smith, Elder, 1885–1906).

35. Glynne Wickham, *Early English Stages, 1300–1660*, 3 vols. (London: Routledge and Kegan Paul, 1959–81), vol. 2:77.

36. Patrick Collinson, *Archbishop Grindal, 1519–1583: The Struggle for a Reformed Church* (Berkeley: University of California Press, 1979), pp. 187–215.

37. *York*, REED, vol. 1:377–78.

38. Ibid., vol. 1:390, 392–93.

39. The suggestion was made by Gardiner, *Mysteries' End*, pp. 77–78.

40. Lumiansky and Mills, *The Chester Mystery Cycle*, p. 190; on the dating of the manuscript from which the extant manuscripts of the play (all late sixteenth and early seventeenth-century antiquarian texts) derive, see pp. 40–48. Uncertainty about the dating of the post-Reformation Banns of the play prevents a more precise indication of when the Wives' Assumption pageant was dropped.

41. Ibid., pp. 190–91, 206–207. In addition the Shoemakers' accounts of 1550 contain a large payment "for bakyng of Godes brede"; after the Bakers' Last Supper was returned to the cycle, the Late Banns instructs them to "caste Godes loves abroad with accustomed cherefull harte." Lumiansky and Mills suggest this had been the Shoemakers' responsibility during the omission of the Bakers' pageant.

42. Lumiansky and Mills, *The Chester Mystery Cycle,* p. 191.

43. *Chester*, REED, pp. 96–97.

44. Richard Emmerson notes that Savage was described as "cold" toward the Elizabethan settlment of religion and would later be charged as a recusant. Though his support of performing the cycle still carried a majority on the Council, the opposition would be strengthened by the challenge from the Privy Council. See Emmerson, "Contextualizing Performance: the Reception of the Chester 'Antichrist'," *JMEMS* 29 (1999): 89–119.

45. Ibid., p. 110; see also Lumiansky and Mills, *Chester Mystery Cycle,* p. 230.

46. *Chester,* REED, pp. 109–110.

47. *Chester,* REED, pp. 96–97, 104–105, 109–117. See also Lumiansky and Mills, *The Chester Mystery Cycle,* pp. 192–94.

48. Writing of York, Alexandra Johnston notes that the plays meant "tourist dollars" for the city. "For over two centuries the community worked together to produce an annual spectacle of great complexity. Then it was no longer there" ("Cycle Drama in the Sixteenth Century," p. 11).

49. *Newcastle Upon Tyne,* REED, ed. J. J. Anderson (Toronto: University of Toronto Press, 1982), pp. xi–xv, 28–29, 55–58, 62–63, 71–72, 132. The Millers' indenture of 1578 instructs the members "to attend upon their said playe in decent manner in euerie place of the said towne where antientlie the same among other plaies usualie hath bene plaied." And two references are made in 1578 and 1579 to "the generall plaies of this towne antientlie in time past called the Corpus Christi plaies" (p. 62). But these do not appear to imply performance in those years.

50. The Assembly Minute Books contain the notation dated May 11, 1547, that the pageants would not be set forth that year, as they had been accustomed, and that the mayor was absolved from legal action for not carrying out this obligation. The records are silent until a notation of April 13, 1565, expressing the agreement that "Souch pagen*tes* as were wonte to go in the type of whitson holydayes shall be Set forth by occupations as in tymes paste haue been vysyd" (David Galloway, *Norwich,* REED [Toronto: Toronto University Press, 1984], 19, 51).

51. "The Norwich Grocers' Play," in *Non-cycle Plays and Fragments,* ed. Norman Davis, EETS (London: Oxford University Press, 1970), p. 11. The main way in which the play has been "accorded" with the Scriptures appears in references to the specific chapters of Genesis in the prologues and God's own glossing of "I am Alpha et homega" to "my Apocalyps." Though the incomplete status of the A text makes comparison uncertain, the revision does not appear notably to Protestantize the play; it seems rather an updating of language and enlivening of the relation between Adam and Eve. On what is known of the circumstances of performance, see Nelson, *The Medieval English Stage,* p. 133.

52. *Coventry,* REED, p. 294.

53. Ian Lancashire, *Dramatic Texts and Records of Britain: A Chronological Topography to 1558* (Cambridge: Cambridge University Press, 1984), p. 120.

54. Not all of the biblical theater that survived into the sixteenth century, of course, ended as late as the 1560s and 1570s. The late 1530s through the late 1540s, the initial period of Reformation, was also a time when some religious theatrical traditions came to an end. At Holbeach, in Lincolnshire, play costumes and properties were sold in 1547. Boston had a Corpus Christi play from at least 1518 until 1546, when the Common Council of the town ordered the suspension of the performance. At Louth, also in Lincolnshire, Corpus Christi plays were not given after the reign of Queen Mary. But it seems that in a few more remote regions—in Lancaster and Preston in Lancashire, at Kendall in Westmoreland, and at Kilkenny (in Co. Kerry, Ireland)— some plays continued on into the early-seventeenth century. See Ian Lancashire, *Dramatic Texts and Records of Britain* under the various locations; for the record of the Lancaster, Preston, and Kendall plays, see also *Lancashire,* REED, ed. David George (Toronto: University of Toronto Press, 1991), pp. xliii, 29.

55. *The Townley Plays,* ed. Martin Stevens and A. C. Cawley, EETS (Oxford: Oxford University Press, 1994), vol. 2:632–33: "The lacuna in the Townley MS is sufficiently large to have comprised a Pentecost play and a series of Mary plays, the latter

perhaps redactions of the very plays that were censured at York. Because this lacuna is not restricted to centre bifolia in a single gathering, as is true of all the other lacunae, it must be assumed that the missing leaves were deliberately cut from the manuscript."

56. Alan H. Nelson, *The Medieval English Stage*, p. 85; see also Gardiner, *Mysteries' End*, pp. 77–79.

57. Lumiansky and Mills, *The Chester Mystery Cycle*, p. 294. The passage paraphrased is as follows:

Of one thinge warne you now I shal:
that not possible it is those matters to be contryved
in such sorte and cunninge and by suche players of price
as at this daye good players and fine wittes coulde devise.

For then shoulde all those persones that as godes doe playe
in clowdes come downe with voyce, and not be seene;
for noe man can proportioun that Godhead, I saye,
to the shape of man—face, nose, and eyne.
But sethence the face-gilte doth disfigure the man, that deme
a clowdye coveringe of the man—a voyce onlye to heare—
and not God in shape or person to appeare.

The banns go on to insist that the plays are played by mere craftsmen and other "meane men" for an audience of common folk and countrymen, and if "better men and finer heades" come to view the plays, they will have to take them or leave them.

58. Munday, *A second and third blast*, p. 104.

59. Northbrooke, *Spiritus est vicarius Christi*, pp. 65–66.

60. Stubbes, *Anatomie of Abuses*, p. 102.

61. See especially John R. Elliott, *Playing God: Medieval Mysteries on the Modern Stage* (Toronto: Toronto University Press, 1989).

62. Walter J. Ong, *The Presence of the Word: Some Prolegomena for Cultural and Religious History* (New Haven: Yale University Press, 1967), p. 269.

63. Ong, *The Presence of the Word*, p. 272. Stephen J. Greenblatt has given a vivid account of the psychological effects of printed books in the religious culture of the 1520s when the force of *sola scriptura* was first felt (*Renaissance Self-Fashioning from More to Shakespeare* [Chicago: University of Chicago Press, 1980], pp. 74–114).

64. Bryan Crockett, *The Play of Paradox: Stage and Sermon in Renaissance England* (Philadelphia: University of Pennsylvania Press, 1995), p. 55.

65. Lumiansky and Mills, *The Chester Mystery Cycle*, pp. 265–66.

66. Stubbes, *Anatomie of Abuses*, p. 102.

67. John Bale, for example, in *King John* similarly conflates the divine Logos with the word of Scripture: "Ye know [God] abydyth not where his word ys refusyd, / For God is his word lyke as Seynt John dothe tell / In the begynnyng of his moste blyssyd gospell" (*The Complete Plays of John Bale*, ed. Peter Happé (Cambridge: D. S. Brewer, 1985], pp. 32–33.

68. "Spectacula, ludos ludiscrosque res id generis, quae ab ethnicorum moribus originem ducunt, disciplinaeque christianae adversantur, perpetuo detestabitur, execrabitur: demonstrabit incommoda, publicasque aerumnas inde in christianum populum dimanare. . . . Scenicae personataeque actiones, unde tamquam e quonam seminario semina malefactorum ac flagitiorum pene omnium existunt, quam a Christianae disciplianae officiis abhorrentes, quam valde cum paganorum institutis convenientes atque diaboli astu inventae, omni officio a populo christiano exterminandae sint, qua maxima

potest religiosa contentione aget" (Ferdinando Taviani, *La Fascinazione del Teatro: la Commedia dell'Arte e la Società Barocca* [Rome: Bulzoni, 1970], p. 13).

69. "Quanto magis in animas quae oculis ipsi aspicimus penetrant, quam quae in libris huiusmodi legimus? Quam gravius adolescentium mentes viva illorum vox ferit, quam mortua, libris insculta?" (Taviani, *La Fascinazione del Teatro*, p. 32).

70. "Quoniam pie introducta consuetudo, repraesentandi populi venerandam Christi Domini Passionem et gloriosa martyrorum certamina, aliorumque sanctorum res gesta, hominum perversitate eo deducta est ut multis offensioni, multis etiam risui et despectui sit, ideo statuimus: ut deinceps Salvatoris passio, nec in sacro nec in profano loco agatur; sed docte et graviter, eatenus a concionatoribus exponatur, ut, qui sunt uberes concionum fructus, pietatem, et lacrymas commoveat auditoribus. Quod adiuvabit proposita Crucifixi Salvatoris imago, coeterique pii actus externi, quos Ecclesiae probatos esse iudicabit" (Taviani, *La Fascinazione del Teatro*, p. 10).

71. See Paolo Prodi, *Richerche sulla teoretica delle arti figurative nella riforma cattolica, estratto dall'archivio italiano per la storia della pietà*, vol. 4 (Roma: Edizione di Storia e Litteratura, 1962), pp. 135–37.

72. Ferdinando Taviani, *La Fascinazione del Teatro*, pp. xcviii–ci.

73. Prodi, *Richerche sulla teoretica delle arti figurative*, pp. 141–80.

74. Louise George Clubb, *Italian Drama in Shakespeare's Time* (New Haven: Yale University Press, 1989), pp. 205–229, esp. p. 218.

75. There are numerous instances in Rome of images being used in polemical ways to counter Reformation doctrine. In the Cappella Paolina of Santa Maria Maggiore, Giovanni Baglione alluded to Protestant iconoclasm in two frescoes (1611) that he was commissioned to paint in the entrance vault; these depict the agonized deaths of two iconoclast emperors of the eighth and ninth centuries, Constantine V Copronymus and Leo V Armenus. Perhaps the best known example is the sculptured allegory by Pierre Legros in the Gesù to the right of the tomb of St. Ignatius: it depicts Holy Religion overcoming two figures representing Heresy thrown back and encircled Loacoön-like by serpents; the figures have the faces of Luther and Calvin, and one holds a book of Luther's works while a putto gleefully rips pages from another book of Protestant heresy. In fact, the subject matter of much religious post-Tridentine painting can be understood as aimed at Protestant doctrinal challenges—for example, the Assumption of the Virgin, St. Luke painting the Virgin, the portrayal of the eucharist in the Last Supper, or portrayals of early Christian martyrs. See Émile Mâle, *L'Art Religieux aprés le Concile de Trente* (Paris: Armand Colin, 1932), especially chapter 2; Thomas Buser, "Jerome Nadal and Early Jesuit Art in Rome," *Art Bulletin* 58 (1976): 424–33; Margaret R. Miles, *Image as Insight*, pp. 95–125.

76. Munday, *A second and third blast*, p. 89; Rankins, *A Mirrour of Monsters*, sig. B.iii^r.

77. Prynne, *Histrio-Mastix*, p. 80; he asserts elsewhere that plays "are the very Nursery of Atheisme, of Paganisme, of Idolatry and profanesse" (p. 551).

78. Prynne, *Histrio-Mastix*: on actors as papists, pp. 72, 142; on Jesuits, p. 117. The attitudes of English Catholics toward the professional drama was in all likelihood no different from those of Anglicans. But one incident does suggest some controversy over playgoing. In March 1618 (n.s.), William Harrison, the Catholic archpriest of England, issued an order forbidding the secular clergy to attend the public playhouses. The reason for the order became evident some weeks later when Thomas Leke, a Catholic priest of London, issued a protest against the prohibition, citing Aquinas in favor of plays which have nothing in them *contra fidem et bonos mores*. Leke and two other priests had been freely attending the London theaters and did not believe they

had scandalized Catholic laity. In spite of a lengthy rejoinder to Leke by John Colleton, assistant to the archpriest, the prohibition was revoked, a fact which suggests support, perhaps general support, of playgoing among the Catholic clergy and laity. The incident is described by I. J. Semper, "The Jacobean Theater through the Eyes of Catholic Clerics," *Shakespeare Quarterly* 3 (1952): 45–51.

79. Crockett, *The Play of Paradox*, p. 81. Crockett suggests that Jonson, alluded to by Milles as "an illiterate bricklayer," may well have got his revenge in the character Zeal-of-the-Land Busy in *Bartholemew Fair* (1614).

80. Gosson, *Plays Confuted*, sig. [E.7.].

81. Prynne, *Histrio-Mastix*, pp. 929–31.

Chapter 2

1. "Qui quod pollicitus sese semper nobiscum fore usque ad consummationem seculi, in his litteris praecipue praestat, in quibus nobis etiamnum vivit, spirat, loquitur, pene dixerim, efficacius quam cum inter homines versaretur" (Desiderius Erasmus, *Omnia Opera*, ed. Joannes Clericus, 6 vols. [Leiden, 1703–1706; reprint, Hildescheim: Georg Olms, 1961], 5:142E).

2. "At hae tibi sacrosanctae mentis illius vivam referunt imaginem, ipsumque Christum loquentem, sanatem, morientem, resurgentem, denique, totum ita praesentem reddunt, ut minus visurus sis, si coram oculis conspicias" (Erasmus, *Omnia Opera*, 5:144D).

3. See also Carlos M. N. Eire, *War Against the Idols*, pp. 28–53: Christ "is not so much God *incarnate*, changing the structure of material reality, but rather a spiritual reflection, temporarily infleshed, whose primary purpose seems to be to point humans in the direction of the spiritual realm. Though he is far from docetic, Erasmus lends an ephem[e]ral quality to Christ's incarnation that comes close to denying the humanity of Jesus. . . . By insisting on the superiority of the spiritual realm, the Word is not so much enfleshed as written" (pp. 40–41).

4. On Erasmus' response to art, see Erwin Panofsky, "Erasmus and the Visual Arts," *JWCI*, 32 (1969): 200–227. His reaction to the iconoclasm in Basel is contained in his letter to Willibald Pirkheimer, *Opus Epistolarum Desiderii Erasmi*, ed. P. S. Allen and H. M. Allen (Oxford: Oxford University Press, 1924), vol. 8: 162: "Tantis autem ludibriis usi sunt in simulacra divorum atque etiam Crucifixi, ut mirum sit nullum illic aeditum miraculum; quum olim tam multa soleant aedere vel leviter offensi divi. Statuarum nihil relictum est, nec in templis nec in vestibulis nec in porticibus nec in monasteriis. Quidquid erat pictarum imaginum, calcea incrustura oblitum est. Quod erat capax ignis, in rogum conjectum est; quod secus, frustulatim comminutum. Nec pretium nec ars impetravit ut cuiquam omnino parceretur."

5. Erasmus, *Omnia Opera*, 5:1189A; *A Playne and godly exposition or declaration of the commune Crede* (London, 1533) sigs. T.viiiᵛ–U.iᵛ.

6. Reginald Pecock, *Repressor of Over Much Blaming of the Clergy,* part 2, chapter 3, in *Rerum Britannicarum Medii Aevi Scriptores*, Rolls Series, vol. 19, ed. Churchill Babington (London: Longman, 1960), pp. 148–49.

7. Thomas More, *Dialogue concerning Heresies*, in *Complete Works of St. Thomas More*, vol. 6, ed. Thomas Lawler, Germain Marc'hadour, and Richard Marius (New Haven: Yale University Press, 1981), part 1, pp. 39–40.

8. Freedberg, *The Power of Images*, p. 245.

9. Marjorie O'Rourke Boyle, *Erasmus on Language and Method in Theology* (Toronto: University of Toronto Press, 1977), p. 83.

10. "Et quidem zelum vos, ne quid manufactum adorari posset, habuisse laudivimus, sed frangere easdem imagines non debuisse indicamus. Idcirco enim pictura in Ecclesiis adhibetur, ut hi qui litteras nesciunt, saltem in parietibus vivendo legant quae legere in Codicibus non valent. Tua ergo fraternitas et illas servare, et ab earum adoratu populum prohibere debuit, quatenus et litterarum nescii haberent unde scientiam historiae colligerent, et populus in picturae adoratione minime peccaret." (*PL*, vol. 77: 1027–28).

11. Stephen Gero, "Byzantine Iconoclasm and the Failure of a Medieval Reformation," in *The Image and the Word*, ed. Joseph Gutmann (Missoula, Mont.: Scholars Press, 1977), p. 54.

12. Jaroslav Pelikan, *The Spirit of Eastern Christendom (600–1700)*, The Christian Tradition: A History of the Development of Doctrine, vol. 2 (Chicago: University of Chicago Press, 1974), pp. 92–93.

13. See Gerhart B. Ladner, "Origin and Significance of the Byzantine Iconoclastic Controversy," in *Images and Ideas in the Middle Ages: Selected Studies in History and Art* (Rome: Edizioni di Storia e Letteratura, 1983), pp. 35–72, esp. pp. 37–44. Ladner notes that the second iconoclast emperor, Constantine V, "even enforced a more intense worship of the imperial icons, while scorning any veneration of the religious ones" and that in many cases the emperor "substituted the cult of the empire for that of the Church" (pp. 52–53). Strikingly similar patterns occur in the English Reformation, particularly under Elizabeth when the royal arms replaced the rood screen in parish churches that had been swept of images. Elizabeth's appropriation of the imagery of the Virgin in her own cult is well known. Peter Brown, in "A Dark-Age Crisis: Aspects of the Iconoclastic Controversy," *English Historical Review* 88 (1973): 1–34, concentrates on the social and psychological aspects of the controversy, seeing in the link between the icons and monasticism a contest for the spiritual allegiance of the lay believer.

14. See in particular Patrick Henry, "What Was the Iconoclast Controversy About?" *Church History* 45 (1976): 16–31. "The Iconoclastic controversy was, among other things, a debate about the meaning of the incarnation for history, about the definition and interpretation of Christian worship, and about conflicting claims to the title of the city of God" (p. 21). Henry's essay is in part a reply to Brown's essay, note 13 *supra*.

15. Augustine makes the distinction between *douleúein* and *latreúein* in *The City of God* X, 1; see *The City of God*, trans. Henry Bettenson (1972; reprint, Harmondsworth: Penguin, 1984), p. 372.

16. John of Damascus, *On the Divine Images*, First Treatise, section 16, trans. David Anderson (Crestwood, N.J.: St. Vladimir's Seminary, 1980), p. 23.

17. Ibid., p. 58; Second Treatise, section 11.

18. Ladner, "Origin and Significance of the Byzantine Iconoclastic Controversy," p. 65. Ladner notes how "a profound spirituality and at the same time an extreme sensualism" inhered in the incarnational ideas which formed the basis for representation for the iconophile theologians" (p. 69).

19. John of Damascus, *On the Divine Images*, pp. 28–29; First Treatise, section 21. Patrick Henry notes that the iconodules refused to admit any sharp distinction between the brief period of Jesus' earthly life and their own time. "All time subsequent to the birth of Christ was time *sub specie incarnationis*, and just as Christ appeared to his disciples with all the attributes of humanity, and was perceived to be divine through the eyes of faith, so now he is discernible in the same way. Once the Word became flesh he did not subsequently become non-flesh. The heart of the iconodule argument against the iconoclast Christological dilemma is the insistence that the paradox of the incarna-

tion cannot be relegated to a period of thirty-three years several centuries ago" ("What Was the Iconoclast Controversy About?" p. 23).

20. The same is true of Nikephoros, patriarch of Constantinople between 806 and 815; a contemporary of Theodore, he similarly saw the necessity of images, and for him word and image provide equivalent access to the incarnation of Christ. See Charles Barber, "The Body Within the Frame: A Use of Word and Image in Iconoclasm," *Word and Image* 9 (1993): 140–53: "For Nikephoros the basis of the possibility of religious imagery was to be found in Christ's body" (p. 150).

21. John of Damascus, *On the Divine Images*, p. 21; First Treatise, section 13.

22. Quoted in Henry, "What Was the Iconoclast Controversy About?" p. 24.

23. John of Damascus, *On the Divine Images*, p. 72; Third Treatise, section 12.

24. Ibid., p. 20; First Treatise, section 11.

25. On the Reformation knowledge and use of the Byzantine Iconoclast Controversy and the Carolingian aftermath, see Margaret Aston, *England's Iconoclasts* pp. 47–61.

26. Rosamond McKitterick, "Text and Image in the Carolingian World," in *The Uses of Literacy in Early Medieval Europe*, ed. Rosamond McKitterick (Cambridge: Cambridge University Press, 1990).

27. W. R. Jones, "Art and Christian Piety: Iconoclasm in Medieval Europe," in *The Image and the Word*, ed. Joseph Gutmann (Missoula, Mont.: Scholars Press, 1977), pp. 75–105, quotation p. 95.

28. Quoted in Jo Ann Hoeppner Moran, *The Growth of English Schooling, 1340–1540* (Princeton, N.J.: Princeton University Press, 1985), p. 20: Thomas More, *The Apology,* in *Complete Works of St. Thomas More*, vol. 9, ed. J. B. Trapp (New Haven: Yale University Press, 1979), p. 13. Moran usefully summarizes the debate about late medieval literacy.

29. F. R. H. Du Boulay, *An Age of Ambition: English Society in the Late Middle Ages* (London: Nelson, 1970), p. 118.

30. Silvia Thrupp, *The Merchant Class of Medieval London* (Chicago: University of Chicago Press, 1948), pp. 156–58.

31. Moran, *The Growth of English Schooling*, pp. 17–20, 150–84. On the basis of an increase in the number of surviving vernacular manuscripts from the period, M. B. Parkes also sees an expansion of literacy in England in the fourteenth and fifteenth centuries but does not venture an estimate of the percentage increase, "The Literacy of the Laity," in *Literature and Western Civilization: The Medieval World*, ed. David Daiches and Anthony Thorlby (London: Aldus, 1973), pp. 555–77.

32. Reginald Pecock, *Repressor*, vol. 19:191–92. Pecock's answer to this was that one mode of knowing does not cancel out another, that "mankinde in this lijf is so freel, that forto make into him sufficient remembraunce of thingis to be profitabli of him remembrid he nedith not oonly heerable rememoratijf signes (as ben Holi Scripture and othere devoute writingis,) but he nedith also therwith and ther to seable rememoratijf signes" (p. 209). The institution of the sacraments bears this out. And while "heerable" signs are useful for things for which "seable" signs are less useful, the converse is also true; sight can be a more efficient way of knowing, for an image can bring into the mind and imagination much information more quickly and easily than the hearing or reading of words can (pp. 212–13).

33. *Selections from English Wycliffite Writings*, ed. Anne Hudson (Cambridge: Cambridge University Press, 1978), pp. 83–84. The text comes from an early-fifteenth-century anthology of works "critical of the contemporary church, though not all overtly heretical" (p. 179).

34. Article 10 of the 37 Conclusions of the Lollards, H. F. B Compston, "The Thirty-Seven Conclusions of the Lollards," *English Historical Review* 26 (1911): 743, noted by Margaret Aston, *England's Iconoclasts*, p. 128.

35. "Treatise on Images and Pilgrimages," in Hudson, *Selections from English Wycliffite Writings*, p. 83.

36. Margaret Aston, *England's Iconoclasts*, p. 113.

37. Margaret Aston, "Lollards and Literacy," in *Lollards and Reformers: Images and Literacy in Late Medieval Religion* (Harmondsworth: Penguin, 1984), pp. 207–208. In 1457 Pecock was convicted of error and was forced to recant; he saw his books burned and spent the rest of his life in seclusion at Thorney Abbey in Cambridgeshire. An account of the incident is given in the introduction by Churchill Babington, editor of *Pecock's Repressor of Over Much Blaming of the Clergy*, in *Rerum Britannicarum Medii Aevi Scriptores*, pp. xxxii–lvii.

38. Hudson, *Selections from English Wycliffite Writings*, p. 13.

39. M. B. Parkes, "The Literacy of the Laity," p. 565.

40. Quoted by Charles Muscatine, *Chaucer and the French Tradition* (Berkeley: University of California Press, 1966), p. 251.

41. Janet Coleman, *Medieval Readers and Writers, 1350–1400* (New York: Columbia University Press, 1981), p. 52.

42. Margaret Deanesly, *The Lollard Bible and Other Medieval Biblical Versions,* (Cambridge: Cambridge University Press, 1920), p. 298.

43. See Deanesly, *The Lollard Bible*, pp. 252–60. Chaucer's *Treatise on the Astrolabe* shows a similar concern for very close literal translation.

44. *The Holy Bible, Containing the Old and New Testaments, with the Apocryphal Books, in the Earliest English Versions Made from the Latin Vulgate by John Wycliffe and his Followers*, ed. Josiah Forshall and Frederic Madden (Oxford: Oxford University Press, 1850), vol. 1:57.

45. Ibid., vol. 1:56–57.

46. Anne Hudson notes that the refusal to honor images of the saints and the related disrespect for pilgrimages "came to be perhaps the commonest Lollard beliefs," though the two questions had been discussed before Wycliffe (*Selections from English Wycliffite Writings*, p. 179). Elsewhere she argues for the centrality of English to Lollardy: "Even the anti-lollard sermons indirectly reflect the importance the Wycliffite movement attached to language: the enemy must be confronted on his own ground. There is then a sense in which it may not be unreasonable to claim lollardy as the heresy of the vernacular, the English heresy" ("Lollardy: The English Heresy?" in *Lollards and Their Books* [London: Hambledon, 1985], p. 163). Interestingly, the first recorded instance of Lollard iconoclasm involved a literate layman, a certain William Smith, a smith of Leicester (Aston, *England's Iconoclasts*, p. 133).

47. See J. C. Dickinson, *An Ecclesiastical History of England: The Later Middle Ages* (London: Adams and Charles Black, 1979), p. 37. Dickinson points to "the intense and widespread appreciation of the visual arts" which characterized every level of medieval society" (p. 411). See also the important final chapter of Gail McMurray Gibson, *The Theater of Devotion: East Anglian Drama and Society in the Late Middle Ages* (Chicago: University of Chicago Press, 1989), pp. 137–77.

48. *New Catholic Encyclopedia* (New York: McGraw-Hill, 1967–1989), s.v. "Relics."

49. On the visual elements of eucharistic practice, see in particular Miri Rubin, *Corpus Christi: The Eucharist in Late Medieval Culture* (Cambridge: Cambridge University Press, 1991), pp. 62–64, 288–90. Rubin mentions that during the interdict of

1376 in Florence, when masses were forbidden, there was pressure for the visual exposition of the eucharist to compensate the public.

50. Beginning with Gerhart B. Ladner, *Ad Imaginem Dei: The Image of Man in Medieval Art* (Latrobe, Pa.: Archabbey Press, 1965), a number of art historians, medievalists, and cultural historians have drawn attention to the new valuation of vision in the twelfth and thirteenth centuries and its effect on the character of religious experience in the late medieval period. See Theresa Coletti, "Spirituality and Devotional Images: The Staging of the Hegge Cycle," (Ph.D. dissertation, University of Rochester, 1975), pp. 37–67; Miles, *Image as Insight*, pp. 63–75, 95–98; Freedberg, *The Power of Images*, pp. 162–74.

51. St. Bonaventure, *De reductione artium ad theologiam*, in *The Works of Bonaventure*, trans. José de Vinck (Paterson, N.J.: St. Anthony Guild Press, 1966), vol. 3: 16–24.

52. Otto von Simson, *The Gothic Cathedral: Origins of Gothic Architecture and the Medieval Concept of Order* (New York: Pantheon, 1956), pp. 35–39.

53. In addition to Von Simson, see George Lesser, *Gothic Cathedrals and Sacred Geometry*, 3 vols. (London: Tiranti, 1957–1964), vol. 1:147–48. An example of the architectural expression of time may be seen in the ceiling bosses of Norwich Cathedral (late-fifteenth century), which portray the events of sacred history from the Creation at the west end to the Last Judgment at the east.

54. Eire, *War Against the Idols*, p. 9. Johan Huizinga's vivid and influential description of medieval piety may be ultimate source of such interpretation:

> The naive religious conscience of the multitude had no need of intellectual proofs in matters of faith. The mere presence of a visible image of things holy sufficed to establish their truth. No doubts intervened between the sight of all these pictures and statues—the persons of the Trinity, the flames of hell, the innumerable saints—and belief in their reality. All these conceptions became matters of faith in the most direct manner: they passed straight from the state of images to that of convictions, taking root in the mind as pictures clearly outlined and vividly colored possessing all the reality claimed for them by the church, and even a little bit more.

His last phrase in particular emphasizes the usual modern assumption about such late medieval religious expression: that it is an excess of the illiterate and the simple, that there exists a distinction between what is assumed to be "popular religion" and that praticed by an intellectual elite (*The Waning of the Middle Ages* [1924; reprint, New York: Doubleday Anchor, 1954]), p. 165.

55. Erasmus went to Walsingham in 1512 and perhaps again in 1514. In the period between he accompanied John Colet to the shrine of Becket at Canterbury. One fruit of these journeys, of course, is the colloquy "A Pilgrimage for Religion's Sake," which satirizes the whole idea of pilgrimage to the images or relics of saints. See Margaret Aston, *England's Iconoclasts*, p. 197; on the role of Colet in the pilgrimage to Canterbury, see John B. Gleason, *John Colet* (Berkeley: University of California Press, 1989), pp. 253–56.

56. Victor Turner and Edith Turner, *Image and Pilgrimage in Christian Culture: Anthopological Perspectives* (New York: Columbia University Press, 1978), p. 145. They suggest that "sermons, homilies, tracts, advice in the confessional, discussions among the laity on religious and ethnic questions, keep fundamental doctrines alive, doctrines which are indeed embedded in the very rituals of the liturgy." The Turners critique Huizinga for taking too simple a view of the relation between signifer and sig-

nified: "What Huizinga did not see was that behind the visible image stood not a single significatum with which it was immediately identified, but an entire semantic field, an area of multivocality, the 'referents' of which were drawn from the most disparate sources." The idea of a split between "popular" and "elite" religion, particularly in the late-medieval period, has come under increasing attack in the past few years. See in particular Eamon Duffy, *The Stripping of the Altars*, pp. 2–3.

57. See in particular Michael Baxandall, *Painting and Experience in Fifteenth Century Italy: A Primer in the Social History of Pictorial Style* (Oxford: Clarendon, 1972), especially his second chapter, in which he emphasizes the sophistication of the perceptual skills by which fifteenth-century people experienced visual art. Vision was understood as the most vivid of the perceptual faculties, most effective in engaging the emotions and thereby exciting an affective understanding of religious truths. As noted in the introductory chapter, much of the polemical edge, both of Freedberg's *Power of Images* and Margaret R. Miles's *Image as Insight,* is directed against the assumption that the modes of thought encountered in periods when visual understanding is ascendant, predominantly from the twelfth through the seventeenth centuries, is primitive, magical, superstitious, or generally less sophisticated than our own verbally grounded modes of thought.

58. See especially the seminal work by Elizabeth L. Eisenstein, *The Printing Press as an Agent of Change: Communications and Cultural Transformations in Early-Modern Europe* (Cambridge: Cambridge University Press, 1979). Walter Ong's *The Presence of the Word* also contains much suggestive analysis of the psychic effects of script and printing.

59. Christensen, *Art and the Reformation*, pp. 42–65. See also Eire, *War Against the Idols,* pp. 65–73, and Rosemarie Bergmann, "A 'tröstich pictura': Luther's Attitude in the Question of Images," *Renaissance and Reformation* 17 (1981): 15–25.

60. Christensen, *Art and the Reformation,* p. 65. In terms of what I have suggested about the significance of printing to humanist attitudes, it is interesting to note that Christensen also stresses the value to Luther of the oral proclamation of the gospel through preaching over the written, printed word. "Printed words are dead," Luther once remarked, "spoken words are living" (p. 63). The written word may preserve the Scriptures, but only in being transposed into the orality of preaching does it become fully an instrument of grace.

61. Eire, *War Against the Idols,* pp. 55–73; Christensen, *Art and the Reformation,* pp. 23–41; Aston, *England's Iconoclasts,* pp. 35–40.

62. Eire, *War Against the Idols,* p. 65.

63. See Charles Garside, *Zwingli and the Arts* (New Haven: Yale University Press, 1966), pp. 33–39, 94; G. R. Potter, *Zwingli* (Cambridge: Cambridge University Press, 1976), p. 71; Eire, *War Against the Idols,* pp. 76–79. Garside believes that Zwingli's opposition to images in worship derives ultimately from his humanism. While Eire admits that Zwingli's initial break with Catholic devotion was inspired by Erasmus, he says that it is clear that Zwingli soon went beyond the humanist critique in his opposition. This is doubtless true, but the significant element shared by both humanism and Zwinglian reform is the concentration upon language as a mode of knowledge.

64. Potter, *Zwingli,* p. 60.

65. Garside, *Zwingli and the Arts,* p. 49.

66. Ibid., pp. 61–62.

67. Eire, *War Against the Idols,* pp. 74–80. Eire notes that Karlstadt's influence is not acknowledged by any of the intelligentsia of the Swiss Reformation but that his

theories appear to have been followed in a concrete manner by the lesser figures, including Haetzer.

68. Garside, *Zwingli and the Arts,* p. 149.

69. Eire, *War Against the Idols,* p. 82.

70. Garside, *Zwingli and the Arts,* pp. 159–60.

71. My account here follows Eire, *War Against the Idols:* on Bern, St. Gall, Toggenburg, Schaffhausen, pp. 108–114; Basel, pp. 114–19; Neuchâtel, pp. 119–21; Geneva, pp. 122–65. On Basel, see also Christensen, *Art and the Reformation,* pp. 93–102.

72. Christensen, *Art and the Reformation,* pp. 66–109.

73. On the development of Calvin's theology of worship, see Eire, *War Against the Idols,* pp. 195–233.

74. See in particular his treatise, *On shunning the Unlawful Rites of the Ungodly, and Preserving the Purity of the Christian Religion,* where he notes that the prohibition of the worship of idols "comprehended the whole of the external worship which the ungodly are wont to bestow" on externals, (*Tracts and Treatises in Defense of the Reformed Faith,* trans. Henry Beveridge [Grand Rapids, Mich.: Eerdmans, 1958], vol. 3: 369).

75. Christensen, *Art and the Reformation,* pp. 66–78.

76. Eire, *War Against the Idols,* pp. 276–80. For an important discussion of the whole pattern of religious violence in France in the 1560s and 1570s, see Natalie Zemon Davis, "The Rites of Violence: Religious Riot in Sixteenth-Century France," *Past and Present* 59 (1973): 51–90.

77. See Phyllis Mack Crew, *Calvinist Preaching,* and David Freedberg, *Iconoclasm and Painting in the Revolt of the Netherlands, 1566–1609* (New York: Garland, 1988).

78. More, *Utopia,* in *The Complete Works of St. Thomas More,* vol. 4, ed. S. J. Edward Surtz and J. H. Hexter, pp. 231–32.

79. On Bilney, see Aston, *England's Iconoclasts,* pp. 161–68; on early iconoclastic incidents, see pp. 210–19.

80. Latimer, *Sermons of Hugh Latimer,* ed. George Elwes Corrie, Parker Society (Cambridge: Cambridge University Press, 1844), pp. 33–58.

81. On the continued role of the late medieval system of devotion, see J. J. Scarisbrick, *The Reformation and the English People* (Oxford: Basil Blackwell, 1984). Eamon Duffy, *The Stripping of the Altars,* pp. 478–564, also assesses the effect of the Reformation on parishes and individual piety.

82. See Hugh Braun, *Parish Churches: Their Architectural Development in England* (London: Faber and Faber, 1970), p. 151; Scarisbrick, *The Reformation,* pp. 12–14. Eamon Duffy estimates that "between a third and a half of the 10,000 or so parish churches of architectural interest in England are mainly or wholly Perpendicular in style," which would mean that they were built in the century and a half before the Reformation. And perhaps as many as two thirds of all English parish churches saw substantial rebuilding in this period (*The Stripping of the Altars,* p. 132).

83. Aston, *England's Iconoclasts,* pp. 222–24; the initial directive came in the sixth of the Ten Articles issued by Convocation on July 11, 1536.

84. Duffy, *The Stripping of the Altars,* p. 451.

85. Phillips, *The Reformation of Images,* pp. 87–89; Aston, *England's Iconoclasts,* pp. 262–77.

86. Phillips, *The Reformation of Images,* p. 96, figs. 24a and 24b. As Aston notes, "where the Reformation was most urgent, image and word were most diametrically

counterposed." The Gregorian idea of images as books of the illiterate could not stand up to this new emphasis, and "there could be no substitute for direct mediation of the word through preaching, teaching, or reading" (*England's Iconoclasts,* p. 258).

87. For a detailed account of the restoration of Catholic ceremonial and its material setting under Mary, see Duffy, *The Stripping of Altars,* pp. 524–64. Duffy emphasizes that the restoration was not simply a return to the status quo ante, but that serious attempts were made, including the use of the press to publish primers and catechetical works, to reestablish the structures of worship and belief prior to Edward's reign.

88. Aston, *England's Iconoclasts,* p. 337.

89. Calvin, *Foure godly sermons agaynst the pollution of Idolatries* (London, 1561).

90. The *Book of Homilies* is, however, commended by the thirty-fifth of the Thirty-nine Articles, as Aston notes (*England's Iconoclasts,* p. 336). Aston suggests that the revisions of the homily "Against Peril of Idolatry," which soften the tone somewhat, are Elizabeth's own (pp. 320–24).

91. William Harrison, *The Description of England,* ed. G. Edelen (Ithaca, N.Y.: Cornell University Press, 1968), pp. 35–36, quoted in Aston, *England's Iconoclasts,* p. 330. Edwardian policy had allowed the parish clergy to remove stained glass, but under Elizabeth only bishops could authorize it.

92. Horton Davies, *Worship and Theology,* pp. 358–59, 370–71.

93. See in particular Ernest Gilman, *Iconoclasm and Poetry.*

94. Baxandall, *Painting and Experience in Fifteenth Century Italy,* esp. ch. 2. Why Italy did not experience iconoclasm, even in places where the Reformation had some influence, is not a question that has, so far as I know, engaged the attention of historians of art or of theology. My own suggestion is that Italian humanism did not take an iconoclastic turn because, by the fifteenth century, it had already established a strong theoretical and practical alliance with the visual arts. As early as Petrarch, who valued Giotto and owned a Madonna by him, Italian humanism appears to have been responsive to painting and sculpture. Increasingly the humanists recognized the analogue between their own concern to revive knowledge of Greek and Roman letters and the concerns of the artists to establish a stylistic rapport with antiquity. Leon Battista Alberti's treatise *Della pittura* (1436; written in Latin 1435) is clearly the most important early chapter of this story, for it treats art as an intellectual activity, grounds it in mathematical laws, and speaks of it in terms of rhetoric. Alberti considers painting as analogous to written history. He views a painting, he says, "with no less delight to my mind than if I was reading a good history; for both are painters, one painting with words and the other with the brush" (quoted by Anthony Blunt, *Artistic Theory in Italy 1450–1600* [Oxford: Clarendon 1940], p. 12). The painter, Alberti insists, must be acquainted with all the branches of knowledge relevant to his art, especially history, poetry, and mathematics. Alberti himself, of course, practiced architecture, and it is this art that in his view unites to the highest degree theoretical and practical knowledge. Already current was the story of how Brunelleschi a generation earlier had rediscovered the principles that enabled him to construct the cupola of the duomo of Florence by assiduous study of Roman remains, a story Vasari would repeat as part of his own account of the growing dignity and prestige of the arts and their practitioners. In Vasari's *Lives* (1550, expanded and revised 1568)—especially in the accounts of Leonardo, Raphael, and Michelangelo—the process by which artists became both equals and collaborators with humanist scholars and poets would reach culmination. If Leonardo could die in the arms of a king, the visual arts were equal in dignity to poetry and history.

The famous *brucciamenti* of Savonarola in 1497 and 1498 may appear examples of iconoclasm, but on closer inspection they have a very different character than the iconoclastic bonfires in Switzerland and Germany three decades later. While paintings and works of sculpture did feed Savonarola's pyres, so did cosmetics, clothes, masks, musical instruments, and books. His purifying fire was not directed toward religious art, but more generally toward worldly vanities. Savonarola in fact supported the religious use of art, and the convent of San Marco, over which he presided as prior, had an artistic tradition reaching back to Fra Angelico and continuing through his own support of Fra Bartolomeo della Porta. See Ronald M. Steinberg, *Fra Girolamo Savonarola, Florentine Art, and Renaissance Historiography* (Athens: Ohio University Press, 1977).

95. On the aesthetic as a semiotic expression of culture, particularly of artistic signs "as modes of thought," see Clifford Geertz, "Art as a Cultural System," *Local Knowledge: Further Essays in Interpretive Anthropology* (New York: Basic Books, 1983), pp. 94–120. "Matisse's color jottings (the word is his own) and the Yoruba's line arrangements do not, save glancingly, celebrate social structure or forward useful doctrines. They materalize a way of expressing, bring a particular cast of mind out into the world of objects, where men can look at it. The signs or sign elements . . . that make up a semiotic system we want, for theoretical purposes, to call aesthetic are ideationally connected to the society in which they are found, not mechanically." On Geertz's aesthetics, see also Giles Gunn, *The Culture of Criticism and the Criticism of Culture* (New York: Oxford University Press, 1987), pp. 93–115.

96. Turner and Turner, *Image and Pilgrimage,* pp. 143–44. Regional and national particularity is the hallmark of the Turners' argument for the continued significance of modern pilgrimage sites, pp. 62–103; see also their comments on the Irish nationalism of the Lough Derg pilgrimage, "St. Patrick's Purgatory," pp. 123–39.

97. On the English devotion to the Virgin and the focus of this cult on Walsingham, see Gibson, *The Theater of Devotion,* pp. 137–77.

98. See Peter Brown, *The Cult of the Saints: Its Rise and Function in Latin Christianity* (Chicago: University of Chicago Press, 1981), esp. pp. 50–68, 86–89.

99. Aston, *England's Iconoclasts,* pp. 234–36. Joseph Gutmann argues for a similar pattern in Josiah's destruction of local shrines and images in a centripetal policy to focus Israel's religion on Jerusalem and the Temple, in "Deuteronomy: Religious Reformation or Iconoclastic Revolution," in *The Image and the Word,* ed. Joseph Gutmann (Missoula, Mont.: Scholar's Press, 1977), 5–25.

100. Mervyn James, "Ritual, Drama and Social Body in the Late Medieval English Town," in *Society, Politics and Culture: Studies in Early Modern England* (Cambridge: Cambridge University Press, 1986), pp. 16–47 (quotation, p. 27).

101. See Paul Whitfield White, *Theatre and Reformation.*

Chapter 3

1. See in particular Steven Mullaney, *The Place of the Stage: Licence, Play, and Power in Renaissance England* (Chicago: University of Chicago Press, 1988), esp. 26–59.

2. Alan H. Nelson, *The Medieval English Stage,* p. 85; see also Gardiner, *Mysteries' End,* pp. 77–79.

3. For a discussion of the incarnational context for drama, see Gail McMurray Gibson, *The Theater of Devotion.*

4. V. A. Kolve, *The Play Called Corpus Christi* (Stanford: Stanford University Press, 1966), pp. 44–50. Kolve did not, however, develop a sense of the relation of the feast to the thematics of the drama. In *The Medieval English Stage* (pp. 1–14), Alan H. Nelson rejected the idea that the feast or its doctrinal undergirding have any essential connection to the development of cycle drama in England.

5. James, *Society, Politics and Culture,* pp. 16–47.

6. Peter W. Travis, *Dramatic Design in the Chester Cycle* (Chicago: University of Chicago Press, 1982), p. 5; see also Travis's important article, "The Social Body of the Dramatic Christ in Medieval England," *Early Drama to 1600, Acta* 13 (1985): 17–35.

7. Sarah Beckwith, "Making the World in York and the York cycle," in *Framing Medieval Bodies,* ed. Sarah Kay and Miri Rubin (Manchester: Manchester University Press, 1994), pp. 254–76, quotations from pp. 254–55. Beckwith has critiqued James's influential article in another important recent study that argues the need for a more nuanced and historical reading of the social relationships articulated in the York play; see "Ritual, Theater, and Social Space in the York Corpus Christi Cycle," in *Bodies and Disciplines: Intersections of Literature and History in Fifteenth-Century England,* ed. Barbara A. Hanawalt and David Wallace (Minneapolis: University of Minnesota Press, 1996), pp. 63–86.

8. Caroline Walker Bynum, *Holy Feast and Holy Fast: the Religious Significance of Food to Medieval Women* (Berkeley: University of California Press, 1987), p. 253. "Physicality as problem and opportunity," she argues, "was a basic theme throughout late medieval religiosity" (p. 258).

9. Bynum, *Holy Feast and Holy Fast,* p. 254; on Mechtild of Hackeborn, see also Bynum's *Jesus as Mother: Studies in the Spirituality of the High Middle Ages* (Berkeley: University of California Press, 1982), 209–227.

10. Bynum, *Holy Feast and Holy Fast,* pp. 252–53. Bynum notes that this concern with body would continue into the succeeding two centuries, that "various late medieval heterodoxies, diverse though they were, seemed to contemporaries to have in common a denigration of the body, a denial that it might be either a source or a recipient of salvation." On the circumstances of the establishment of the feast Corpus Christi, see also Miri Rubin, *Corpus Christi,* pp. 164–85.

11. A belief that drama arose from pre-Christian rituals was succeeded by a scholarship that saw the drama as emerging in an evolutionary fashion from the liturgical pattern of the *Quem quaeritis* trope for Easter, the former understanding most fully expressed in E. K. Chambers, *The Medieval Stage* (Oxford: Clarendon, 1903), the latter in Karl Young's *The Drama of the Medieval Church.* In Young's account, the dramatic suggestiveness of the trope gradually inspired a more elaborated portrayal until true dramatic representation finally emerged. But this formulation has been challenged by O. B. Hardison, Jr., on the grounds that there is little evidence of an evolutionary growth toward drama: Hardison also challenged the distinction between ritual and drama and advanced other rites, rather than the tropes, as bases for the dramatic structures (*Christian Rite and Christian Drama in the Middle Ages: Essays in the Orgin and Early History of Medieval Drama* [Baltimore, Md.: Johns Hopkins University Press, 1965]). More recently Walter Cohen has employed a Marxist paradigm to attempt to link monastic drama to the emergence of feudalism (*The Drama of a Nation: Public Theater in Renaissance England and Spain* [Ithaca, N.Y.: Cornell University Press, 1985], pp. 33–81), but the uncertain provenance of many of the plays and the difficulties of establishing the conditions of feudalism create inevitable problems for such an argument; while Cohen can find appropriations of feudal language within the plays, the larger question of why drama as a phenomenon should emerge when it does, or how

the phenomenon itself relates to fuedalism, remains resistant to such explanation. Most recently, Jody Enders has suggested that the rhetorical tradition, especially as played out in forensic disputation, offers another way of understanding the origins of medieval drama in *Rhetoric and the Origins of Medieval Drama* (Ithaca, N.Y.: Cornell University Press, 1992).

12. Sandro Sticca, *The Latin Passion Play: Its Origins and Development* (Albany: State University of New York Press, 1970), pp. 3–19; Richard Axton (*European Drama of the Early Middle Ages* [London: Hutchinson, 1974], pp. 24–26) believes there was some understanding of Terence as a theatrical text. On the evidence for the survival of traditions of mime, see William Tydeman, *The Theatre in the Middle Ages: Western European Stage Conditions, 800–1576* (Cambridge: Cambridge University Press, 1978), pp. 26–27. As Tydeman notes, Hrosthvitha, abbess of Gandersheim (c. 935–c. 1002), offers the one possible exception to the judgment of a twelfth-century new beginning of European drama; she wrote six Latin comedies, Christian imitations of Terence, but with no indications of theatrical auspices or that they were intended for performance (pp. 27–28).

13. Andrew Hughes notes the difficulty in establishing the precise date and provenance of the liturgical drama. The plays are transmitted in liturgical manuscripts which frequently cannot be dated more closely than within a century or more ("Liturgical Drama," in *The Theatre of Medieval Europe*, ed. Eckhard Simon [Cambridge: Cambridge University Press, 1991], pp. 42–62).

14. On twelfth-century thought in relation to the visual arts, see Ladner, *Ad Imaginem Dei*, pp. 51–66; Robert Grinnell, "Iconography and Philosophy in the Crucifixion Window at Poitiers," *The Art Bulletin* 28 (1946): 171–96.

15. *De Unione Corporis et Spiritus* in Ugo di S. Vittore, *I tre giorni dell'invisibile luce; l'unione del corpo e dello spirito*, ed. Vincenzo Liccaro (Florence: Sansoni, 1974), p. 212.

16. "Summum est corpus [ignis] et spirituali naturae proximum, quod per se semper moveri habet, extra nunquam cohiberi habet; quod quidem, in quantum sensum praestat, imitatur rationalem vitam, in quantum imaginationem format, vitalem sapientiam" (pp. 216–18). It is important to realize that "imagination," by which I have rendered *imaginatio*, does not have its modern English meaning, but something closer to the "power of imaging," since it appears to be the perceptual power which organizes the data of sense; in Hugh's usage it is a power shared with non-rational animals.

17. *Hugh of St. Victor on the Sacraments of the Christian Faith*, trans. Roy J. Deferrari (Cambridge, Mass.: The Medieval Academy of America, 1951), pp. 226–27.

18. In noting Bernard's role in stimulating the gothic art of the later twelfth century, Gerhardt B. Ladner suggests that his strictures against artistic luxury may have had the half-animal, half-human monsters of Romanesque sculpture in mind, that Bernard could not have known "the fuller humanism of late twelfth- and early-thirteenth-century art," *Ad Imagination Dei*, p. 61.

19. "Venit in carne, ut vel sic carnalibus exhiberetur et apparente humanitate benignitas agnosceretur. Ubi enim Dei innotescit humanitas, jam benignitas latere non potest. In quo enim magis commendare poterat benignitatem suam, quam suscipiendo carnem meam? Meam, inquam, non carnem Adam, id est non qualem ille habuit ante culpam. Quid tantopere declaret ejus misericordiam, quam quod ipsam suscepit miseriam? Quid ita pietate plenum, quam quod Dei Verbum propter nos factus est fenum? [note rhyme] . . . Magna plane et manifesta benignitas Dei et humanitas! et magnum benignitatis indicium declaravit, qui humanitati addere nomen Dei curavit." (*PL*, vol. 183:143.)

20. "Amplexatus est nos Dominus Jesus per laborem et dolorem nostrum; amplectamur eum nos quoque vicariis quibusdam amplexibus propter justitiam et ad justitiam suam, actiones ad justitiam dirigendo, passiones propter justitiam sustinendo" (In feria IV Hebdomadae Sanctae Sermo, *PL,* vol. 183:270.)

21. *Bernard of Clairvaux: Selected Works,* trans. G. R. Evans, (New York: Paulist Press, 1987), p. 216; the Latin reads "Sit os osculans, Verbum assumens; osculatum, caro quae assumitur; osculum vero, quod pariter ab osculante et osculato conficitur, persona ipsa scilicet ex utroque compacta, mediator Dei et hominum homo Christus Jesus" (*PL,* vol. 183:790).

22. *PL,* vol. 183:218–19; "Securus suscipio mediatorem Dei Filium, quem agnosco et meum. Minime plane jam mihi suspectus erit: frater enim et caro mea est. Puto enim, spernere me jam non poterit, os de ossibus meis, et caro de carne mea" (*PL,* vol. 183:792).

23. "Monstrabat autem postea eis altiorem amoris gradum, cum diceret: Spiritus est qui vivificat, caro non prodest quidquam (Joan. VI, 46). Puto, hunc ascenderat jam qui dicebat: Etsi cognovimus Christum secundum carnem, sed nunc jam non novimus (II Cor. V, 16). Fortassis et nihilominus propheta in hoc ipso stabat, cum diceret: Spiritus ante faciem nostram Christus Dominus. Nam quod subjungit: Sub umbra eius vivemus inter gentes (Thren. IV, 20), mihi videtur ex persona incipientium addidisse, ut quiescant saltem in umbra, qui solis ferre ardorem minus validos se sentiunt; et carnis dulcedine nutriantur, dum necdum valent ea percipere quae sunt Spiritus Dei. Umbram siquidem Christi, carnem reor esse ipsius, de qua obumbratum est et Mariae (Luc. I, 55), ut ejus objectu fervor splendorque Spiritus illi temperaretur" (*PL,* vol. 183:870).

24. Licet vero donum, et magnum donum Spiritus sit istiusmodi erga carnem Christi devotio; carnalem tamen dixerim hunc amorem, illius utique amoris respectu, quo non tam Verbum caro jam sapit, quam Verbum sapientia, Verbum justitia, Verbum veritas, Verbum sanctitas, pietas, virtus; et si quid aliud quod sit, hujusmodi dici potest. . . . An tibi aeque et uno modo affecti videntur, is quidem qui Christo passo pie compatitur, compungitur, et movetur facile ad memoriam honorum quae pertulit, atque istius devotionis suavitate pascitur, et confortatur ad quaeque salubria, honesta, pia; itemque ille, qui justistiae zelo semper est accensus, qui veritatem ubique zelat, qui sapientiae fervet studiis; cui amica sanctitas vitae, et morum disciplina; cujus mores erubescunt jactantiam, abhorent detractionem, invidiam nesciunt, superbiam detestantur, omnem humanam gloriam non solum fugiunt, sed et fastidiunt et contemnunt; omnem in se carnis et cordis impuritatem vehementissime abominantur et persequuntur; omne denique tanqam naturaliter et malum respuunt, et quod bonum est amplectuntur? Nonne si compares utriusque affectiones, constat quodam modo illum superiorem, respectu quidem hujus, amare quasi carnaliter?" (*PL,* vol. 183:871).

25. "Quid tu times, o homo? quid trepidas a facie Domini, quia venit? . . . Noli fugere, noli timere. . . . Ecce infans est, et sine voce. Nam vagientis vox magis miseranda est, quam tremenda." *In Nativitate Domini* I, 1–4 (*PL,* vol. 183:116). "Et ego certe agnosco mea esse Nativitatis hujus tempus et locum, infantilis corporis teneritudinem, parvuli vagitus et lacrymas; sed et ipsorum quibus primo annuntiatur nativitas Salvatoris, paupertatem pastorum atque vigilias" (*PL,* vol. 183:123).

26. "Carnalis homo non percipit ea quae sunt Spiritus Dei: sed jam capiat et carnalis, quia verbum factum est caro. Si nihil praeter carnem novit, ecce Verbum caro factum est; audiat illud vel in carne. O homo, in carne tibi exhibetur Sapientia; illa quondam occulta, ecce jam trahitur de occultis, et ipsis sese ingerit sensibus carnis tuae. . . . Hoc tibi praedicat stabulum istud hoc praesepe clamat, hoc membra illa infantilia manifeste loquuntur. hoc lacrymae et vagitus evangelizant" (*PL,* vol. 183:124).

27. "Hodie enim magi ab Oriente venerunt, ortum Solum justitiae requirentes,

cum de quo legitur: Ecce vir Oriens nomen illi. Hodie adoraverunt novum Virginis partum, sequentes novi sideris ductum" (*PL,* vol. 183:144–45).

28. "Luximus his diebus, compunctioni et orationi, gravitati et abstinentiae dediti, caeterorum negligentias temporum sacro hoc quadragenario redimere et diluere cupientes" (*PL,* vol. 183:281).

29. *Ad Faciendum Similitudinem Dominici Sepulcri,* in *Medieval Drama,* ed. David Bevington (Boston: Houghton Mifflin, 1975), p. 40.

30. *Ad Repraesentandum Conversionem Beati Pauli Apostoli,* in Bevington, *Medieval Drama,* p. 165.

31. *Ordo and Peregrinum in Secunda Feria Pasche and Vesperas,* in Bevington, *Medieval Drama,* p. 45.

32. *Ludus de Passione,* in *Medieval Drama,* Bevington, p. 220.

33. Rosemary Woolf notes that the vernacular was considered the language of lament in particular and that lamentations in French, Provençal, German, and Italian occur in the Latin musical dramas (*The English Mystery Plays,* pp. 43–44).

34. Sarah Beckwith, *Christ's Body: Identity, Culture and Society in Late Medieval Writings* (London: Routledge, 1993), p. 52.

35, Thomas of Celano, "First Life of St. Francis," in *St. Francis of Assisi, Writings and Early Biographies,* ed. Marion A. Habig (Chicago: Franciscan Herald Press, 1975), pp. 299–301.

36. While identified with St. Francis in medieval art, the stigmata were experienced primarily by women ascetics from the twelfth to the sixteenth centuries, according to Caroline Bynum, *Holy Feast and Holy Fast,* pp. 200, 210.

37. *Il Teatro Italiano: Dalle Origini al Quattrocento,* ed. Emilio Faccioli (Turin: Einaudi, 1975), vol. 1:45; subsequent citations are to pages in this volume; translation is mine.

38. Gail McMurray Gibson had pointed out to me that the textual source of this popular tradition is the *Meditationes Vitae Christi* of Pseudo-Bonaventure.

39. *La rappresentazione della Conversione di Santa Maria Maddalena,* stanza 86; in *Sacre Rappresentazioni del Quattrocento,* ed. Luigi Banfi (Turin: Unione Tipografica-Editrice Torinese, 1968), p. 222.

40. Leo Steinberg, *The Sexuality of Christ in Renaissance Art and in Modern Oblivion* (New York: Pantheon, 1983).

41. A similar use of familiar and erotic language occurs in the contemporaneous *Book of Margery Kempe,* for example when Margery reports Christ speaking to her as her lover and husband: "Therefore most I nedys be homly wyth the & lyn in thi bed wyth the. Dowtyr, thow desyrest gretly to se me, & the mayst boldy, whan thu are in thi bed, take me to the as for thi weddyd husbond, as thy derworthy derlyng, & as for thy swete sone, for I wyl be louyd as a sone shuld be louyd with the modyr and wil that thu loue me, dowtyr as a good wife oweth to loue hir husbonde, & therfor thu mayest boldly take me in the armys of thi sowle and kyssen my mowth, my hed, & my fete as swetly as thow wylt." *The Book of Margery Kempe,* ed. Sanford Meech and Hope Emily Allen, EETS o.s. 212 (Oxford: Oxford University Press, 1940), p. 90.

42. *A Tretise of Miraclis Pleyinge,* ed. Clifford Davidson, Early Drama, Art, and Music Monograph Series, 19 (Kalamazoo, Mich.: Medieval Institute Publication, 1993); on the dating of the *Tretise,* see note 1, pp. 34–35; on its provenance, see Paul A. Johnston, Jr., "The Dialect of *A Tretise of Miraclis Pleyinge,*" pp. 53–84, of Davidson's edition. On the basis of manuscript and dialect influence, the area between Northampton, Peterborough, and Huntingdon appears the most likely region of authorship.

43. See Davidson's introduction, *Tretise of Miraclis PLeyinge,* p. 2.

44. York is probably the oldest among the surviving cycles, having talen something like its subsequent shape as early as 1415, when the *Ordo Paginarum* in the city's "A/Y Memorandum Book" listed the guilds and the content of the plays assigned to them; however, it was revised and expanded until the third quarter of the fifteenth century, the date of the manuscript register containing the cycle. See Beadle, *The York Plays,* pp. 19–28. As described in chapter one, however, this register was subject to considerable revision right to the time of its final performance in 1569. Martin Stevens argues that Wakefield is a "second generation" cycle, dating from the last third of the fifteenth century, its manuscript dated around 1500 (*Four Middle English Mystery Cycles: Textual, Contextual, and Critical Interpretations* [Princeton, N.J.: Princeton University Press, 1987], pp. 113–18). *N-Town,* now generally seen as more compilation than integrated cycle, is least susceptible to secure dating; its manuscript is dated between c. 1468 and the early-sixteenth century (*The N-Town Play,* ed. Stephen Spector, EETS s.s. 11 [Oxford: Oxford University Press, 1991], p. xvi. The Chester cycle, though performed as early as 1422 (and perhaps 1376), was transformed substantially between 1505 and 1532, especially after it was shifted from a one-day performance at Corpus Christi to Whitsunday by 1521 and to a three-day performance in Whitsuntide week by 1532. Because of its more extensive manuscript record (five manuscripts and a sixth with two pageants and a fragment), Chester offers the most evidence for the revision, expansion, and transformation of any of the English cycles; for an account of this complex process, see Travis, *Dramatic Design in the Chester Cycle,* pp. 30–69, and Lumiansky and Mills, *The Chester Mystery Cycle,* pp. 165–202.

45. Arguing for the economic and social subversiveness of the representation of bodily suffering in the plays, Claire Sponsler has recently drawn attention to the very excessiveness of that representation. She suggests that the plays seem "to encourage spectators to enjoy the attacks on Christ's body as moments of undisguised sadistic delight in the inflicting of bodily pain. In these scenes, which develop the torture of Christ's body into a long and grotesque drama focusing on whips, wounds, and bloodshed, a highly charged erotics is revealed as the nearly naked, brutalized body of Christ is scourged by other men's hands. In the process, violence refuses to be limited to safe cultural zones" (*Drama and Resistance: Bodies, Goods, and Theatricality in Late Medieval England, Medieval Cultures,* vol. 10. [Minneapolis: University of Minnesota Press, 1997], pp. 136–60, quotation p. 152).

46. *Mirrour of the Blessed Lyf of Jesu Christ* by Pseudo-Bonaventure, trans, Nicholas Love, ed. Lawrence F. Powell (Oxford: Oxford University Press, 1907), p. 216.

47. Peter Womack, "Medieval Drama," in *English Drama: A Cultural History,* ed. Simon Shepherd and Peter Womack (Oxford: Blackwell, 1996), p. 11.

48. Beadle, *The York Plays,* p. 49; subsequent citations of the York plays are to pages in this edition. (I have silently substituted *th* for the Middle English letter thorn and *gh* for yogh.)

49. B. M. Bonansea, *Man and His Approaches to God in John Duns Scotus* (Lanham, Md.: University Press of America, 1983), pp. 47–48. Rosemary Woolf first noticed that this is a Franciscan doctrine, but she dismisses it, mistakenly in my view, as "the relic of an older version, or introduced by the injudicious vagary of a later redactor" and suspects "the hand of a polemical Franciscan" (*The English Mystery Plays,* p. 116). On Franciscan involvement generally with medieval English drama, see David L. Jeffrey, "Franciscan Spirituality and the Rise of Early English Drama," *Mosaic* 8 (1975): 17–46; Jeffrey does not, however, mention this passage.

50. In fact, the post-Reformation banns of the Chester play suggests that just such a change to an offstage voice would more properly render the majesty of God. See chapter 1, this volume, p. 27, and note 57.

51. Elaine Scarry, *The Body in Pain,* p. 216.

52. John Elliot notes that the scenes of torture appear to have been among the strongest reasons why the plays encountered difficulty in achieving production earlier in this century, *Playing God,* pp. 42–70. Modern productions, however, as Peter Travis indicates, have not portrayed the wounded, tortured Christ that medieval performance required, but have remained "sanitized and civil" ("The Social Body of the Dramatic Christ in Medieval England," p. 27).

53. On the whole issue of the expressibility of pain, see especially Scarry, *The Body in Pain,* pp. 3–23.

54. Davidson, *Tretise of Miraclis Pleyinge,* p. 102. Davidson suggests that weeping at the Passion was a particular form of Northern piety (p. 16); the critique of emotionalism as empty and therefore false is the same charge that was constantly laid against the crying out and weeping of Marjorie Kempe.

55. Beckwith, *Christ's Body,* pp. 56–63. *The Prickynge of Love* is an anonymous translation of the Franciscan *Stimulus Amoris,* once attributed to Bonaventure, now to James of Milan. Beckwith describes this influential text as "at once exemplary and extraordinary for the way it examines the construction and dissolution of identity in relation to the body of Christ" (p. 57).

56. Travis, "The Social Body of the Dramatic Christ in Medieval England," p. 33.

57. For example, Robert Weiman, *Shakespeare and the Popular Tradition in the Theater: Studies in the Social Dimension of Dramatic Form and Function,* ed. Robert Schwartz (Baltimore, Md.: Johns Hopkins University Press, 1978), pp. 49–97; Martin Stevens has a brief but suggestive discussion of the significance of typology for generating multiple dramatic plots in his *Four Middle English Mystery Cycles,* pp. 244–57.

58. See Michael O'Connell, "Vital Cultural Practices: Shakespeare and the Mysteries," *JMEMS* 29 (1999): 149–68, esp. 160–64.

Chapter 4

1. Paul Whitfield White, *Theatre and Reformation.*

2. See, in particular, Ritchie D. Kendall, *The Drama of Dissent: The Radical Poetics of Nonconformity, 1380–1590* (Chapel Hill: University of North Carolina Press, 1986): "Repeatedly in the nonconformist canon, the reader encounters the products of an inherently theatrical imagination. Dialogues, dramatic satires, saints' lives animadversions, and fictionalized records of prelatical examinations—all are attempts to dramatize the soul's awakening to its idealized self through a ritualistic encounter with its spiritual adversaries" (p. 8). On the development of this sense of psychological drama from John Bale to Foxe, see especially pp. 122–31.

3. Bryan Crockett, *The Play of Paradox,* pp. 8–9.

4. Martha Tuck Rozett notes the popularity of sermon-going and the explosion in the numbers of sermons preached and printed during this period; see *The Doctrine of Election and the Emergence of Elizabethan Tragedy* (Princeton, N.J.: Princeton University Press, 1984), pp. 15–20.

5. See Peter Burke, *Popular Culture in Early Modern Europe* (London, 1978; reprint, New York: Harper and Row, 1978), pp. 178–243.

6. Glynne Wickham speaks of "the wholesale emasculation of the theatre in the provinces in the late-sixteenth and early-seventeenth centuries": "The work of the Ecclesiastical Commissions, in suppressing local religious plays during the reign of Elizabeth I, followed by the steady withdrawal of touring professional companies between the accession of James I and the outbreak of the Civil War, succeeded in divorcing provincial towns and villages from all previously maintained standards of play writing and play-production: and unlike London the provinces failed to regain a professional theatre at the Restoration" (*The Medieval Theatre*, 3rd ed. [Cambridge: Cambridge University Press, 1987], p. 147). Cf. also his *Early English Stages, Volume Two: 1576 to 1660*, part 1 (London: Routledge and Kegan Paul, 1963), p. 96. Louis Montrose characterizes the historical shift as "from a culture focused upon social dynamics within the local community to one that incorporates the local within the national framework and subordinates it to the political and cultural center" (*The Purpose of Playing: Shakespeare and the Cultural Politics of the Elizabethan Theatre* [Chicago: University of Chicago Press, 1996], p. 23).

7. For Bale's life, I rely on Honor C. McCusker, *John Bale: Dramatist and Antiquary* (1942; reprint, Freeport, N.Y., 1971), pp. 1–28, and Peter Happé's introduction to his edition, *The Complete Plays of John Bale*, vol. 1:2–9.

8. Bale, *Complete Plays of John Bale*, vol. 1:8.

9. McCusker, *John Bale*, p. 14. See also White, *Theatre and Reformation*, pp. 12–41; on the basis of known performances by the players under Cromwell's patronage, White works out conjectural itineraries for "Bale and his fellows."

10. Peter Womack, "Medieval Drama," in Shepherd and Womack, *English Drama*, p. 7.

11. Kendall notes that Bale shared with the Lollards "a deep mistrust for the apotheosis of the holy child" (*Drama of Dissent*, p. 96; see also pp. 130–31).

12. Bale, *Complete Plays of John Bale*, vol. 1:12.

13. A minor qualification of this point would be the opening of *The Three Lawes*, where, as Kendall points out, Deus Pater begins by insisting that he is "a substance invisible" and therefore, "To angel and man . . . incomprehensible" (*Drama of Dissent*, p. 101).

14. Mark Breitenberg also notes that Bale ends up creating plays with dialogue very close to sermons "in order to lessen the visual and theatrical aspects of his own plays in favor of their language" ("Reading Elizabethan Iconicity: *Gorboduc* and the Semiotics of Reform," *English Literary Renaissance* 18 [1988]: 194–217, quotation p. 196).

15. Bale, *Complete Plays of John Bale*, vol. 2:26.

16. Ibid., p. 58.

17. Ibid., p. 54.

18. Paul Whitfield White suggests that the broom here makes Infidelitas a version of Robin Goodfellow in the folk plays (*Theatre and Reformation*, p. 31).

19. My colleague Robert Potter, who directed what may be the only modern production of *King Johan,* has suggested to me the stage worthiness of certain speeches and scenes in the play.

20. *The Resurrection of Our Lord*, ed. J. Dover Wilson and Bertram Dobell, The Malone Society Reprints (Oxford: Oxford University Press, 1912).

21. The textual source of this tradition is the *Meditationes Vitae Christi* of Pseudo-Bonaventure.

22. Lewis Wager, *The Life and Repentaunce of Marie Magdalene*, ed. Frederick Ives Carpenter (Chicago: University of Chicago Press, 1902).

23. *Reformation Biblical Drama in England: The Life and Repentaunce of Mary Magdalene; The History of Jacob and Esau,* ed. Paul Whitfield White (New York: Garland, 1992), p. 64.

24. On the record of Ashton's plays at Shrewsbury and on the immense theater in the quarry where these and other plays were performed, see J. Alan B. Somerset's *Shropshire*, REED (Toronto: University of Toronto Press, 1994), vol. 1:204, 207–212, 214–15, 243; vol. 2:379–80, 387–88, 661–64, and his "Local Drama and Playing Places at Shrewsbury: New Findings in the Borough Records," in *Medieval and Renaissance Drama in England*, ed. J. Leeds Barroll (New York: AMS Press, 1985), pp. 1–31. Somerset notes that the record is clouded by the unreliability of the antiquarian accounts, among them the "Escutcheons of the Bailiffs," which uniquely records the playing of the passion. He concludes that Ashton produced "as few as three or as many as seven plays," though some of seven would have been produced before it is likely that Ashton took up residence in Shrewsbury as headmaster of the school; town records, not complete, corroborate only three of the productions. He suggests that "it is not over the fact of play productions that one must be cautious, but over the play titles given in 'Escutcheons' and other details given there" (vol. 2:381). A large-scale production of the Passion by a humanist-educated, Protestant schoolmaster in the decade leading to the ending of the civic cycles in the North, while not perhaps impossible, would indeed be a prodigy.

25. *The Commody of the most vertuous and Godlye Susanna,* ed. B. Ifor Evans and W. W. Greg, The Malone Society Reprints (Oxford: Oxford University Press, 1937), p. v.

26. The *Interlude of Kyng Daryus* (1565; reprint, in 1577) shares with *Godly Susanna* both a source in the Apocrypha and a grafting of that source onto a morality pattern, but *Kyng Daryus* is far thinner theatrically and stylistically. The biblical narrative, itself of limited dramatic value, is tucked into the final quarter of the interlude, and consists mainly of a slanging match between vices and virtues. It is not easy to see why the work was reprinted in 1577, by which time it must have seemed theatrically quite out of date.

27. Theodore de Bèze's *A Tragedie of Abrahams Sacrifice,* trans. Arthur Golding, ed. Malcolm W. Wallace, University of Toronto Studies, philological series (Toronto: University of Toronto Press, 1906).

28. Ibid., p. xxxviii.

29. Leicester Bradner, "A Test for Udall's Authorship," *Modern Language Notes* 42 (1927): 378–80. William Hunnis, choirmaster of Elizabeth's Chapel Royal from 1568, has also been proposed as the playwright; see N. E. Pasachoff, *Playwrights, Preachers, and Politicians: A Study of Four Tudor Old Testament Dramas* (Salzburg: Institut für Englische Sprache und Litertur, 1975), pp. 16–50, and Paul Whitfield White, *Theatre and Reformation*, pp. 118–19. The case for Hunnis rests primarily on what Pasachoff sees as the revolutionary sentiments in the play and Hunnis's involvement in plots to overthrow Queen Mary. But the case for those sentiments seems seriously overdrawn, and I am not persuaded that a play arguing for resistance and rebellion could have been published in 1568.

30. See Paul Whitfield White, *Theatre and Reformation*, pp. 118–23, and *Reformation Biblical Drama*, pp. xxxix–xliii. White sees the topic of predestination as the central topic of the play and would assign its composition to the Edwardian period. But the references to election and reprobation are surprisingly mild and non-polemical, and there is little that would have offended Catholic sensibilities in Mary's reign.

31. Murray Roston makes the point of the dual tradition of the play and suggests

that the relation of Ragau and Esau "comes straight out of the Wakefield cycle" in its resemblance to that of Garcio and Cain, *Biblical Drama in England* (London: Faber and Faber, 1968), p. 77. The link is probably not as direct as that, but the play seems no less indebted, in a general way, to the vernacular tradition of biblical drama.

32. DeBèze, *A Tragedie of Abrahams Sacrifice*, p. 34.

33. Munday, *A second and third blast*, p. 104.

34. Stubbes, *Anatomie of Abuses*, p. 102.

35. The play was first printed in 1594, but with no indication of the company who had performed it or when it was first performed. Henslowe's diary indicates that it was performed on March 8, 1592, and on four other occasions in 1592 by Lord Strange's men, but this may have been a revival. As the play seems generally indebted to *Tamburlaine,* a date of composition between 1588 (the presumed date of *Tamburlaine*) and 1592 is as close as one can come. Greene's avowal in 1589–1590 that he will devote himself to serious matters ("sero sed serio") may indicate the time of his involvement. See the introduction to the edition by George Alan Clugston, Thomas Lodge, and Robert Greene, *A Looking Glasse for London and England* (New York: Garland, 1980).

36. One quite specific instance is Adam's comment "ecce signum" as he draws forth a joint of beef and a bottle of beer from his slops. Falstaff repeats this when he displays his hacked dagger in *Henry IV, Part 1,* 2.4.170.

37. *Henslowe's Diary,* ed. R. A. Foakes and R. T. Rickert (Cambridge: Cambridge University Press, 1961), pp. 20–21.

38. Ibid., p. 217.

39. Ibid., pp. 185–86; the first payment of ten shillings was made to William Haughton in May 1600 in earnest for the book of the play, but Haughton seems not to have completed the project (p. 135).

40. Malone made this suggestion; see *Henslowe's Diary,* p. 319.

41. Pasachoff, *Playwrights, Preachers, and Politicians,* p. 100. Albert Braunmuller notes that the play produces "an ironic, albeit external, vision of the central figure" (*George Peele* [Boston: G. K. Hall, 1983], p. 118).

42. George Peele, *David and Bethsabe,* ed. Elmer Blistein, in *The Dramatic Works of George Peele* (New Haven: Yale University Press, 1970), p. 254.

43. See Roston, *Biblical Drama in England,* pp. 226–32, and Elliott, *Playing God,* pp. 8–24.

44. *Wits Miserie, and the Worlds Madness: Discovering the Deuils Incarnat of this Age* [London, 1596], in *The Complete Works of Thomas Lodge* (New York: 1893; reprint, Russell and Russell, 1963), vol. 4:40; quoted by Roston, *Biblical Drama in England,* p. 112.

45. *Canons and Decrees of the Council of Trent,* ed. H. J. Schroeder (London: Herder, 1941), p. 20.

46. Henry Crosse, *Vertues Common-wealth: or the Highway to Honour* (London, 1603), sig. P3r. Crosse goes on to reprehend the staging of kings and "auntient Fathers and Pastors of the Church," suggesting that he himself links the staging of biblical and Protestant martyr plays. Crosse in fact is the significant exception to Jean Howard's judgment that the antitheatricalists' preoccupation with the visual allure of theater "blocked any thought that the theater itself might breed a certain form of iconoclasm" (*The Stage and Social Struggle,* p. 30). With more experience of the power of theater than the first generation of antitheatricalists, Crosse clearly saw the iconoclastic potential of the representation of monarchs and Protestant heroes.

47. Richard Helgerson, *Forms of Nationhood: The Elizabethan Writing of England* (Chicago: University of Chicago Press, 1992), pp. 195–245.

48. See Judith Doolin Spikes, "The Jacobean History Play and the Myth of the Elect Nation," *Renaissance Drama*, n.s. 8 (1977): 117–49; one might quarrel with the "Jacobean" in her title, as the performance of these plays seems to have spanned the two reigns and indeed to have intersected, in Shakespeare's *Henry IV, Parts 1 and 2*, and *Henry V*, with the earlier "type" of history play, centered on dynastic conflict. But the plays she considers do indeed appear an alternative type of history play designed to appeal to distinct audience interests. I am indebted to my colleague Richard Helgerson for suggesting the relevance of these plays to the puzzle of the biblical plays of 1602.

Chapter 5

1 See Wickham, *Early English Stages*, vol. 2.1:75–97.

2. Jean Howard has recently used the antitheatrical tracts to elicit the class and gender anxieties that appear in relation to the public theaters and to consider the way those anxieties shape theatrical practice, in *The Stage and Social Struggle*.

3. Ernest B. Gilman, *Iconoclasm and Poetry*, p. 11.

4. *The Poems of Sir Philip Sidney*, ed. William A. Ringler, Jr. (Oxford: Clarendon, 1962), p. 167.

5. Lucy Gent, *Picture and Poetry, 1560–1620* (Leamington Spa: James Hall, 1981), pp. 12–13. Huston Diehl makes the claim that "[f]ar from suppressing the visual, sixteenth-century religious reform provides a stimulus for the production of images," *Staging Reform, Reforming the Stage: Protestantism and Popular Theater in Early Modern England* (Ithaca, N.Y.: Cornell University Press, 1997), p. 46. If true for England, it is true only of engravings and woodcuts appearing in printed books, where they are under the interpretive sway of texts. The English images Diehl adduces are illustrations of Foxe's *Actes and Monuments*; for paintings, she must go to continental examples, where one does find, in the Low Countries and in Germany, examples of the production of Reformed visual art.

6. Leonard Barkan, "Making Pictures Speak: Renaissance Art, Elizabethan Literature, Modern Scholarship," *Renaissance Quarterly* 48 (1995): 331–32.

7. Stephen Gosson, *Playes Confuted* (1582?), sig. E.i.

8. Peter Stallybrass, "Worn Worlds: Clothes and Identity on the Renaissance Stage," in *Subject and Object in Renaissance Culture,* ed. Margreta de Grazia, Maureen Quilligan, and Peter Stallybrass (Cambridge: Cambridge University Press, 1996), 289–320.

9. Andrew Gurr, *The Shakespearean Stage, 1574–1642*, 3rd ed. (Cambridge: Cambridge University Press, 1992), pp. 194–96, quotes Henslowe's list of costumes.

10. Glynne Wickham, *Early English Stages* vol. 2.1:38; John Coldewey, "The Last Rise and Final Demise of Essex Town Drama," *MLQ* 36 (1975): 239–60, esp. 254–57. Records from Bungay in Suffolk mention players' gowns and coats made from old copes; see *Records of Plays and Players in Norfolk and Suffolk*, ed. David Galloway and John Wasson, The Malone Collections (Oxford: The Malone Society, 1980), vol. 11:146. Several of the REED volumes offer further instances of the sale of vestments for players' costumes: see *Cambridge*, ed. Alan H. Nelson, vol. 1:153, 180, 181; *Lancashire*, ed. David George, pp. 40, 323; and *Shropshire*, ed. J. Alan B. Somerset, vol. 1:212–13, 663.

11. See chapter 1, p. 18.

12. Barnish, *The Anti-Theatrical Prejudice*, p. 132.

13. Richard Helgerson, *Self-Crowned Laureates: Spenser, Jonson, Milton, and the Literary System* (Berkeley: University of California Press, 1983), pp. 101–184. See also, "The Fair, the Pig, Authorship," in Peter Stallybrass and Allon White, *The Politics and Poetics of Trangression* (Ithaca, N.Y.: Cornell University Press, 1986), esp. pp. 66–79.

14. On Erasmus' emphasis on the textual nature of Christ's body, see chapter 2, pp. 36–37.

15. Ben Jonson, *The Staple of News*, ed. Devra Rowland Kifer, Regents Renaissance Drama Series (Lincoln: University of Nebraska Press, 1975), p. 9.

16. Jonson, *The Alchemist*, ed. Alvin B. Kernan (New Haven: Yale University Press, 1974), p. 103 (III.2.89–90).

17. Clifford Davidson details how the Smithfield fair at the feast of St. Bartholomew could be associated with the themes of idolatry and iconoclasm, "Judgment, Iconoclasm, and Anti-Theatricalism in Jonson's *Bartholomew Fair*," *Papers on Language and Literature* 25 (1989): 349–63.

18. Laura Levine argues interestingly that the puppet's response is not so much to defend theater, or to argue that gender is safe from costume, "but to present a world devoid of gender to begin with," and that eroticism is precisely what Jonson eliminates from the puppet version of Marlowe's poem. "The puppet, as much as Marlowe's mangled text, is Jonson's vision of a world which has met the demands of the anti-theatricalist" (*Men in Women's Clothing*, pp. 89, 100).

19. See George E. Rowe, *Distinguishing Jonson: Imitation, Rivalry, and the Direction of a Dramatic Career* (Lincoln: University of Nebraska Press, 1988), p. 143. Rowe gives a splendid reading of the ambiguous subtlety of *Bartholomew Fair* (pp. 139–58).

20. Laura Levine, *Men in Women's Clothing*, p. 106.

21. Peter Stallybrass and Allon White suggest that "with its enormities, abominations, and its intimacy with the 'low' forms, it would certainly have compromised the haughty individuation of the classical to which Jonson so avidly aspired" (*Politics and Poetics*, p. 78). Leah S. Marcus makes a complementary argument about the paradoxical importance of the "low" to Jonson's imagination, particularly in *Bartholomew Fair*, in "Of Mire and Authorship," in *The Theatrical City: Culture, Theatre and Politics in London, 1576–1649*, ed. David L. Smith, Richard Strier, and David Bevington (Cambridge: Cambridge University Press, 1995), pp. 170–81; she also makes a point similar to mine about Jonson's proximity to Puritan language when he comments on theatricality.

22. Bryan Crockett makes an interesting complementary argument that "the explosion of interest in edifying knowledge that grew out of the Protestant Reformation" involves both Jonson and his Puritan opponents. He suggests that "self-consciously or not, a playwright like Ben Jonson partakes in the very mentality he denounces. In his adaptation of classical forms to current situations, he participates in the Puritan interest in epistemology even as he inveighs against Puritanism" (*The Play of Paradox*, p. 81).

23. The principle study of Shakespeare's relation to iconoclasm is James R. Siemon's *Shakespearean Iconoclasm*, from which my own argument will differ in significant ways. Siemon treats the icon and the image as rhetorical elements of Shakespeare's poems and plays and iconoclasm as the challenge to a unitary way of construing the meaning of images thus understood. In this he responds to the multifarious way in which "idol" and "image" were understood in the Reformation debate. My own approach throughout has been to insist on the literal character of the image and on theater as, in part, a visual art. To this end I concentrate on the plays' insistence on the significance of sight and the ways in which we can imagine this was played in the visual images of his theater.

24. I quote throughout from *The Riverside Shakespeare,* ed. G. Blakemore Evans (Boston: Houghton Mifflin, 1974); act, scene, and line references correspond to this addition. I have, however, silently modernized words that the *Riverside Shakespear* eccentrically leaves in their original form.

25. Cf. Jean E. Howard's reading of *Much Ado* as self-conflicted in its presentation of truth and illusion; the play dramatizes a world "in which truth is discursively produced" and remains unknowable outside theatrical practices, but at the same time it does not enable the viewer to distinguish between the falsity of Hero's dramatic construction by Don John and the "truth" of Beatrice and Benedick's love also constructed by illusionary practice (*The Stage and Social Struggle,* pp. 57–72). I find her argument persuasive, but my own reading differs in seeing the play as wanting to delineate thematic differences between the two sets of lovers; whether these thematic differences are dramatically convincing is, of course, another question. See also the earlier version of Howard's argument, "Renaissance Antitheatricality and the Politics of Gender and Rank in *Much Ado about Nothing,*" in *Shakespeare Reproduced: The Text in History and Ideology,* ed. Jean E. Howard and Marion F. O'Connor (New York: Methuen, 1987), pp. 163–87.

26. Folly says that she would be recognized even if she were not speaking, and speech, "oratio," is the "least deceptive mirror of the mind," "minime mendax animi speculum" (*Erasmus, Omnia Opera* [Amsterdam: North Holland Publishing, 1979], vol. 4:3, 74).

27. For a discussion of the extent of the synesthesia in the language of the play, see Garrett Stewart, "Shakespearean Dreamplay," *ELR* 11 (1981):44–69.

28. Robert Weimann, "Mimesis in *Hamlet,*" in *Shakespeare and the Question of Theory,* ed. Patricia Parker and Geoffrey Hartman (New York: Methuen, 1985), p. 282.

29. Huston Diehl argues that "[t]hrough the character of Hamlet, Shakespeare self-consciously addresses the central concerns of the reformers when they critique plays, players, playwrights, and playgoers" (*Staging Reform,* p. 82). She suggestively links Hamlet's scorn for the spectacular dimension of theater to Calvin's for those dazzled by ceremonial pomp. But it may be that she identifies Hamlet too closely with Shakespeare's designs in the play, particularly in the play-within-the-play, which she sees functioning just as Hamlet says it should. See also her "Observing the Lord's Supper and the Lord Chamberlain's Men: The Visual Rhetoric of Ritual and Play in Early Modern England," *Renaissance Drama* n.s. 22 (1991): 147–74.

30. Gurr, *The Shakespearean Stage, 1574–1642,* p. 190.

31. For example, the experiments of The Living Theater in the late 1960s were frequently "pre-verbal"; see also Antonin Artaud, *The Theater and Its Double,* trans. Mary Caroline Richards (New York: Grove, 1958), pp. 37–41, 86–87.

32. Diehl, *Staging Reform,* pp. 81–92.

33. Barbara Hodgdon, "He Do Cressida in Different Voices," *English Literary Renaissance* 20 (1990): 254–86.

34. Johnson, *Bartholomew Fair,* p. 32.

35. In exploring the tradition of the metamorphosis of sculpture into persons (and the reverse), Leonard Barkan emphasizes that Shakespeare has gone to considerable trouble—and dramatic risk—to fashion the recognition scene *as* apparent transformation of a statue ("'Living Sculptures': Ovid, Shakespeare, and *The Winter's Tale,*" *ELH* 48 [1981]: 639–67).

36. Graham Holderness, "*The Winter's Tale*: Country into Court," in *Shakespeare: Out of Court: Dramatizations of Court Society* ed. Graham Holderness, Nick

Potter, and John Turner (Basingstoke: Macmillan, 1990), pp. 195–235, quotations from pp. 209–211.

37. T. G. Bishop, *Shakespeare and the Theatre of Wonder* (Cambridge: Cambridge University Press, 1996), p. 171.

38. Louis Montrose, "The Purpose of Playing: Reflections on a Shakespearean Anthropology," *Helios*, n.s. 7 (1980): 62. In a recent revision of this work, Montrose drops this discussion and in a note says he wants "to disassociate [his] secularist perspective" from what he takes to be my own "recuperation" of Shakespeare's theater "for an aesthetic of late-medieval Catholic spirituality" (*The Purpose of Playing*, p. 32). In this Montrose appears to misunderstand my original position in "The Idolatrous Eye: Iconoclasm, Anti-theatricalism, and the Image of the Elizabethan Theater," *ELH* 52 (1985): 279–310. Rather than a "recuperation," my argument there was groping towards what T. G. Bishop has recently termed a "theater of wonder." In Bishop's formulation, Shakespeare reworked "a dramaturgy of wonder" in the service of what Bishop calls "a poetics of incarnation": "This idea of Shakespeare's work as a consistent seeking of the world, using the force of wonder to register both the difficulty and the promise of that quest, sees him running counter to the strong transcendentalizing use of wonder and the sublime which dominated the medieval dramaturgy." Bishop understands the plays as "instinct above all with a desire to restore or refurbish a world that has somehow gone wrong, that has resisted or refused the touch of our need. Wonder in such terms is a mark not of subjection but of an overcoming and satisfaction that 'delivers' us into the world (the term is a favorite of Shakespeare's)—at once like a message, a captive, and a child" (*Shakespeare and the Theatre of Wonder*, pp. 15–16). Stanley Cavell, while not satisfied to find the scene "a translated moment of religious resurrection," believes that such a translation will have to find its place within an understanding of the scene, and finds this theater in a sense in competition with religion, as if displacing it. "A transformation is being asked of our conception of the audience of the play, perhaps a claim that we are no longer spectators, but something else, more, say participants" (*Disowning Knowledge in Six Plays of Shakespeare* [Cambridge: Cambridge University Press, 1987], p. 218).

39. Diehl, "Observing the Lord's Supper," p. 267; *Staging Reform*, p. 111. But in the latter work, she revises somewhat her reading of the play-within-the-play to suggest that "Hamlet imagines a theater in which word and image reinforce each other."

40. Barish, *The Antitheatrical Prejudice*, p. 151.

Bibiliography

Anderson, J. J., ed. *Newcastle Upon Tyne*. REED. Toronto: University of Toronto Press, 1982.

Artaud, Antonin. *The Theater and Its Double*. Translated by Mary Caroline Richards. New York: Grove, 1958.

Aston, Margaret. *Lollards and Reformers: Images and Literacy in Late Medieval Religion*. London: Hambledon, 1984.

———. *England's Iconoclasts*. Oxford: Clarendon, 1988.

Augustine. *The City of God*. Translated by Henry Bettenson. Harmondsworth, England: Penguin, 1984.

Axton, Richard. *European Drama of the Early Middle Ages*. London: Hutchinson, 1974.

Bale, John. *The Complete Plays of John Bale*. Vol. 1. Edited by Peter Happé. Cambridge: D. S. Brewer, 1985.

Banfi, Luigi, ed. *Sacre Rappresentazioni del Quattrocento*. Turin: Unione Tipografica-Editrice Torinese, 1968.

Barber, Charles. "The Body Within the Frame: A Use of Word and Image in Iconoclasm." *Word and Image* 9 (1993): 140–53.

Barish, Jonas. *The Antitheatrical Prejudice*. Berkeley: University of California Press, 1981.

Barkan, Leonard. "'Living Sculptures': Ovid, Shakespeare, and *The Winter's Tale*." *ELH* 48 (1981): 639–67.

———. "Making Pictures Speak: Renaissance Art, Elizabethan Literature, Modern Scholarship." *Renaissance Quarterly* 48 (1995): 331–32.

Baxandall, Michael. *Painting and Experience in Fifteenth Century Italy: A Primer in the Social History of Pictorial Style*. Oxford: Clarendon, 1972.

Beadle, Richard, ed. *The York Plays*. London: Edward Arnold, 1982.

Beckwith, Sarah. *Christ's Body: Identity, Culture, and Society in Late Medieval Writings*. London: Routledge, 1993.

———. "Making the World in York and the York cycle." In *Framing Medieval Bodies*. Edited by Sarah Kay and Miri Rubin, pp. 254–76 Manchester: Manchester University Press, 1994.

———. "Ritual, Theater, and Social Space in the York Corpus Christi Cycle." In *Bodies and Disciplines: Intersections of Literature and History in Fifteenth-Century England*. Edited by Barbara A Hanawalt and David Wallace. Minneapolis: University of Minnesota Press, 1996.

Bergmann, Rosemarie. "A 'tröstlich pictura': Luther's Attitude in the Question of Images." *Renaissance and Reformation* 17 (1981): 15–25.

Bernard of Clairvaux. *Bernard of Clairvaux: Selected Works*. Translated by G. R. Evans. New York: Paulist, 1987.

Bevington, David, ed. *Medieval Drama*. Boston: Houghton Mifflin, 1975.

Bible, The Wycliffite. *The Holy Bible, Containing the Old and New Testaments, with the Apocryphal Books, in the Earliest English Versions Made from the Latin Vulgate by John Wycliffe and his Followers*. Edited by Josiah Forshall and Frederic Madden. Oxford: Oxford University Press, 1850.

Bills, Bing D. "The 'Suppression Theory' and the English Corpus Christi Play: A Reexamination." *Theater Journal* 32 (1980): 157–68.

Bishop, T. G. *Shakespeare and the Theatre of Wonder*. Cambridge: Cambridge University Press, 1996.

Blunt, Anthony. *Artistic Theory in Italy, 1450–1600*. Oxford: Clarendon, 1940.

Bonansea, B. M. *Man and His Approaches to God in John Duns Scotus*. Lanham, Md.: University Press of America, 1983.

Bonaventure. "De reductione artium ad theologiam." In *The Works of Bonaventure*, vol. 3. Translated by José de Vinck. Paterson, N.J.: St. Anthony Guild Press, 1966.

Bouwsma, William. "The Two Faces of Humanism: Stoicism and Augustinianism in Renaissance Thought." In *Intinerarium Italicum: The Profile of the Italian Renaissance in the Mirror of its European Transformation*. Studies in Medieval and Reformation Thought. Vol. 14. Edited by Heiko A. Oberman and Thomas A. Brady, Jr. Leiden: E. J. Brill, 1975.

Boyle, Marjorie O'Rourke. *Erasmus on Language and Method in Theology*. Toronto: University of Toronto Press, 1977.

Bradner, Leicester. "A Test for Udall's Authorship." *Modern Language Notes* 42 (1927): 378–80.

Braun, Hugh. *Parish Churches: Their Architectural Development in England*. London: Faber and Faber, 1970.

Braunmuller, Albert. *George Peele*. Boston: G. K. Hall, 1983.

Breitenberg, Mark. "Reading Elizabethan Iconicity: *Gorboduc* and the Semiotics of Reform." *English Literary Renaissance* 18 (1988): 194–217.

Brown, Peter. "A Dark-Age Crisis: Aspects of the Iconoclastic Controversy." *English Historical Review* 88 (1973): 1–34.

———. *The Cult of the Saints: Its Rise and Function in Latin Christianity*. Chicago: University of Chicago Press, 1981.

Bucer, Martin. *Melancthon and Bucer*. Edited and translated by Wilhelm Pauck. Library of Christian Classics. Philadelphia: Westminster, 1969.

Burke, Peter. *Popular Culture in Early Modern Europe*. London, 1978. Reprint, New York: Harper and Row, 1978.

Buser, Thomas. "Jerome Nadal and Early Jesuit Art in Rome." *Art Bulletin* 58 (1976): 424–33.

Bynum, Caroline Walker. *Holy Feast and Holy Fast: The Religious Significance of Food to Medieval Women*. Berkeley: University of California Press, 1987.

———. *Jesus as Mother: Studies in the Spirituality of the High Middle Ages*. Berkeley: University of California Press, 1982.

Calvin, John. *Foure godly sermons agaynst the pollution of Idolatries*. London, 1561.

———. *On Shunning the Unlawful Rites of the Ungodly, and Preserving the Purity of the Christian Religion*. In *Tracts and Treatises in Defense of the Reformed Faith*, vol. 3. Translated by Henry Beveridge. Grand Rapids, Mich.: Eerdmans, 1958.

Cavell, Stanley. *Disowning Knowledge in Six Plays of Shakespeare.* Cambridge: Cambridge University Press, 1987.

Chambers, E. K. *The Elizabethan Stage.* 4 vols. Oxford: Clarendon, 1923.

———. *The Medieval Stage.* Oxford: Clarendon, 1903.

Christensen, Carl C. *Art and the Reformation in Germany.* Athens: Ohio University Press, 1979.

Clopper, Lawrence M., ed. *Chester.* REED. Toronto: University of Toronto Press, 1979.

Clubb, Louise George. *Italian Drama in Shakespeare's Time.* New Haven: Yale University Press, 1989.

Clugston, George Alan. Introduction to *A Looking Glasse for London and England,* by Thomas Lodge and Robert Greene. New York: Garland, 1980.

Cohen, Walter. *The Drama of a Nation: Public Theater in Renaissance England and Spain.* Ithaca, N.Y.: Cornell University Press, 1985.

Coldewey, John. "The Last Rise and Final Demise of Essex Town Drama." *MLQ* 36 (1975): 239–60.

Coleman, Janet. *Medieval Readers and Writers, 1350–1400.* New York: Columbia University Press, 1981.

Coletti, Theresa. "Spirituality and Devotional Images: The Staging of the Hegge Cycle." Ph.D. dissertation, University of Rochester, 1975.

Collinson, Patrick. *Archbishop Grindal, 1519–1583: The Struggle for a Reformed Church.* Berkeley: University of California Press, 1979.

Compston, H. F. B. "The Thirty-Seven Conclusions of the Lollards." *English Historical Review* 26 (1911): 738–49.

Crew, Phyllis Mack. *Calvinist Preaching and Iconoclasm in the Netherlands, 1544–1566.* Cambridge: Cambridge University Press, 1978.

Crewe, Jonathan V. "The Theatre of the Idols: Marlowe, Rankins, and Theatrical Images." *Theatre Journal* 36 (1984): 321–33.

Crockett, Bryan. *The Play of Paradox: Stage and Sermon in Renaissance England.* Philadelphia: University of Pennsylvania Press, 1995.

Crosse, Henry. *Vertues Common-wealth: or the Highway to Honour.* London, 1603.

Davidson, Clifford, ed. *A Tretise of Miraclis Pleyinge.* Early Drama, Art, and Music Monograph Series, 19. Kalamazoo, Mich.: Medieval Institute Publication, 1993.

———. "Judgment, Iconoclasm, and Anti-Theatricalism in Jonson's *Bartholomew Fair.*" *Papers on Language and Literacy* 25 (1989): 349–63.

Davies, Horton. *Worship and Theology in England from Cranmer to Hooker, 1534–1603.* Princeton, N.J.: Princeton University Press, 1970.

Davis, Natalie Zemon. "The Rites of Violence: Religious Riot in Sixteenth-Century France." *Past and Present* 59 (1973): 51–90.

Davis, Norman, ed. *Non-cycle Plays and Fragments.* EETS. London: Oxford University Press, 1970.

———. "Spectacula Christiana: A Roman Christian Template for Medieval Drama." *Medieval English Theater* 9 (1987): 125–52.

De Bèze, Theodore. *A tragedie of Abrahams Sacrifice.* Translated by Arthur Golding. Edited by Malcolm W. Wallace. Toronto: University of Toronto Press, 1906.

Deanesly, Margaret. *The Lollard Bible and Other Medieval Biblical Versions.* Cambridge: Cambridge University Press, 1920.

Dickinson, J. C. *An Ecclesiastical History of England: The Later Middle Ages.* London: Adams and Charles Black, 1979.

Dictionary of National Biography. Edited by Leslie Stephen and Sidney Lee. New York: Macmillan; London: Smith, Elder, 1885–1906.

Diehl, Huston. "Observing the Lord's Supper and the Lord Chamberlain's Men: The Visual Rhetoric of Ritual and Play in Early Modern England." *Renaissance Drama* n.s. 22 (1991): 147–74.

———. *Staging Reform, Reforming the Stage: Protestantism and Popular Theater in Early Modern England.* Ithaca, N.Y.: Cornell University Press, 1997.

Du Boulay, F. R. H. *An Age of Ambition: English Society in the Late Middle Ages.* London: Nelson, 1970.

Duffy, Eamon. *The Stripping of the Altars: Traditional Religion in England, 1400–1580.* New Haven: Yale University Press, 1992.

Eire, Carlos M. N. *War Against the Idols: The Reformation of Worship from Erasmus to Calvin.* Cambridge: Cambridge University Press, 1986.

Eisenstein, Elizabeth L. *The Printing Press as an Agent of Change: Communications and Cultural Transformations in Early-Modern Europe.* Cambridge: Cambridge University Press, 1979.

Elliott, John R. *Playing God: Medieval Mysteries on the Modern Stage.* Toronto: Toronto University Press, 1989.

Ellul, Jacques. *The Humiliation of the Word.* Translated by Joyce Main Hanks. Grand Rapids, Mich.: Eerdmans, 1985.

Enders, Jody. *Rhetoric and the Origins of Medieval Drama.* Ithaca, N.Y.: Cornell University Press, 1992.

Erasmus, Desiderius. *The Godly Feast.* London, 1522.

———. *Moriae Encomium, Id Est Stultitia Laus.* Edited by Clarence Miller. In *Opera Omnia.* Amsterdam: North Holland Publishing, 1979.

———. *Omnia Opera.* Edited by Joannes Clericus. 6 vols. Leiden, 1703–1706. Reprint, Hildescheim: Georg Olms, 1961.

———. *Opus Epistolarum Desiderii Erasmi.* Vol. 8. Edited by P. S. Allen and H. M. Allen. Oxford: Oxford University Press, 1924.

———. *A Playne and godly exposition or declaration of the commune Crede.* London, 1533.

Evans, B. Ifor, and W. W. Greg, eds. *The Commody of the most vertuous and Godlye Susanna.* The Malone Society Reprints. Oxford: Oxford University Press, 1937.

Faccioli, Emilio, ed. *Il Teatro Italiano: Dalle Origini al Quattrocento.* Turin: Einaudi, 1975.

Foakes, R. A., and R. T. Rickert, eds. *Henslowe's Diary.* Cambridge: Cambridge University Press, 1961.

Freedberg, David. *Iconoclasm and Painting in the Revolt of the Netherlands, 1566–1609.* New York: Garland, 1988.

———. *The Power of Images: Studies in the History and Theory of Response.* Chicago: University of Chicago Press, 1989.

Galloway, David, ed. *Norwich.* REED. Toronto: Toronto University Press, 1984.

Galloway, David, and John Wasson, eds. *Records of Plays and Players in Norfolk and Suffolk.* The Malone Collections, vol. 11. Oxford: The Malone Society, 1980.

Gardiner, Harold C. *Mysteries' End: An Investigation of the Last Days of the Medieval Religious Stage.* New Haven: Yale University Press, 1946.

Garside, Charles. *Zwingli and the Arts.* New Haven: Yale University Press, 1966.

Geertz, Clifford. *Local Knowledge: Further Essays in Interpretive Anthropology.* New York: Basic Books, 1983.

———. *The Interpretation of Cultures.* New York: Basic Books, 1973.

Geneva Bible. 1560. Madison: University of Wisconsin Press, 1969.

Gent, Lucy. *Picture and Poetry, 1560–1620.* Leamington Spa: James Hall, 1981.

George, David, ed. *Lancashire*. REED. Toronto: University of Toronto Press, 1991.

Gero, Stephen. "Byzantine Iconoclasm and the Failure of a Medieval Reformation." In *The Image and the Word*. Edited by Joseph Gutmann. Missoula, Mont.: Scholars Press, 1977.

Gibson, Gail McMurray. *The Theater of Devotion: East Anglian Drama and Society in the Late Middle Ages*. Chicago: University of Chicago Press, 1989.

Gilman, Ernest B. *Iconoclasm and Poetry in the English Reformation: Down Went Dagon*. Chicago: University of Chicago Press, 1986.

Gleason, John B. *John Colet*. Berkeley: University of California Press, 1989.

Gombrich, E. H. *Art and Illusion*. Princeton, N.J.: Princeton University Press, 1956.

Goodman, Nelson. *The Languages of Art: An Approach to a Theory of Symbols*. 2nd ed. Indianapolis, Ind.: Bobbs-Merril, 1968.

Gosson, Stephen. *Playes Confuted in five Actions*. London, 1582?.

Grabar, André. *Early Christian Art: From the Rise of Christianity to the Death of Theodosius*. Translated by Stuart Gilbert and James Emmons. New York: Odyssey, 1968.

Greenblatt, Stephen J. *Renaissance Self-Fashioning from More to Shakespeare*. Chicago: University of Chicago Press, 1980.

Grinnell, Robert. "Iconography and Philosophy in the Crucifixion Window at Poitiers." *The Art Bulletin* 28 (1946): 171–96.

Gross, Kenneth. *Spenserian Poetics: Idolatry, Iconoclasm, and Magic*. Ithaca, N.Y.: Cornell University Press, 1985.

Gunn, Giles. *The Culture of Criticism and the Criticism of Culture*. New York: Oxford University Press, 1987.

Gurr, Andrew. *The Shakespearean Stage, 1574–1642*. 3rd ed. Cambridge: Cambridge University Press, 1992.

Gutmann, Joseph. "Deuteronomy: Religious Reformation or Iconoclastic Revolution." In *The Image and the Word*. Edited by Joseph Gutmann. Missoula, Mont.: Scholar's Press, 1977.

Hardison, O. B., Jr. *Christian Rite and Christian Drama in the Middle Ages: Essays in the Origin and Early History of Modern Drama*. Baltimore, Md.: Johns Hopkins University Press, 1965.

Harris, Max. *Theatre and Incarnation*. Basingstoke, Hants.: Macmillan, 1990.

Harrison,William. *The Description of England*. Edited by G. Edelen. Ithaca, N.Y.: Cornell University Press, 1968.

Hart, Roderick P. *Seducing America: How Television Charms American Voters*. New York: Oxford University Press, 1994.

Heidegger, Martin. *Poetry, Language, Thought*. Translated by Albert Hofstadter. New York: Harper and Row, 1975.

Helgerson, Richard. *Forms of Nationhood: The Elizabethan Writing of England*. Chicago: University of Chicago Press, 1992.

———. *Self-Crowned Laureates: Spenser, Jonson, Milton, and the Literary System*. Berkeley: University of California Press, 1983.

Henry, Patrick. "What Was the Iconoclast Controversy About?" *Church History* 45 (1976): 16–31.

Hodgdon, Barbara. "He Do Cressida in Different Voices." *English Literary Renaissance* 20 (1990): 254–86.

Holderness, Graham. "*The Winter's Tale*: Country into Court." In *Shakespeare: Out of Court: Dramatizations of Court Society*. Edited by Graham Holderness, Nick Potter, and John Turner. Basingstoke, Hants.: Macmillan, 1990.

Howard, Jean E. "Renaissance Antitheatricality and the Politics of Gender and Rank in *Much Ado About Nothing*." In *Shakespeare Reproduced: The Text in History and Ideology*. Edited by Jean E. Howard and Marion F. O'Connor. New York: Methuen, 1987.

————. *The Stage and Social Struggle in Early Modern England*. London: Routledge, 1994.

Hudson, Anne, ed. *Selections from English Wycliffite Writings*. Cambridge: Cambridge University Press, 1978.

————. *Lollards and Their Books*. London: Hambledon, 1985.

Hugh of St. Victor. "De Unione Corporis et Spiritus." In *I tre giorni dell'invisibile luce; l'unione del corpo e dello spirito*. Edited by Vincenzo Liccaro. Florence: Sansoni, 1974.

————. *Hugh of St. Victor on the Sacraments of the Christian Faith*. Translated by Roy J. Deferrari. Cambridge, Mass.: The Medieval Academy of America, 1951.

Hughes, Andrew. "Liturgical Drama." In *The Theatre of Medieval Europe*. Edited by Eckhard Simon. Cambridge: Cambridge University Press, 1991.

Huizinga, Johan. *The Waning of the Middle Ages* [1924]. Reprint, New York: Doubleday Anchor, 1954.

Ingram, R. W., ed. *Coventry*. REED. Toronto: University of Toronto Press, 1981.

Interlude of King Darius. London, 1565. Reprinted 1577.

Jacob and Esau. In *Reformation Biblical Drama in England*. Edited by Paul Whitfield White. New York: Garland, 1992.

James, M. R. *The Sculptures in the Lady Chapel at Ely*. London: D. Nutt, 1895.

James, Mervyn. *Society, Politics and Culture: Studies in Early Modern England*. Cambridge: Cambridge University Press, 1986.

Jameson, Frederic. *Signatures of the Visible*. New York: Routledge, 1990.

Jay, Martin. "The Rise of Hermeneutics and the Crisis of Ocularcentrism." In *The Rhetoric of Interpretation and the Interpretation of Rhetoric*. Edited by Paul Hernadi. Durham, N.C.: Duke University Press, 1989.

————. *Downcast Eyes: The Denigration of Vision in Twentieth-Century French Thought*. Berkeley: University of California Press, 1993.

Jeffrey, David L. "Franciscan Spirituality and the Rise of Early English Drama." *Mosaic* 8 (1975): 17–46.

John of Damascus. *On the Divine Images*. Translated by David Anderson. Crestwood, N.J.: St. Vladimir's Seminary Press, 1980.

Johnston, Alexandra F. "Cycle Drama in the Sixteenth Century: Texts and Contexts." In *Early Drama to 1600*. Edited by Albert H. Tricomi. Acta, vol. 13. Center for Medieval and Early English Studies. Binghamton: State University of New York, 1987.

————, and Margaret Rogerson, eds. *York*. REED. Toronto: University of Toronto Press, 1979.

Johnston, Paul A., Jr. "The Dialect of *A Tretise of Miraclis Pleyinge*." In *A Tretise of Miraclis Pleyinge*. Edited by Clifford Davidson. Early Drama, Art, and Music Monograph Series, 19. Kalamazoo, Mich.: Medieval Institute Publications, 1993.

Jones, William R. "Art and Christian Piety: Iconoclasm in Medieval Europe." In *The Image and the Word*. Edited by Joseph Gutmann. Missoula, Mont.: Scholars Press, 1977.

Jonson, Ben. *Bartholomew Fair*. Edited by Eugene M. Waith. New Haven: Yale University Press, 1963.

————. *The Alchemist*. Edited by Alvin B. Kernan. New Haven: Yale University Press, 1974.

————. *The Staple of News*. Edited by Devra Rowland Kifer. Regents Renaissance Drama Series. Lincoln: University of Nebraska Press, 1975.

Kempe, Margery. *The Book of Margery Kempe*. Edited by Sanford Meech and Hope Emily Allen. EETS. Oxford: Oxford University Press, 1940.

Kendall, Ritchie D. *The Drama of Dissent: The Radical Poetics of Noncomformity, 1380–1590*. Chapel Hill: University of North Carolina Press, 1986.

Kitzinger, Ernst. "The Cult of Images in the Age before Iconoclasm." *Dumbarton Oaks Papers*. Vol. 8. Cambridge, Mass.: Harvard University Press, 1954.

Kolve, V. A. *A Play Called Corpus Christi*. Stanford: Stanford University Press, 1966.

Ladner, Gerhart B. *Ad Imaginem Dei: The Image of Man in Medieval Art*. Latrobe, Pa.: Archabbey Press, 1965.

————. "Origin and Significance of the Byzantine Iconoclastic Controversy." In *Images and Ideas in the Middle Ages: Selected Studies in History and Art*. Rome: Edizioni di Storia e Letteratura, 1983.

Lancashire, Ian. *Dramatic Texts and Records of Britain: A Chronological Topography to 1558*. Cambridge: Cambridge University Press, 1984.

Latimer, Hugh. *Sermons of Hugh Latimer*. Edited by George Elwes Corrie. Parker Society. Cambridge: Cambridge University Press, 1844.

Lesser, George. *Gothic Cathedrals and Sacred Geometry*. 3 vols. London: Tiranti, 1957–64.

Levine, Laura. *Men in Women's Clothing: Anti-Theatricality and Effeminization, 1579–1642*. Cambridge: Cambridge University Press, 1994.

Lodge, Thomas, and Robert Greene. *A Looking Glasse for London and England*. Edited by George Alan Clugston. New York: Garland, 1980.

————. *Wits Miserie, and the Worlds Madness: Discovering the Deuils Incarnat of this Age* [London, 1596]. In *The Complete Works of Thomas Lodge*, vol. 4. New York, 1893. Reprint, Russell and Russell, 1963.

Lumiansky, R. M., and David Mills, eds. *The Chester Mystery Cycle: Essays and Documents*. Chapel Hill: University of North Carolina Press, 1983.

Mâle, Émile. *L'Art Religieux aprés le Concile de Trente*. Paris: Armand Colin, 1932.

Mander, Jerry. *Four Arguments for the Elimination of Television*. New York: William Morrow, 1978.

Marcus, Leah S. "Of Mire and Authorship." In *The Theatrical City: Culture, Theatre and Politics in London, 1576–1649*. Edited by David L. Smith, Richard Strier, and David Bevington. Cambridge: Cambridge University Press, 1995.

McCusker, Honor C. *John Bale: Dramatist and Antiquary*. 1942. Reprint, Freeport, N.Y., 1971.

McKitterick, Rosamond. "Text and Image in the Carolingian World." In *The Uses of Literacy in Early Medieval Europe*. Edited by Rosamond McKitterick. Cambridge: Cambridge University Press, 1990.

Meredith, Peter. "John Clerke's Hand in the York Register." *Leeds Studies in English* 12 (1981): 245–71.

Migne, J. P. *Patrologia Latina*. Vols. 77 and 183. Paris, 1878–90.

Miles, Margaret R. *Image as Insight: Visual Understanding in Western Christianity and Secular Culture*. Boston: Beacon, 1985.

Mitchell, W. J. T. *Iconology: Image, Text, Ideology*. Chicago: University of Chicago Press, 1986.

Montrose, Louis. *The Purpose of Playing: Shakespeare and the Cultural Politics of the Elizabethan Theatre*. Chicago: University of Chicago Press, 1996.

————. "The Purpose of Playing: Reflections on a Shakespearean Anthropology." *Helios* 7 (1980): 51–74.

Moran, Jo Ann Hoeppner. *The Growth of English Schooling, 1340–1540.* Princeton, N.J.: Princeton University Press, 1985.

Morgan, David. *Visual Piety: A History and Theory of Popular Religious Images.* Berkeley: University of California Press, 1998.

More, Thomas. *Utopia.* In *The Complete Works of St. Thomas More.* Vol. 4. Edited by S. J. Edward Surtz and J. H. Hexter. New Haven: Yale University Press, 1964.

————. *Dialogue concerning Heresies.* In *The Complete Works of St. Thomas More.* Vol. 6. Edited by Thomas Lawler, Germain Marc'hadour, and Richard Marius. New Haven: Yale University Press, 1981.

————. *The Apology.* In *The Complete Works of St. Thomas More.* Vol. 9. Edited by J. B. Trapp. New Haven: Yale University Press, 1979.

Mullaney, Steven. *The Place of the Stage: Licence, Play, and Power in Renaissance England.* Chicago: University of Chicago Press, 1988.

Munday, Anthony. *A second and third blast of retrait from plaies and Theaters.* London, 1580.

Murray, Sister Charles. "Art and the Early Church." *Journal of Theological Studies* 28 (1977): 303–345.

Muscatine, Charles. *Chaucer and the French Tradition.* Berkeley: University of California Press, 1966.

Nelson, Alan H. *Cambridge.* REED. Toronto: University of Toronto Press, 1989.

————. *The Medieval English Stage: Corpus Christi Pageants and Plays.* Chicago: University of Chicago Press, 1974.

New Catholic Encyclopedia. Edited by an editorial staff at Catholic University of America. New York: McGraw-Hill, 1967–89.

Nichols, Aidan. *The Art of God Incarnate: Theology and Image in Christian Tradition.* New York: Paulist, 1980.

Northbrooke, John. *Spiritus est vicarius Christi in terra: A Treatise wherein Dicing, Dauncing, Vaine playes or Enterludes . . . are reproved.* London, 1577?

Oberman, Heiko A., and Thomas A. Brady, Jr., eds. *Itinerarium Italicum: The Profile of the Italian Renaissance in the Mirror of its European Transformation.* Studies in Medieval and Reformation Thought. Vol. 14. Leiden: E. J. Brill, 1975.

O'Connell, Michael. "The Civic Theater of Suffering: Hans Memling's Passion and Late Medieval Drama." In *European Iconography: East and West.* Edited by Gyorgy Szonyi. Symbola et Emblemata. Leiden: E. J. Brill, 1996.

————. "The Idolatrous Eye: Iconoclasm, Antitheatricalism, and the Image of the Elizabethan Theater." *ELH* 52 (1985): 279–310.

————. "Vital Cultural Practices: Shakespeare and the Mysteries." *JMEMS* 29 (1999): 149–68.

Ong, Walter J. *The Presence of the Word: Some Prolegomena for Cultural and Religious History.* New Haven: Yale University Press, 1967.

Orgel, Stephen. *Impersonations: The Performance of Gender in Shakespeare's England.* Cambridge: Cambridge University Press, 1997.

————. "Nobody's Perfect: Or, Why Did the English Stage Take Boys for Women?" *The South Atlantic Quarterly* (Winter 1989): 7–29.

Panofsky, Erwin. "Erasmus and the Visual Arts." *Journal of Warburg and Courtald Institute* 32 (1969): 200–227.

Parkes, M. B. "The Literacy of the Laity." *Literature and Western Civilization: The*

Medieval World. Edited by David Daiches and Anthony Thorlby. London: Aldus, 1973.

Pasachoff, Naomi E. *Playwrights, Preachers, and Politicians: A Study of Four Tudor Old Testament Dramas*. Salzburg: Institut für Englische Sprache und Literatur, 1975.

Pecock, Reginald. *Repressor of Over Much Blaming of the Clergy*. In *Rerum Britannicarum Medii Aevi Scriptores*. Rolls Series, vol. 19. Edited by Churchill Babington. London: Longman, 1960.

Peele, George. *David and Bethsabe*. Edited by Elmer Blistein. In *The Dramatic Works of George Peele*. New Haven: Yale University Press, 1970.

Pelikan, Jaroslav. *The Spirit of Eastern Christendom, 600–1700*. The Christian Tradition: A History of the Development of Doctrine. Vol. 2. Chicago: University of Chicago Press, 1974.

Phillips, John. *The Reformation of Images: Destruction of Art in England, 1535–1660*. Berkeley: University of California Press, 1973.

Potter, G. R. *Zwingli*. Cambridge: Cambridge University Press, 1976.

Prodi, Paolo. *Richerche sulla teoretica delle arti figurative nella riforma cattolica, estratto dall'Archivio italiano per la storia della pietà*. Vol. 4. Roma: Edizione di Storia e Litteratura, 1962.

Prynne, William. *Histrio-Mastix, the players scourge, or, actors tragoedie*. London, 1633. Reprint, New York: Garland, 1973.

Pseudo-Bonaventure. *Mirrour of the Blessed Lyf of Jesu Christ*. Translated by Nicholas Love. Edited by Lawrence F. Powell. Oxford: Oxford University Press, 1907.

Rahner, Karl. *The Foundations of Christian Belief*. Translated by Willian V. Dych. New York: Seabury, 1978.

Rainolds, John. *Th'overthrow of Stage-playes*. London, 1599.

Rankins, William. *A Mirrour of Monsters*. London, 1587.

The Resurrection of Our Lord. Edited by J. Dover Wilson and Bertram Dobell. The Malone Society Reprints. Oxford: Oxford University Press, 1912.

Roston, Murray. *Biblical Drama in England*. London: Faber and Faber, 1968.

Rowe, George E. *Distinguishing Jonson: Imitation, Rivalry, and the Direction of a Dramatic Career*. Lincoln: University of Nebraska Press, 1988.

Rozett, Martha Tuck. *The Doctrine of Election and the Emergence of Elizabethan Tragedy*. Princeton, N.J.: Princeton University Press, 1984.

Rubin, Miri. *Corpus Christi: The Eucharist in Late Medieval Culture*. Cambridge: Cambridge University Press, 1991.

Scarisbrick, J. J. *The Reformation and the English People*. Oxford: Basil Blackwell, 1984.

Scarry, Elaine. *The Body in Pain: The Making and Unmaking of the World*. New York: Oxford University Press, 1985.

Schroeder, H. J., ed. *Canons and Decrees of the Council of Trent*. London: Herder, 1941.

Semper, I. J. "The Jacobean Theater through the Eyes of Catholic Clerics." *Shakespeare Quarterly* 3 (1952): 45–51.

Shakespeare, William. *The Riverside Shakespeare*. Edited by G. Blakemore Evans. Boston: Houghton Mifflin, 1974.

Sidney, Sir Philip. *The Poems of Sir Philip Sidney*. Edited by William A. Ringler, Jr. Oxford: Clarendon, 1962.

Siemon, James R. *Shakespearean Iconoclasm*. Berkeley: University of California Press, 1985.

Somerset, J. Alan B. "Local Drama and Playing Places at Shrewsbury: New Findings in the Borough Records." In *Medieval and Renaissance Drama in England.* Edited by J. Leeds Barroll. New York: AMS Press, 1985.

———, ed. *Shropshire.* REED. Toronto: University of Toronto Press, 1994.

Spector, Stephen, ed. *The N-Town Play.* EETS. Oxford: Oxford University Press, 1991.

Spikes, Judith Doolin. "The Jacobean History Play and the Myth of the Elect Nation." *Renaissance Drama* n.s. 8 (1977): 117–49.

Sponsler, Claire. *Drama and Resistance: Bodies, Goods, and Theatricality in Late Medieval England.* Medieval Cultures, vol. 10. Minneapolis: University of Minnesota Press, 1997.

Stallybrass, Peter. "Worn Worlds: Clothes and Identity on the Renaissance Stage." In *Subject and Object in Renaissance Culture.* Edited by Margreta de Grazia, Maureen Quilligan, and Peter Stallybrass. Cambridge: Cambridge University Press, 1996.

Stallybrass, Peter, and Allon White. *The Politics and Poetics of Transgression.* Ithaca, N.Y.: Cornell University Press, 1986.

States, Bert O. *Great Reckonings in Little Rooms: On the Phenomenology of Theater.* Berkeley: University of California Press, 1985.

Steinberg, Leo. *The Sexuality of Christ in Renaissance Art and in Modern Oblivion.* New York: Pantheon, 1983.

Steinberg, Ronald M. *Fra Girolamo Savonarola, Florentine Art, and Renaissance Historiography.* Athens: Ohio University Press, 1977.

Stevens, Martin. *Four Middle English Mystery Cycles: Textual, Contextual, and Critical Interpretations.* Princeton, N.J.: Princeton University Press, 1987.

Stevens, Martin, and C. A. Cawley, eds. *The Townley Plays.* EETS. Oxford: Oxford University Press, 1994.

Stewart, Garrett. "Shakespearean Dreamplay." *ELR* 11 (1981): 44–69.

Sticca, Sandro. *The Latin Passion Play: Its Origins and Development.* Albany: State University of New York Press, 1970.

Stubbes, Philip. *The Anatomie of Abuses.* London, 1583.

Taviani, Ferdinando. *La Fascinazione del Teatro: La Commedia dell'Arte e la Società Barocca.* Rome: Bulzoni, 1970.

Tertullian. *De Spectaculis.* Translated by T. R. Glover. Loeb Classical Library. Cambridge, Mass.: Harvard University Library, 1931.

Thomas of Celano. "First Life of St. Francis." In *St. Francis of Assisi, Writings and Early Biographies.* Edited by Marion A. Habig. Chicago: Franciscan Herald Press, 1975.

Thrupp, Silvia. *The Merchant Class of Medieval London.* Chicago: University of Chicago Press, 1948.

Travis, Peter W. *Dramatic Design in the Chester Cycle.* Chicago: University of Chicago Press, 1982.

———. "The Social Body of the Dramatic Christ in Medieval England." *Early Drama to 1600, Acta* 13 (1985): 17–35.

A Tretise of Miraclis Pleyinge. Edited by Clifford Davidson. With Commentary on the Dialect by Paul A. Johnston, Jr. Early Drama, Art, and Music Monograph Series, 19. Kalamazoo, Mich.: Medieval Institute Publications, 1993.

Turner, Victor, and Edith Turner. *Image and Pilgrimage in Christian Culture: Anthropological Perspectives.* New York: Columbia University Press, 1978.

Tydeman, William. *The Theatre in the Middle Ages: Western European Stage Conditions, c. 800–1576.* Cambridge: Cambridge University Press, 1978.

Vasari, Giorgio. *Lives of the Artists.* Translated by George Bull. 2 vols. Harmondsworth: Penguin, 1987.

Von Simson, Otto. *The Gothic Cathedral: Origins of Gothic Architecture and the Medieval Concept of Order.* New York: Pantheon, 1956.

Wager, Lewis. *The Life and Repentaunce of Marie Magdalene.* Edited by Frederick Ives Carpenter. Chicago: University of Chicago Press, 1902.

Weiman, Robert. *Shakespeare and the Popular Tradition in the Theater: Studies in the Social Dimension of Dramatic Form and Function.* Edited by Robert Schwartz. Baltimore, Md.: Johns Hopkins University Press, 1978.

———. "Mimesis in *Hamlet.*" In *Shakespeare and the Question of Theory.* Edited by Patricia Parker and Geoffrey Hartman. New York: Methuen, 1985.

White, Paul Whitfield, ed. *Reformation Biblical Drama in England: The Life and Repentaunce of Mary Magdalene; The History of Jacob and Esau.* New York: Garland, 1992.

———. *Theatre and Reformation: Protestantism, Patronage, and Playing in Tudor England.* Cambridge: Cambridge University Press, 1993.

Wickham, Glynne. *Early English Stages, 1300–1660.* 3 vols. London: Routledge and Kegan Paul, 1959–81.

———. *The Medieval Theatre.* 3rd ed. Cambridge: Cambridge University Press, 1987.

Wirth, Jean. "Théorie et practique de l'image sainte à la veille de la réforme." *Bibliothèque d'Humanisme et Renaissance* 48 (1986): 319–58.

Womack, Peter, "Imagining Communities: Theatres and the English Nation in the Sixteenth Century." In *Culture and History, 1350–1600: Essays on English Communities, Identities and Writing.* Edited by David Aers. Detroit, Mich.: Wayne State University Press, 1992.

———. "Medieval Drama." In Simon Shepherd and Peter Womack, *English Drama: A Cultural History.* Oxford: Blackwell, 1996.

Woolf, Rosemary. *The English Mystery Plays.* Berkeley: University of California Press, 1972.

The York Play: A Facsimile of British Library MS Additional 35290. Introduction by Richard Beadle and Peter Meredith. Leeds: University of Leeds School of English, 1983.

Young, Karl. *The Drama of the Medieval Church.* Oxford: Clarendon, 1933.

Index

Abraham and Isaac (Brome), 28, 74, 105
Abraham Sacrifiant, 103, 104–105,
"Abram and Lot" (lost play), 108, 112
Admiral's Men, 91, 108, 109, 112, 113
Alberti, Leon Battista, 162 n. 94
Angelico, Fra, 163 n. 94
Annas (in mystery cycles), 81, 84, 98
Anne of Bohemia, 44
Anti-Christ (Tegernsee), 67
anti-visual attitudes, 4–6, 19–20, 117–18,
    121
antitheatricalism, 11, 99, 101
    in early church, 16, 19
    Elizabethan and Jacobean, 3, 12, 13,
        14–30, 63, 116, 143, 144
    and iconoclasm, 17–27, 33, 127
    medieval, 77–78
    in Milan, 30–32, 144
    "scurrility" of biblical plays, 27–28,
        29
Apocrypha, plays drawn from, 12, 91,
    101–02, 107, 108, 111, 112
Artaud, Antonin, 87, 175 n. 31
Arundel, Thomas, 44
Ashton, Thomas, 101, 171 n. 24
Aston, Margaret, 46, 57, 145 n. 2, 148
    n. 13, 157 n. 25, 159 n. 55, 161
    n. 79, n. 83, n. 85, 161–62 n. 86,
    162 n. 90, n. 91, 163 n. 99
audience, role of, 81, 83, 84–85, 86, 124,
    141
Augustine, Saint, 39, 89, 156 n. 15
Auto de los Reyes Magos, 67
Axton, Richard, 165 n. 12

Baglione, Giovanni, 154 n. 75
Bale, John, 12, 21, 90, 92–97, 100, 114,
    153 n. 67, 170 n. 7, n. 11, n. 14

Barber, Charles, 157 n. 20
Barish, Jonas, 15–17, 120, 148 n. 11, 149
    n. 18
Barkan, Leonard, 118, 119, 175 n. 35
baroque period, 32
Barthe, Roland, 93
Bartolommeo, Fra, della Porta, 163 n. 94
Baxandall, Michael, 59, 160 n. 57
Beadle, Richard, 151 n. 28, 168 n. 44
Becket, Saint Thomas, shrine of, 56, 60
Beckwith, Sarah, 64, 65, 72, 85, 164 n. 7
Belcari, Feo, 74, 75, 105
Benediktbeuern plays, 67, 71, 72
Bergmann, Rosemarie, 160 n. 59
Bernard of Clairvaux, Saint, 67, 69–71,
    72, 76, 165 n. 18
Bèze, Théodore de, 103, 104–105, 106
Bible
    and Lollards, 43
    in medieval culture, 28
    New Testament, 29, 45, 46, 96,
        97–101, 102
    Old Testament, 6, 29, 40, 147 n. 17
    profaned by stage representation,
        27–30, 106
    prohibition of idolatry in second com-
        mandment, 9, 14, 33, 37, 46, 53
    in Reformation, 51, 52
    representation of, 8, 28, 31, 93
    Vulgate, 45
    Wycliffite translation, 44–45
    See also biblical drama *and individual
        books of the Bible*
biblical drama, 15–17, 29, 89
    end of in seventeenth century, 112–14
    Italian, 30–32, 73–77
    from Old Testament, 12, 21, 27, 31,
        74, 94–95, 103–105, 107, 108, 111

biblical drama (*continued*)
  Protestant 89, 90, 91, 92–115
  in public theaters, 107–115
  See also mystery cycles; liturgical
    theater
Bills, Bing D., 150, n. 24
Bilney, Thomas, 55, 161 n. 79
Binham, St. Mary's Priory, 57
Bird, William, 111
Bishop, T. G., 141–42, 176 n. 38
blood
  of Christ, 72, 78, 79, 84–85, 86, 87
  in Shakespeare's tragedies, 87–88
  See also body
body, 7, 40, 47
  of Christ, 10, 12, 27, 72, 73, 78–87,
    114, 168 n. 45
  idea and practice of, 12, 32–33, 63–88
  and incarnation, 68
  rejected by Catharism, 65–66
  textualizing of, 12, 89–115, 120
  in theater, 11, 19–20, 29, 32, 77, 124,
    137, 144, 149 n. 22
  See also blood; Eucharist; humanity of
    Christ; incarnation
Bonansea, B. M., 168, n. 49
Bonaventure, St., 48, 78
Book of Common Prayer, 16, 22, 56
Borne, William, 109
Borromeo, Federico, 31–32
Borromeo, Saint Carlo, 30–32
Bottom, 123, 131–32
Bouwsma, William, 148 n. 11
Boxley (Kent), rood of, 60
Boyle, Marjorie O'Rourke, 37
Bradner, Leicester, 171 n. 29
Braun, Hugh, 161 n. 82
Braunmuller, Albert, 172 n. 41
Brecht, Bertolt, 98
Breitenberg, Mark, 170 n. 14
Brown, Peter, 156 n. 13, n. 14, 163 n. 98
Brunelleschi, Filippo, 162 n. 94
Bucer, Martin, 21, 27, 101
Buchanan, George, 34
Burbage, James, 15
Burke, Peter, 169 n. 5
Buser, Thomas, 154 n. 75
Bynum, Caroline Walker, 65, 164 n. 8,
    n. 9, n. 10, 167 n. 36
Byzantine iconoclasm. *See* Iconoclast
    Controversy

Caiaphas
  in mystery cycles, 81, 82, 84, 88, 98
  in public theater, 109

Calvin, Jean, 54, 57, 105, 161 n. 73, n. 74
Calvinism, 23, 61, 89, 103, 105
Carmelites, 93
Castellano Castellani, 74
Catharism, 12, 65–66, 67, 69
Catholic Reform, 30–33, 144
Catholicism, 30, 89, 112, 144
  incarnational structures of, 22, 37–38,
    46–50
  late-medieval worship of, 47, 49
  in mystery cycles, 16, 21
  worship of, as idolatry, 14–15, 33
  worship of, restored under Mary, 57
  See also Catholic Reform
Cavell, Stanley, 176 n. 38
Cawley, A. C., 152–53, n. 55
Chamberlain's Men, 112, 113
Chambers, E. K., 150 n. 25, 164 n. 11
Chester Plays, 61, 65, 92, 149 n. 23, 168
    n. 44
  Abraham and Isaac, 28
  Banns of, 24, 27, 169 n. 50
  Last Judgment, 78, 79
  revision of, 24
  suppression of, 22, 24–25, 91
Chettle, Henry, 111, 113
Christensen, Carl C., 51, 145 n. 2, 160
    n. 60, 161 n. 71, n. 72, n. 75
Christology. *See* incarnation
Christos Pantocrator, 48
Cistercians, 49, 69
Clerke, John, 21, 150 n. 27, 150–51,
    n. 28
Clubb, Louise George, 32
Clugston, George Alan, 172 n. 35
Cohen, Walter, 164–65 n. 11
Coldeway, John, 119, 173 n. 10
Coleman, Janet, 158 n. 41
Colet, John, 159 n. 55
Coletti, Theresa, 159 n. 50
Colleton, John, 155 n. 78
Collier, Jeremy, 15
Collinson, Patrick, 151 n. 36
commedia dell'arte, 30
Constantine V, 156 n. 13
corporeality. *See* body
Corpus Christi (feast), 26, 47, 61, 64, 92,
    106
  See also Eucharist
costume, 119, 120, 132–33, 134, 173 n. 10
Counter-Reformation. *See* Catholic
    Reform
Coventry Plays, 25, 61, 77, 80, 87, 91,
    92, 149 n. 23
Cranmer, Thomas, 21, 56, 93

Creed Play (York), 22
Crew, Phyllis Mack, 145 n. 2, 161 n. 77
Crewe, Jonathan V., 149 n. 16
Crockett, Bryan, 29, 34, 90, 155 n. 79, 174 n. 22
Cromwell, Thomas, 21, 56
cross-dressing, 17–18, 122
Crosse, Henry, 15, 112, 113, 114, 172 n. 46

Daniel (Beauvais), 67
David and Bethsabe, 12, 91, 108, 109–111, 112, 113, 115
Davidson, Clifford, 168 n. 43, 169 n. 54, 174 n. 17
Davies, Horton, 151 n. 33, 162 n. 92
Davis, Natalie Zemon, 161 n. 76
Davis, Norman, 149 n. 18
Deanesly, Margaret, 158 n. 43
Dekker, Thomas, 106, 109, 111, 113
Derfel Gadarn, 60
Destruction of Ierusalem (Coventry), 26
Deuteronomy, Book of, 9–10, 96
Dickinson, J. C., 158 n. 47
Diehl, Huston, 143, 173 n. 5, 175 n. 29, 176 n. 39
Disciplinati of Umbria, 73
docetism, 68
Du Boulay, F. R. H., 42
Duffy, Eamon, 56, 145 n. 2, 148 n. 13, 160, n. 56, 161 n. 81, n. 82, 162 n. 87
dulia, 39, 41
Duns Scotus, 80

ear. *See* language
East Anglian drama, 25, 92, 93, 94, 96, 100
Edward VI, reign of, 21, 22, 24, 57, 61, 99, 162 n. 87, n. 91
Eire, Carlos M. N., 48–49, 52, 145 n. 2, 155 n. 3, 160 n. 59, n. 61, n. 63, 160–61 n. 67, 161 n. 69, n. 71, n. 73, n. 76
Eisenstein, Elizabeth L., 160 n. 58
Elizabeth I
    reign of, 22, 24, 104, 170 n. 6
    and iconoclasm, 57, 61, 156 n. 13
    and Edmund Grindal, 90
    as Protestant saint, 113
Elliott, John R., 153 n. 61, 169 n. 52
Ellul, Jacques, 5–6, 7, 9, 146 n. 8, n. 9
Ely Cathedral, Lady Chapel, 3, 56
Emmerson, Richard, 151 n. 44
Enders, Jody, 165 n. 11
English vernacular, 44–46

epistemology
    and perceptual faculties, 17, 30, 128–30, 143, 144, 174 n. 22
    of theater, 125, 130, 133
    See also religious aesthetics
Erasmus, Desiderius
    privileging of verbal texts, 11, 36–38, 120, 128, 175 n. 26
    and "incarnational" religious structures, 49, 52, 155 n. 3, n. 4, 159 n. 55, 160 n. 63
Eucharist, 27, 37, 47–48, 50, 64–65
    in Chester Plays, 24
    devotion of "forty hours," 31
    in York plays, 22, 86
    See also blood; body; Corpus Christi
eye. *See* images; vision; visual art

Faerie Queene, The. See Spenser, Edmund
fall of humanity, in York Plays, 79–80
Falstaff, 20, 107, 113, 172 n. 36
Famous History of Sir Thomas Wyat, 113
Fleury plays, 67, 71–72
Florence, 32, 74–77
Fortune (theater), 114
Foxe, John, 90, 113
Francis, Saint, 70, 72, 167 n. 36
Franciscans, 12, 65, 70, 72, 73, 80, 98
    and theater, 72, 168 n. 49
Frankfort, Council of, 41
Freedberg, David, 7–9, 37, 147 n. 14, 159 n. 50, 160 n. 57, 161 n. 77

Gardiner, Howard C., 150, n. 23, n. 24, n. 25, 151 n. 39, 153 n. 56, 163 n. 2
Garside, Charles, 53, 160 n. 63, n. 65, 161 n. 68, n. 70
Garter, Thomas, 101–102, 103
Geertz, Clifford, 163 n. 95
Gent, Lucy, 118
George, David, 152 n. 54
Gerhoh of Reichersberg, 148 n. 10
Gero, Stephen, 39
Gibson, Gail McMurray, 158 n. 47, 163 n. 97, n. 3, 167 n. 38
Gilman, Ernest, 117, 118, 145 n. 2, 148 n. 13, 162 n. 93
Giotto, 162 n. 94
Gleason, John B., 159 n. 55
Godlye Susanna, Comedy of, 101–102, 103, 104, 171 n. 26
Golding, Arthur, 103, 104, 105, 106
Gombrich, E. H., 4
Goodman, Nelson, 146 n. 11

Gosson, Stephen, 14, 15, 19, 34, 118, 119
gothic architecture, 48
Gray, Lady Jane, 113
Greccio, 72
Greenblatt, Stephen J., 153 n. 63
Greene, Robert, 12, 91, 106, 107–108, 114, 172 n. 35
Gregory I (the Great), Pope Saint, 38, 41, 43, 161 n. 86
Gregory Nazianus, Saint, 34
Grindal, Edmund, 23, 24, 25, 30, 90
Grinnell, Robert, 165, n. 13
Gross, Kenneth, 148 n. 13
Gunn, Giles, 163 n. 95
Gurr, Andrew, 173 n. 9
Gutmann, Joseph, 163 n. 99

Haetzer, Ludwig, 53, 161 n. 67
Hankey, John, 24, 25
Happé, Peter, 170 n. 7
Hardison, O. B., Jr., 164 n. 11
Harris, Max, 149 n. 22
Harrison, William (antiquary), 58
Harrison, William (Catholic archpriest of England), 154–55 n. 78
Hart, Roderick P., 145–46 n. 6, 147 n. 16
Haughton, William, 172 n. 39
Haydocke, Richard, 118
Heidegger, Martin, 20, 149 n. 22
Helgerson, Richard, 112, 120, 173 n. 48
Henry, Patrick, 156 n. 14, 156–57 n.19
Henry VIII, 56, 57, 113
Henslowe, Philip, 12, 91, 106, 108, 111–14, 119, 172 n. 35
Herod (in mystery cycles), 79, 81, 82, 83, 84, 88
Herrad of Landsberg, 148 n. 10
"Hester and Ahasuerus" (lost play), 108, 112
Heywood, Thomas, 113, 116
Hiereia, Council of, 41
Higden, Ranulph, 44
Hilarius, 67, 72
Hilton, Walter, 49
Hodgdon, Barbara, 135
Holderness, Graham, 139
Homilies, Book of, 90, 162 n. 90
Homily "Against Peril of Idolatry," 58
homosexuality, fear of, 17–18
Hope (playhouse), 123
Horace, 4
Howard, Jean, 148 n. 12, n. 14, 172 n. 46, 173 n. 2, 175 n. 25
Hrosthvitha of Gandersheim, 165 n. 12

Hudson, Anne, 44, 157 n. 33, 158 n. 46
Hugh of St. Cher, 65
Hugh of St. Victor, 67–69
Hughes, Andrew, 165 n. 13
Huizinga, Johan, 159 n. 54
humanism, 105, 125, 130, 131, 132, 135, 138, 144
  in Italy, 162–63 n. 94
  and late-medieval devotion, 60, 160 n. 63
  and print culture, 11, 36–37, 51, 58
  See also Erasmus, Desiderius
humanity of Christ, 39–40, 47, 65, 66, 67–71, 72–73, 75–77
  See also body; incarnation
Hunnis, William, 171 n. 29
Huntington, Earl of, 25
Hutton, Matthew, 22–23, 26, 27, 151 n. 34

iconoclasm
  attitude toward body, 9
  contemporary scholarly interest in, 5
  and culture of image in Italy, 32, 154 n. 75, 162–63 n. 94
  figurative, 135–38
  Reformation, 3–4, 11, 17, 50, 51–58, 60, 106, 116, 125, 143, 174 n. 17
  and Shakespeare, 128, 139, 141
  sixth-century, 38
  and texts, 117–18
  and theater, 11, 17–19, 87, 90, 114
  in England, 55–58, 61
  in France, 55
  in Germany, 54
  in Netherlands, 55
  in Scotland, 54–55
  in Zurich and Switzerland, 52–54, 155 n. 4
  See also Iconoclast Controversy; idolatry; images; representation, of God
Iconoclast Controversy (Byzantine), 11, 38–41, 42, 49, 50, 154 n. 75
idea, and image, 10
idolatry
  anxiety about, 37, 38, 58, 78, 105, 118, 121
  Catholicism charged with, 30
  in Hebraic thought, 10
  Shakespeare and discourse of, 126, 128, 135–36, 141
  theater as, 3, 11, 14–20, 26, 33, 34–35, 61, 63, 143, 174 n. 17
  See also iconoclasm; images; representation

If You Know Not Me You Know Nobody,
  113
images
  affective power of, 5, 6, 19
  anxiety about, 4, 8, 32, 143
  challenge and opposition to, 38–41,
    43–46, 51–58, 63
  in culture of Catholic Reform, 32, 144,
    154 n. 75
  defense of, 6–9
  development of, 33
  efficacy of, 7–8
  epistemology of, 17
  erotic response to, 8
  Gregorian defense of, 38, 42, 43
  in Hebrew Scriptures, 10, 147 n. 17
  Hellenic sense of, 10
  humans as "quick" images, 43–44, 46,
    126
  Lollard attitude toward, 43–44, 45–46
  miraculous, 9
  plays as, 125, 134
  in relation to language 4–7, 11, 35,
    36–37, 42, 46, 58, 157 n. 32,
    161–61 n. 86, 173 n. 5
  Shakespeare's use of term, 126–27
  theory of, 11, 37, 38, 39, 41, 59
  in *Troilus and Cressida*, 135–38
  use of, 7–8, 46
  in verbal discourse, 117–18
  See also iconoclasm; idolatry; lan-
    guage; representation
incarnation
  and image, 10, 11, 36–37
  and theater, 12, 63–88, 94, 114
  theology of, 6, 39–40, 47–48, 50, 65,
    67–71, 79–80, 155 n. 3
  See also body; Eucharist; humanity of
    Christ; incarnational mode of reli-
    gious experience
incarnational mode of religious experi-
    ence, 22, 37–38, 46–50, 58, 60, 89
  See also incarnation; images
Internet, 5
Islam, 39

Jacob and Esau, 103–104, 106, 107
Jacomot, Jean, 103
James, M. R., 145 n. 1
James I, 170 n. 6
James, Mervyn, 61, 64, 65, 164 n. 7
Jameson, Frederic, 4, 145 n. 3
Jansenists, 15
Jay, Martin, 146 n. 8
Jeffrey, David L., 168 n. 49

"Jephthah" (lost play), 91, 106, 111, 112
Jesuits, 33
Jeu d'Adam, 67
John of Damascus, 39–41, 50
John, Gospel of, 29, 48, 67, 100
Johnston, Alexandra F., 150 n. 24, 152
  n. 48
Johnston, Paul A., Jr., 167 n. 42
Jonah, 108
Jones, W.R., 41
Jones, Inigo, 121
Jonson, Ben, 12, 34, 119–25, 138–39,
  143, 144, 174 n. 22
  antitheatricalism of, 120
  and costume, 120–21
  and humanist culture, 12, 120
  and Puritans, 116, 121–22, 123, 124
  The Alchemist, 18, 110, 121
  Bartholomew Fair, 13, 14, 18, 116,
    122–25, 138, 174 n. 18, n. 22
  Catiline, 120
  Cynthia's Revels, 120
  Everyman Out of His Humour, 125
  The New Inn, 120
  Poetaster, 122
  The Staple of News, 121
  Volpone, 110, 120
Josephus, Flavius, 111
"Joshua" (lost play), 91, 111
"Judas" (lost play), 91, 109, 111, 112,
  172 n. 39
Judges, Book of, 111
Juliana of Liège, 65

Karlstadt, Andreas Bodenstein von,
  51–52, 160–61 n. 67
Kempe, Margery, 167 n. 41, 169 n. 54
Kendall, Ritchie D., 169 n. 2, 170 n. 11,
  n. 13
King Darius, 103, 106, 171 n. 26
Kings, Book of, 95
Kolve, V. A., 64, 164 n. 4

La Seinte Resureccion, 67
Ladner, Gerhart B. 156 n. 13, n. 18, 159
  n. 50, 165 n. 14, n. 18
Lancashire, Ian, 152 n. 53, n. 54
language
  in doctrinal formulation, 11
  hegemony over image, 7, 57
  in relation to image, 4–6, 11, 30,
    34–35, 36–37, 42, 46, 57, 97, 121,
    139–40
  and Jonson, 121–22, 125
  and ornamentation, 117

language (*continued*)
  in relation to silence, 82
  thematized by Shakespeare, 129,
    139–40
  as vehicle of biblical revelation, 9
  violence through, 84
Lateran Council, Fourth, 47, 65
Latimer, Hugh, 55
latria, 39, 41
Laud, William, 57
laude drammatiche, 12, 73–74, 80
Laus pro nativitate domini, 73
Legros, Pierre, 154 n. 75
Leke, Thomas, 154–55 n. 78
Leland, John, 93
Lesser, George, 159 n. 53
Levine, Laura, 124–25, 148 n. 14, 174
  n. 18
Libri Carolini, 41
light, 48
Lincoln plays, 25
literacy, 42–44, 131; and images, 38, 44
liturgical theater, 12, 64, 66–67, 71–72, 73
liturgical vestments, turned into players'
  costumes, 119
Living Theater, The, 175 n. 31
Lodge, Thomas, 12, 106, 107–108, 112,
  114, 172 n. 35
logocentricity, 6, 11, 28–29
  privileging of, 8, 36–38, 58, 63
logolatry, 29–30
Logos, 6, 68, 71
  as Scripture, 29–30
Lollards, 158 n. 34, 170 n. 11
  and images, 41–42, 43–46, 50, 51,
    158 n. 46
  and literacy, 42–43
  and vernacular, 44–46, 158 n. 46
  and theater, 16, 77
Lomazzo, Giovanni Paolo, 118
*Looking Glasse for London and England,
  A*, 12, 91, 106, 107–108, 112, 114,
  172 n. 35
Love, Nicholas, 78, 82
Lucifer, in York Plays, 79–80
  See also Satan, in John Bale's play
Luke, Saint
  Gospel of, 98, 99, 100, 154 n. 78
  painting Virgin, 9
Lumiansky, R. M., 149 n. 23, 151 n. 40,
  n. 41, 153 n. 57
Luther, Martin, 51, 52, 160 n. 60

Mâle, Émile, 154 n. 75
Malone, Edmund, 172 n. 40

Mander, Jerry, 146 n. 6
Manichaeism, 40, 66
  See also Catharism
Mankind, 97
Marcus, Leah, 174 n. 21
Marlowe, Christopher, 15, 33, 107, 149
  n. 16
  Tamburlaine, 108, 172 n. 35
martyrs. *See* saints
Mary Magdalene (Digby), 100
Mary Tudor, reign of, 22, 57, 61, 94, 162
  n. 87, 171 n. 29, n. 30
Mary Magdalene, 71, 75–77, 98, 99–101
masque, court, 121
Mass, derided as theater, 14–15, 33, 71
  See also Catholicism; Eucharist
Matthew, Gospel of, 52
McKitterick, Rosamund, 41
Mechtild of Hackborn, 65, 164 n. 9
*Meditationes Vitae Christi. See Mirrour
  of the Blessed Lyf of Jesu Christ*
mendicant orders, 12, 72
  See also Franciscans
Merciless Parliament, 44
Meredith, Peter, 150 n. 27, 151 n. 30
metadrama. *See* self–reflexivity
Miles, Margaret, 7, 146 n. 11, 154 n. 75,
  159 n. 50, 160, n. 57
Milles, Robert, 34
Mills, David, 149 n. 23, 151 n. 40, n. 41,
  153, n. 57
*Mirrour of the Blessed Lyf of Jesu Christ
  (Meditationes Vitae Christi)*, 78–79,
  167 n. 38, 170 n. 21
Mitchell, W. J. T., 4
Molière, 15
monasteries, dissolution of, 55
Montecassino Passion, 67
Montrose, Louis, 142, 170 n. 6, 176 n. 38
moral interludes, 90, 100, 102
Moran, Jo Ann Hoeppner, 42, 157 n. 28
More, (St.) Thomas, 37, 42, 55
Morgan, David, 146 n. 11
Mullaney, Steven, 163 n. 1
Munday, Anthony, 15, 18, 19, 27, 28, 33,
  106, 111, 113, 119
Muscatine, Charles, 158 n. 40
music, 52–53, 141
mystery cycles, 11, 27, 47, 50, 101, 108
  and Corpus Christi, 64–65
  in modern performance, 79, 87
  regional particularity of, 60
  and Shakespeare, 87
  suppression of, 15–16, 17, 20–27, 28,
    61, 89, 91, 114, 152 n. 54

and *Tretise of Miraclis Pleyinge,*
77–79
See also Chester Plays; Coventry
Plays; Newcastle-upon-Tyne Plays;
Norwich Plays; N-Town Plays; York
Plays; Wakefield Plays

N-Town Plays, 84, 93, 94, 98, 168 n. 44
Nativity, St. Bernard on, 70–71
"Nebuchadnezzar" (lost play), 108, 112
Nelson, Alan H., 149–50, n. 23, 152 n.
51, 153 n. 56, 163 n. 2, 164 n. 4
Newcastle-upon-Tyne Plays, 25, 61, 152
n. 49
Nicean Council, Second, 39, 41
Nichols, Aidan, 146 n. 10, 147 n. 17
Nicodemus, Gospel of, 82, 111
Nikephoros, Patriarch, 157 n. 20
Northbrooke, John, 15, 19, 28, 30
Norwich Plays, 25, 61, 91, 152 n. 50,
n. 51

O'Connell, Michael, 169 n. 58, 176 n. 38
Oldcastle. See Sir John Oldcastle, Part 1
Ong, Walter, 28, 29, 160 n. 58
orality, 28–29
Orgel, Stephen, 148–49 n. 14
origins of medieval drama, 64, 66–73
Orthodoxy, Greek, 6, 38–41

Palleoti, Gabriele, 31
Panofsky, Erwin, 155 n. 4
parish churches, 55
Parkes, M. B., 157 n. 31
particularity, 59–61, 92
Pasachoff, Naomi, 109–110, 171 n. 29
Passion of Christ. *See* suffering of Christ
Paternoster Play (York), 22
Paul, Saint, 14, 40, 69, 89, 98, 100, 122,
132
Pecock, Reginald, 37, 43, 44, 49, 157
n. 32
Peele, George, 12, 91, 108, 109–111,
112, 113, 115
Pelikan, Jaroslav, 156 n. 12
perceptual faculties, 17, 28–29, 38, 41,
128
See also epistemology; religious aes-
thetics
Peregrinus (Beauvais), 67, 71
Petrarch, 162 n. 94
Phillips, John, 3, 145 n. 2, 148 n. 13, 161
n. 85, 161–62 n. 86
physicality. *See* body; spectacle, theatri-
cal

pictorialism, 117–18
Pilate (in mystery cycles), 79, 81, 82, 83,
84, 98
pilgrimage, 43, 46, 48, 49, 53, 56, 60, 61
See also incarnational mode of reli-
gious experience; particularity
Pius V, 32
Plato, 15
"Pontius Pilate" (lost play), 91, 109, 111
Potter, G. R., 160 n. 63, n. 64
Potter, Robert, 170 n. 19
poverty, 73
preaching, 18, 29, 35, 90, 144, 160 n. 60,
169 n. 4
in competition with theater, 28, 30–31,
34
Prickynge of Love, 85, 169 n. 55
printing and print culture, 11, 13, 22–29,
36–37, 51, 58
Privy Council (Elizabethan), 25
Prodi, Paolo, 154 n. 71, n. 73
Protestantism. *See* Reformation
Prynne, William, 14, 17, 18, 19, 30, 33,
34, 116, 154 n. 77, n. 78
puppets, 122–23
Puritanism, and theaters, 11, 34, 63, 112,
113, 174 n. 22
See also Jonson, Ben

Queen Anne's Men, 113
Quem quaeritis trope, 66

Racine, Jean, 15
Rahner, Karl, 146 n. 10
Ralph Roister Doister, 103
Rankins, William, 15, 33, 149 n. 16
Ranworth (Norfolk), 56
Rappresentazione del Figliuol Prodigo,
74
Rappresentazione di Abramo e Isacco,
74, 105
*Rappresentazione del Martirio de' Ss.
Giovanni e Paolo,* 31
*Rappresentazione della conversione di
Santa Maria Maddelena,* 75–77,
100
realism, and representation, 8–9
Reformation
and *Abraham Sacrifiant,* 105
adaptation of Catholic rites, 16, 22
and biblical theater, 89–115
as centripetal force, 60, 92
dramatic character of, 89–90, 169 n. 2
and humanism, 11, 50–52
and iconoclasm, 4, 6, 11, 17, 29, 143

Reformation (*continued*)
　and Iconoclast Controversy, 39, 41
　modern scholarship of, 38, 48–50,
　　58–59
　revision of mystery cycles, 21–22
　and *sola scriptura*, 29, 52
　and theater, 14, 16, 89–115
Refutation of the Apologie for Actors,
　116
relics, 39, 46, 47, 48, 49, 50, 58
　See also incarnational mode of reli-
　　gious experience; pilgrimage; saints,
　　cult of
religious aesthetics, 17, 27, 29, 38, 47,
　　51, 58, 64, 89, 163 n. 95
　See also epistemology; image; repre-
　　sentation
Repentaunce of Mary Magdalen, 99–101,
　　102, 103, 114
representation, 69
　anxiety about, 90, 116
　of God, 10–11, 12, 26–27, 28, 36–37,
　　39–40, 94, 95, 99–101, 104, 108,
　　114, 116
　and Franciscans, 72
　and realism, 8–9
　technologies of, 5, 6, 11, 33, 38,
　　42–46, 51–52
　and theater, 9, 15, 18, 20, 26–27, 64,
　　70
　visual, 4, 7, 27, 33, 63
Resurrection of Our Lord, The, 97–99,
　　114
Revolt of Northern earls (1569), 26
Richard II, 44
Rogers, David, 29
Rolle, Richard, 85
rood screens, 56, 57
Rose (theater), 114
Roston, Murray, 171–72 n. 31, 172 n. 43
Rowe, George E., 174 n. 19
Rowley, Samuel, 109, 111, 113
Rozett, Martha Tuck, 169 n. 4
Rubin, Miri, 158–59 n. 49, 164 n. 10

sacre rappresentazioni, 12, 74–77
　opposed by Borromeo, 30–31, 32
　See also laude drammatiche
sacri monti, 8
saints, cult of, 39, 40, 43–44, 46, 47, 50,
　　58, 60, 102
　See also incarnational mode of reli-
　　gious experience; pilgrimage; relics
Sallman, Warner, 146 n. 11
"Samson" (lost play), 91, 111

Samuel, Books of, 109, 110
Sandys, Edwin, 22
Satan, in John Bale's play, 95
　See also Lucifer
Saussurian linguistics. *See* signifier and
　　signified
Savage, John, 24, 25
Savanarola, Girolamo, 163 n. 94
Scarisbrick, J. J., 161 n. 81, n. 82
Scarry, Elaine, 10, 81, 88, 169 n. 53
self-reflexivity, 122–23, 124, 125,
　　130–35, 136, 139–42, 143, 144
Semper, I. J., 155 n. 78
sensus, sensualitas, 67
sentience, 11, 81, 84–85, 86, 87, 88
　See also body; suffering of Christ
Shakespeare, 12, 15, 19, 87, 115, 125–44
　and mystery cycles, 87
　All's Well that Ends Well, 126
　Antony and Cleopatra, 144
　Cymbeline, 139
　Hamlet, 13, 87, 125, 126, 132–35,
　　143, 175 n. 29
　Henry IV, Part 1, 20, 110, 113, 126–27
　Henry IV, Part 2, 113, 127
　Henry VI, Part 2, 126
　King Lear, 87, 88
　Love's Labor's Lost, 131, 134
　Macbeth, 88
　Measure for Measure, 126
　Midsummer Night's Dream, 13, 123,
　　130–32, 134
　Much Ado About Nothing, 128–30,
　　131, 143, 175 n. 25
　Othello, 88, 144
　Richard III, 126
　The Tempest, 90, 123, 138
　Troilus and Cressida, 13, 135–38, 144
　Two Gentlemen of Verona, 127–28
　Venus and Adonis, 126
　The Winter's Tale, 13, 127, 138,
　　139–42, 144, 176 n. 38
Sidney, Sir Philip, 117, 118
Siemon, James R., 148 n. 13, 174 n. 23
sight. *See* vision
signifier and signified, 8, 29, 37
silence, 82
Simpson, Otto von, 48
Sir John Oldcastle, Part 1, 113
Smith, John, 26
Smithfield, 123, 124
Solomon, 9
Somerset, J. Alan B., 171 n. 24
Song of Songs, St. Bernard's sermons on,
　　69, 70, 76

Southwold (Suffolk), 56
spectacle, theatrical, 121, 123, 125,
    133, 134, 135, 138, 142, 143,
    144
    See also theater, phenomenology of;
    vision
Spenser, Edmund, 117–18, 130
Spikes, Judith Doolin, 173 n. 48
spirit, in relation to flesh, 67–71
Sponsler, Claire, 168 n. 45
stained glass, 56, 58
Stallybrass, Peter, 119, 174 n. 13, 174
    n. 21
States, Bert O., 20
Steinberg, Leo, 76–77
Steinberg, Ronald, 163 n. 94
Stevens, Martin, 152–53 n. 55, 167 n. 44,
    169 n. 57
Stewart, Garrett, 175 n. 27
Sticca, Sandro, 165 n. 12
stigmata, 72, 167 n. 36
Strange's Men, 172 n. 35
Straten, Dirik van der, 93
Stubbes, Philip, 14, 15, 29, 106
suffering of Christ, 65, 68, 70, 78–79,
    81–87
    See also blood; body; sentience
synesthesia, 131–32, 175 n. 27

Taviani, Ferdinando, 31, 32
Tertullian, 19, 149 n. 18
textuality, 29, 95–96, 98–99, 110, 114,
    115
    and body of Christ, 12, 36–37, 52,
    120
    See also Erasmus, Desiderius; lan-
    guage; printing and print culture
theater
    biblical, 11, 15–17, 71–87, 89, 90–115
    in competition with preaching, 18, 28,
    34
    and iconoclasm, 11, 17–19
    as idolatry, 14–19, 29, 33–34, 61–62,
    141
    phenomenology of, 9, 12, 15, 18,
    19–20, 34–35, 62, 64, 86, 130,
    131–35, 142–43, 144, 149 n. 22
    power of, 18
    status of, 63
    visual and sensual appeal of, 11, 13,
    19–20, 30, 34, 118–19, 121
    See also liturgical drama; mystery
    plays; moral interludes
Theater, The (playhouse), 15
theaters, closing of, 11, 17, 18, 116

Theodore of Studios, 39–40, 50
theology
    of image 6, 10, 38–41, 47–48, 50
    of God's name, 9–10
    See also iconoclasm; incarnation;
    incarnational mode of religious
    expression
Thomas of Celano, 72
Thomas Lord Cromwell, 113
Thrupp, Silvia, 42
Titian, 117
Tobias play (Lincoln), 25
"Tobias" (lost play), 91, 111
torture. *See* suffering of Christ
touch. *See* sentience
tragedia sacra, 32
translation, 45
transubstantiation. *See* Eucharist
Travis, Peter W., 64, 65, 86, 164 n. 6, 168
    n. 44, 169 n. 52
Trent, Council of, 30, 31, 112
Tretise of Miraclis Pleyinge, 16, 77–78,
    84, 167 n. 42
Trevisa, John, 44
Turin, shroud of, 9
Turner, Victor and Edith, 49, 59, 159–60
    n. 56, 163 n. 96
"twelfth-century renaissance," 67
Tydeman, William, 165 n. 12
Tyndale, William, 55, 57

Udall, Nicholas, 103, 171 n. 19
Urban IV, Pope, 47

Vasari, Giorgio, 162 n. 94
verisimilitude. *See* images; realism, and
    representation
vernacular. *See* English vernacular
Veronica, napkin of, 9
Virgin Mary, 68, 70, 94
    in liturgical drama, 71, 72
    in mystery cycles, 21, 22, 26, 27,
    80–81
    in Umbrian *Laus pro nativitate do-*
    mini, 73
    in *sacre rappresentazioni,* 74–75, 98
    shrines of, 46, 48, 56, 60
vis ignea, 67
vision, 41, 159 n. 50, 160 n. 57
    as active power, 68
    anxiety about, 4, 12, 32–33, 116–18
    in Christian theology, 10–11, 40, 47
    in Shakespeare, 128–30
    and theater, 3, 19–20, 30, 32, 34–35,
    115, 130, 131, 133, 135–38, 139–40

visual art, 48, 50, 58–59, 77, 115, 160
     n. 57
  in Catholic Reform, 31, 36–37
  Flemish and Northern European, 43,
     47, 84
  in Italy, 59, 117, 162–63 n. 94
  medieval English, 118
  portraiture, 118
  in relation to language, 36–37, 46,
     58
  theater as, 125, 130, 144
Wager, Lewis, 99–101, 102, 103, 114
Wakefield Plays, 26, 27, 61, 80, 88, 91,
     104, 149 n. 23, 168 n. 44, 172
     n. 31
Webster, John, 113
Weimann, Robert, 132, 169 n. 57
Wentworth, Thomas, Lord, 92
When You See Me You Know Me, 113
White, Allon, 174 n. 13, n. 21
White, Paul Whitfield, 89, 150 n. 25, 163
     n. 101, 170 n. 9, n. 18, 171 n. 29,
     n. 30
Wickham, Glynne, 119, 151 n. 35, 170
     n. 6, 173 n. 1
Wirth, Jean, 147 n. 15
Womack, Peter, 79, 93
wonder, 140, 176 n. 38

Woolf, Rosemary, 147 n. 10, 167 n. 33,
     168 n. 49
Worcester's Men, 112, 113
word. *See* language
Word. *See* Logos
Wycliffites. *See* Lollards

York Plays, 27, 61, 77, 79–87, 92, 149
     n. 23, 168 n. 44
  Agony and Betrayal, 82
  Christ before Annas and Caiaphas, 82
  Christ before Herod, 83
  Christ before Pilate 2, 82
  Christ's Appearance to Mary Mag-
     dalen, 85
  Crucifixion, 83–84
  Dream of Pilate's Wife, 83
  Fall of Angels, 79
  Fall of Man, 80
  Flight into Egypt, 80–81
  Incredulity of Thomas, 85
  revision of, 21–24
  suppression of, 21–24, 91
Young, Karl, 147 n. 10, 164 n. 11

Zurich, 52–54
Zwilling, Gabriel, 52
Zwingli, Huldrych, 51–54, 160 n. 63